THE INNER WORLD OF MAN

THE INNER WORLD
OF MAN

FRANCES G. WICKES

Second Edition

SIGO PRESS
BOSTON

Copyright © 1950, 1988 by Frances G. Wickes

All rights reserved. No part of this book may be reproduced or transmitted in any form or by any means, electronic or mechanical including photocopying, recording or by any information storage and retrieval system, without permission in writing from the publisher.

SIGO PRESS
25 New Chardon Street, #8748
Boston, Massachusetts 02114

Publisher and General Editor: Sisa Sternback

Library of Congress Cataloging-in-Publication Data

Wickes, Frances G. (Frances Gillespy), 1875–1967.
  The inner world of man.
  Reprint. Originally published: London : Methuen, 1950.
  1. Psychoanalysis. 2. Jung, C. G. (Carl Gustav), 1875–1961. I. Title.
BF173.W545   1988   150.19'54   88-15825
ISBN 0-938434-34-9 (pbk.)

Printed in the United States of America

Cover illustration: *Soap Bubbles* by Thomas Couture, reproduced by permission of The Metropolitan Museum of Art, Bequest of Catharine Lorillard Wolfe, 1887. Catharine Lorillard Wolfe Collection (87.15.22).

TABLE OF CONTENTS

Introduction   3
- I. The Inner World   7
- II. The Appearance of Images   21
- III. Parental Images   36
- IV. The Ego   51
- V. The Persona   65
- VI. The Shadow   78
- VII. The Anima   89
- VIII. The Animus   103
- IX. The Self   116
- X. A Brief Experience in Analysis   135
- XI. Dreams of Mother and Anima   145
- XII. Dream Analysis in Later Life   164
- XIII. Phantasy   221
- XIV. Visions   239
- XV. Drawing
  - Introduction   248
  - Part 1   268
  - Part 2   279
  - Part 3   290
  - Psychological Drawings and Paintings   323

ACKNOWLEDGEMENTS

I wish to express my gratitude to those persons who so generously permitted the use of their dreams and other analytical material, and particularly to those who made available the material appearing in the six final chapters. In every case, their careful reading and checking of this material has been of the greatest assistance.

All the work in this book has been illumined by the theories of Dr. C.G. Jung. In particular, certain definitions—the Persona, the Shadow, the Anima, and the Animus—and, in general, the fundamental concepts underlying the analytical procedure, are derived from my work with him.

F. G. W.

New York City
July 1st, 1938

INTRODUCTION

Two PEOPLE who lived their lives deeply and consciously often come to my mind, and I am struck both by their dissimilarity and by their inherent likeness. One was a great physician and scientist, the other a washerwoman in a frontier town. The dissimilarity lay in circumstances and outer opportunity, in gifts and natural ability. The similarity lay in their attitude towards experience; in their ability to live deeply in whatever came to them, and to see the true drama of life as something not produced by circumstance or Fate, but by the inner relation to events. In each of them one felt, as the dominant quality, a life wisdom which, while drawn from the daily experience, yet penetrated deeper to a level where the inner being of the spirit was revealed and the moment became a part of a greater reality. In each the judgment of an act was tempered by a form of charity which, always acknowledging its own limitations, was willing to give to others an understanding that helped to cast out fear, so that bewildered people could see themselves more clearly and, through this understanding, accept themselves.

One of these two people, operating in the world of science, contributed not only to the healing of individual lives, but also to the greater knowledge of mankind; the other, operating in a small pioneer town, contributed new courage and understanding to the lives of many. In both were present an almost fierce integrity and self-scrutiny, which, turned upon their own acts, gave them clarity of vision in judging the acts of others. In thinking of them I have often remembered the parable of the talents and the judgment of "Well done, thou good and faithful servant" —a judgment as right for the possessor of two talents as for the one to whom ten had been given.

To each of these people the word "individual" can be applied, for the individual is one who, from the chaos of inner confusion and the assault of outer reality, separates that undefinable individual nucleus which makes him a unique being. This individual self may be very simple or infinitely complex—the essential quality is the acceptance of its own reality and its own true relation to life.

Such individuality cannot be obtained without a recognition of the need for understanding one's own inner life. A new technique for this understanding has come into being through the revelations of modern psychology, though the validity and the importance of the inner life are no new discovery.

The activity of this inner world is not confined to the so-called spiritual realm. It operates in our lives at every period and in every act. This realization was first brought home to me clearly when I was teaching little children and found that the absent-minded child was indeed absent from the class-room, but very present in another realm, that of phantasy, which to him was more important, more nearly related to his psychological need, than unimportant multiplication tables. The imaginary companion was not just a bit of playful imagination, but a vital element of the self finding its life through this incorporeal body. Childish descriptions of people bore bizarre qualities which made one know that an image lived in the depth of the child's unconscious and that it was this image whom he perceived instead of the actual person. And then came the realization that these parents whose "images" the child described were themselves ruled by inner forces of which they were quite unaware. They, too, had their "ideas" of people, their phantasies of themselves, their hidden motives, their preconceptions. The children had learned to conceal their phantasies from older people, but the older people had learned to conceal them from themselves. And so this inner world was a more and more deeply hidden world until to most it became almost unknown.

When, after many years of study, my work moved into the field of adult analysis, I saw how in many cases the unrealized parts of the self still lived in a buried phantasy life, a life of hidden images moving in a world below the level of consciousness. If they received attention, they became visible in dream or vision, for a vision can come to the ordinary person who is intensely aware of the inner activity—it is not merely the heritage of the saint or the obsession of the insane. The vision and the great dream, which we ordinarily know only in their historical aspects, do come to us today, and, when they come, they do penetrate deeper than the merely personal. Through their connection with racial experience they remove one from the purely personal interpretation of life. The horizons widen, the proportions change; one is no longer caught in the details of daily living. Those details may of necessity remain, but ore has a new relation to them.

As analysis after analysis revealed the workings of the unconscious, I saw with reverence how the inner experience illuminated the apparently ordinary human life and made of it a drama unperceived by others. It is true that such a drama produces deep changes, but they are inner changes of attitude and motivation which, in themselves, appear undramatic.

From time to time, over a period of some twenty years, the material in this book was with the utmost generosity placed in my hands. The long analysis was edited and put into form first. It was laid away for many years. Other chronicles were added. Gradually an idea grew, the idea of incorporating in a volume a few of these records which would illustrate some of the infinite variations of the experience of the inner image.

As the material was arranged for possible publication, so much psychological theory was needed to define necessary terms that the human narrative often had to be broken for the sake of theoretical explanations. It seemed wise, therefore, to write an introductory chapter, explaining these terms already so familiar to readers of Dr. C. G. Jung. This was conceived of as perhaps some twenty or thirty pages which would introduce the reader to the Anima, the Animus, the Persona and the Shadow, terms old in themselves, but in their modern use and definition clearly Dr. Jung's own and part of his enormous contribution to modern psychology. But this material could not be confined to twenty or thirty pages. The images could not be treated with such brevity and so, with that growing independence which children—even brain children—must be permitted to assume, the book changed its own form and resolved itself into a volume on analytical psychology based on Jung's concepts of the nature of the psyche. The original material then fell into place as illustrations of these concepts.

From these illustrations it becomes apparent that analysis starts a new life process which makes possible a continued connection with the inner world. It is not an end in itself, it does not "finish," though it may be ended in its professional aspects. The problems of life are never solved; but when new problems arise, as they will so long as life lasts, the connection with this inner source of understanding is still open. One is more aware of one's own motives, one's dark aspects and creative potentials. As one turns back to the material of the unconscious, dreams and phantasies are activated, and with each step in integration comes an increased understanding with which to meet the demand of life.

F. G. W.

I. THE INNER WORLD

THE INTRUSION of the unexpected into our daily lives is so usual an occurrence that we are apt to take it for granted. This is especially true of ideas or impulses which take us by surprise and seem to come from nowhere.

"The idea just came to me;" everybody has had this experience. The idea may be trivial or amusing, it may be illuminating, or it may be an idea that has such intensity that we speak of being "carried away" by it.

Or an impulse or emotion may arise within us bringing with it a dynamic energy, an energy which stimulates us to an act of which we felt ourselves incapable, or which finds an expression contradictory to our conscious intention. But we rarely ask ourselves where the idea or impulse comes from, or what gives it its energy.

Again, most of us have been obliged to say at some time or other, "I was not myself when I said that," or "I don't know what possessed me to do it." We may then dismiss the matter without inquiring who this speaker was whom we have disavowed or what it was that possessed us.

I have a vivid memory of an old woman of unpredictable impulses, of sudden and lavish generosity or violent hates. Her black cook once said to me, "The trouble with Mis' Eliza is that she's still got her nature with her but she just don't rightly know she's got it!" The woman was speaking not only for Mis' Eliza but for all of us. The manifestations of Mis' Eliza's "nature" were, it is true, somewhat exaggerated, but all of us have still got our nature with us, and few of us rightly know we've got it. There are times when we feel that we do not know ourselves as well as we supposed we did; that there is an unexplored region within the self, a region below the threshold of our conscious life, a place where life is apparently living itself without our knowledge.

We realize that the psyche is greater than consciousness, that it includes a totality of all the known and unknown factors.

All the contents of the psyche of which we are unaware at any given moment (that is, these unknown factors), make up this substratum known as "the unconscious." There is no definite line which can be drawn between the conscious and the unconscious, for the boundaries are always changing; we may be vividly aware today of something which tomorrow will be remote or incomprehensible or forgotten, that is, dropped completely into the unconscious. This forgotten element has then become part of the unconscious; the conscious attention is focussed elsewhere. Yet when some event or emotion recalls this forgotten element, it will emerge again into consciousness. It has not ceased to exist; it has temporarily descended into a subliminal region from which it reappears, perhaps with an increased emotional intensity.

The relation of the conscious to the unconscious is not a fixed and stable one, for both the conscious and the unconscious continually change and shift. An experience becomes conscious when it has reached a degree of intensity which makes us aware of its existence. Thus, when the forces of consciousness are directed elsewhere or their emotional intensity is altered, material of which we have been conscious (even acutely conscious), may become unconscious. But it still exists within the psyche. As a revolving light brings first one object, then another, into the field of vision, so the light of consciousness may bring now one, now another, part of the psyche into the field of inner perception.

But the unconscious is not merely a storehouse of experiences once conscious, now forgotten. It is the source of many elements in the conscious mind. Intuitions, phantasies, images, vague concepts, appear as we say "from nowhere" but their appearance is not accidental. For the unconscious is also a living, moving stream of energy from which rise those impulses and tendencies, those phantasies and ideas, which gradually emerge into consciousness and there take on definite form. It is as though the light penetrated into the deep waters and there revealed life of which we had no previous knowledge. Or, to use another analogy, the unconscious is the "mother lode" out of which the ore of the conscious is slowly mined. It contains not only forgotten or repressed elements, but other potentials which have not yet reached consciousness.

We must also differentiate in regard to the material which has once been conscious. Forgetting is of two kinds. Many things are forgotten because they are unimportant; to remember them would overburden the conscious with a weight of trivialities. But other things are forgotten because they are disturbing, unpleasant, or self-revealing. They are purposely forgotten, "repressed." Once disposed of, they can be recalled only with difficulty and the emotional reaction caused by remembering them often seems out of all proportion to the actual event or circumstance. Remembering them would interfere with our believing what we like to believe about ourselves, and so they must be kept out of sight.

But these repressed experiences have an energy greater than that of the experiences which are forgotten merely because they are unimportant, and this energy seeks an outlet. It may live in phantasy, daydream, vaguely disturbing mood, or it may return to consciousness in new emotional forms, as though, being denied admittance in their own right, these buried experiences and emotions masquerade as other characters and so steal their way back into the upper world of consciousness. They may come as fears, inhibitions, intolerant attitudes, arrogant assumptions, dislikes, or sudden intensities of warm emotion.

For instance, if we have injured someone and a sense of shame becomes attached to this memory, we may succeed in forgetting the special act, we may repress all memory of it, but it becomes unpleasant to us to see the person we injured. We begin to find reasons for disliking him. The emotion properly belonging to our own sense of shame reappears wearing the garb of dislike. In this new form we can place the blame on the one disliked. We can make him the scapegoat carrying the burden of our repressed memory. Our emotion, we believe, comes from *his* act, not our own.

Again, if another person has injured us, we "forget" it, but later we have an unreasonable distrust of a new acquaintance. If we examine our "unconscious" reactions we may find that in some way he suggests our former experience. We are predisposed to mistrust him. Or perhaps a memory of some childhood love suddenly stirs at the sight of a stranger and we find ourselves apparently magically involved with him. In such a case we are apt to demand that he should "live up to" our expectations—that is, that he should live out our idea of him instead of his own reality. When he refuses to embody this idea of ours, we feel that he has failed us, not that we have been indiscriminating.

This process of putting upon another person the burden of our own repressed emotion is commonly known as *projection*. Whenever we are obsessively bound to any person whether it be through love or hate, so that *we cannot seem to escape* from him, we may feel sure that this overintensive quality of the emotion is a form of projection. Thus we remain unconscious of much of our own inner experience, our emotions, prejudices, dominating ideas, through the assumption that the forces which determine our life lie outside ourselves instead of within us.

Another form of unconsciousness which stands between us and a knowledge of who and what we really are is known as *identification*. Identification is a process whereby ideas, attitudes, and ambitions which we have absorbed from without and taken into our psychic system reappear as though they were our own. They are not subjected to conscious scrutiny, they are not questioned, their appearance is spontaneous, effortless, and therefore assumed to have originated within ourselves. For instance, admiration, gratitude, love for another person may make us feel that what the object of these emotions does is what we should do. We accept his pattern of life as the desirable one without subjecting it to criticism. We swallow the other person's beliefs and prejudices whole; we "identify with" him. Only when confronted by a conflict between old, accepted ideas and desires and emotions aroused by a new situation or by a sudden failure in our work or our emotional life which brings us face to face with the realization that this excellent idea has not worked—only then do we begin to wonder whether, psychologically speaking, we have eaten some food that did not agree with us.

Our concepts of life are combinations of objective reality and subjective attitude. In this way our world becomes peopled not by human beings as they really are, but by images of our own conceiving. Two daughters may describe a mother in such varying terms that you feel they must be talking of two different individuals. They have described not the parent but a parental image. Two people (a golfing friend and an employee) describe a man to us, and their descriptions bear little resemblance to each other. We meet him and the image we form of him differs from either of the others. Which is the image of reality? Where does the truth lie?

We realize that in each case the person is telling the truth *as he sees it*, he is describing an image that *to him* expresses the reality of the person. Our personal experiences and our temperamental prejudices are continually at work forming images, not only of people but of ideals and concepts, by which we judge, evaluate and determine much of our conscious life. Nor is the image a mere psychic reproduction of an objective reality. Into its formation enter the emotions, the personal reactions, and the imaginative concepts about the object. All these elements combine to form an image which is a blending of the objective and the subjective. How much this image conforms to outer reality depends upon the psychic background of the individual.

The images which owe their origin to our own personal experience, and move in the region of the *personal* unconscious, are also determined by the impact of ideas, values, and attitudes imposed upon us by the social collective milieu. We cannot escape the impressions of the time and place in which we live, they are all around us, permeating the very air we breathe. We take them for granted, much as we do sun and rain. It is not until a conflict arises that we begin to question them. Even then it is difficult for us to judge and evaluate them. Only very slowly do we submit them to conscious scrutiny. From these collective social ideas we derive our ideas of good and evil. And these concepts, regarded as fundamental, early become part of our unconscious reactions to life. A "good woman" in the Victorian era was quite different from a good woman today. The ideas and ideals of our own generation, our own social class, are to a greater or less extent taken as our own. To the extent that they are an accepted part of life, they color all our judgments and choices. The concepts which we take as a matter of course have come to us ready-made as a part of our environment and inheritance. They are collective ideas, not sufficiently appraised by individual consciousness to be made our own.

All collective ideas deal with generalities, and therefore they may serve only as refuges from thought. As soon as one takes over a moral or social code or creed, swallows it whole, the power of discrimination is lost. It becomes an *a priori* truth which no longer needs to be tested by its relation to the reality of the immediate situation. If we have become identified with a collective ideal, a thing is good or bad, desirable or undesirable, not in accordance with its actual value in the special instance, but in accordance with its conformity to the accepted code, and people are good or bad as they conform to the ideal image created by the code.

A social collective ideal, which has been swallowed whole, such as unselfishness, self-sacrifice, a "gentleman's word," and so on, lives very contentedly in the unconscious, and from there may direct conscious activity with silent but autonomous authority. Hence the great confusion when we find that what seemed the right act has produced the wrong result. Since the act was ideal, the blame must be laid elsewhere, on the other fellow, or on the injustice of life. Yet sometimes a suspicion arises. Was something perhaps wrong inside ourselves? Have we taken the trouble to think out this situation for ourselves? Or has our concept, our image, of a social collective ideal been doing the thinking for us? At such a time, common sense may come to the rescue, and show us how unmindful we have been of the real demands of the situation. Or it may be that the unconscious will give us some information; for it is in the unconscious, after all, that the image lives, and it is from the unconscious that we may obtain a picture of what it is really doing.

A woman who was truly anxious to help a youth in a difficult position learned that he had been offered an opportunity which he felt would enable him to enter his chosen field of work. To accept this opportunity, he would have to give up the uninteresting job on which he depended for his self-support. She studied the situation carefully and decided that by practicing certain self-denials she would be able to furnish him with money enough to support him during the interim. She also thought very carefully about the situation from his point of view. She felt quite sure the opportunity was one in which he could develop his talent and achieve success, and her own sacrifice seemed meritorious. She decided therefore upon the "unselfish" course and went to sleep satisfied. But a strange dream intruded:

She was standing in a large bare room. At her feet was a gleaming two-edged sword. In front of her stood the youth naked, and as she looked at him a voice said, "You can cut off his testicles if you want to."

She woke with a shock—the dream seemed remote and barbarous, yet it was too vivid to dismiss. It touched her too deeply to be disregarded. Was this then what her "unselfishness" might do?—take from him his virility, rob him of his ability to be a man? —destroy his own independence and so leave him dependent upon her? Had her unselfishness any hidden motive of power? All these questions came as she faced the images that the dream portrayed. What realities had she forgotten when she made her unselfish decision? She recalled small instances of his too-easy acceptance of help, of his reluctance to face difficult realities, of his insistence upon the potential that he was to bring forth in the future rather than upon the present achievement. She had consciously concentrated upon his talent and its demands—she had repressed her intuitions of his need of struggle and independence as a man. She saw repressed desires within herself that had made her wish to hold him, through ties of gratitude, to a childish relation to her, desires she had disposed of by permitting the ideal image to swallow them up. So the unconscious had showed her the forgotten elements of the situation and, looking upon her unselfish act in relation to these, she reversed her decision and realized that what might seem ruthless selfishness might serve life better than any apparent selflessness.

We think of the dream as something which takes us away from reality into an irrational and phantastic world. Yet quite clearly the value of this dream was that it brought the dreamer face-to-face not only with the subjective elements, but with the reality of the objective situation. In her concentration upon a theory of life very good in general, she had forgotten to look at what was just in front of her nose—the real young man, his real situation, and his real need at that particular time. The dream was mercilessly factual. It showed how she had "identified" with the collective ideal of the unselfish person, and how that ideal image had dominated her conscious choice.

But though this dream applied directly to the dreamer's personal situation, and though its meaning showed her the conflict between the collective ideal and the individual values involved, the images in it were not ones derived from personal experiences. The dream conveyed to her a sense of remoteness, as though it had been evoked from a far distant past; and she realized that her experience was not unique but one which had, in one form or another, been faced by many people in many times. The symbols used in this dream were certainly not ones which she would have arrived at through a process of conscious thought, and quite as certainly they did not relate to forgotten personal experience. They expressed a modern experience in images natural to primitive man, to ancient religions. The testicles here denoted the container of the seed, the virility, the creative energy which is inherent in the masculine psyche. As such a symbol they appear in old religious rites and in primitive attitudes. Through this energy (this seed) the youth creates his own life and manhood.

The sword is also an ancient symbol—a symbol of destructive power, not merely in its negative form, but in the positive and creative form of the destruction of evil. To her the two-edged sword symbolized a great idea, a truth which could cleave through darkness and so destroy the old, the regressive. In the dream she was struck by the beauty of this gleaming sword; that is, the idea of sacrifice, the giving up of an old desired value to set free a greater value, was essentially beautiful. But in her hands, if used indiscriminately, this idea could be destructive. For should her act of sacrifice deprive this youth of independence, it would also deprive him of the essential side of his own masculine being. It would destroy him as a man.

The perception, supplied by the dream, of the issues involved in this immediate situation connected her with something far deeper than that moment of personal experience. She had been shown a picture of the essential values contained in a typical human experience. Through this she was able to perceive that she was confronted with an eternal question—what do you do when you assume the responsibility for another person's life? Is your decision based upon a theory or upon a consideration of immediate values? Her identification with a superimposed ideal had destroyed her perception and she was about to fall into an age-old trap; that of believing oneself to be generous while one is actually at the mercy of an unconscious power motive which would destroy the independence of another person.

When a dream pictures a problem which is ancient, yet constantly recurring, it frequently uses symbols which are outside the personal experience, and which come from a region which has been termed the collective unconscious, collective because common to all mankind. The personal unconscious is made up of repressed memories, emotional complexes, forgotten experiences, and subliminal impressions never intense enough to have become conscious—all of which are part of the purely personal psychic life. But in the collective unconscious are all the supra-personal psychic elements which are common to everyone. It is part of our inheritance. It is a congenital psychic background.

The images arising spontaneously from this source appear within the psyche in many times and many places. They have been built up by countless experiences, throughout many ages—and each one of them, therefore, embodies the essential meaning of a typical human experience. As a matter of fact, we are already familiar with them in mythology and folklore. In these, gods, demons, witches, magicians, all appear as embodiments of instinctive traits (hate, love, power, etc.), and the movement of the myth is a dramatization of some problem common to all mankind. We think of these myths as belonging to a far-distant past, but when we study dreams we find these same images reappearing within the psyche and the movement of the dream again repeats the dramatization of the problem.

The problem may be unmistakably one which though personal must be met by every human being. For instance, the child must give up his dependence and accept adult responsibility. This means that he must cease to turn to the mother for guidance, for otherwise the love she gives him becomes a menace to his growing manhood. He begins to have resentments toward her, fear of her authority, for he vaguely feels it is *she* who wishes to rule him. In countless dreams of adolescents, the mother has appeared as witch, or ogress, or as a dragon which must be overcome.

When the adolescent dreams in this way there is a merging of the personal aspects of his problem with something more general, more universal, something which appears to be part of the collective experience of mankind. The archaic images of his dream are clearly derived from ancient human experience.

Whether or not such an image makes its appearance in dreams, it is usually in the emotional background. We become aware of its existence when we discuss the problem in a way which we consider factual and practical. We may see the youth who longs for his adult freedom beset by conscientious doubts—his mother has done so much; she loves him; she is really so good and unselfish—after all, she is Mother. As he talks we see the image of the Divine Mother, the Mother of Compassion hovering in the background. Then the thought of his own necessity intrudes. He speaks of her eternal demands on him, the way she intrudes into all his affairs, how he wishes she would not always be asking him to do things because she loves him, or for his own good. She smothers the life out of him. The mental picture has shifted, a new image has appeared. Such a young man cannot be reasonable and fair-minded because the intensity of the emotional situation is too great. But if he can see his situation as a universal psychological experience he can recognize it as being essentially his own inner battle—a conflict with the forces of the unconscious.

In such general situations, therefore, there is always a merging of the personal and collective aspects of the problem. It is as though behind the personal images move these greater ones. Behind the father is the Jehovah God, behind the teacher is the Wise Old Man, behind the mother is the Terrible Mother or the image of divine compassion. To understand those images means to understand ourselves as part of the greater impersonal life of humanity. Through them we can perceive meanings which are hidden to us when we regard ourselves as isolated individuals and our life as merely personal. Out of those events of our personal life which have a root in universal experience, we can learn to accept universal meanings. The images which embody those meanings have been termed the archetypes, or *representations collectives;* they are personifications of the typical in psychic experience.

These archetypes may appear in supra-personal form, as god or demon, witch, magician, child-savior, imp or dwarf. Or they may be contained in a symbol which stirs in man a sense of some meaning of life not yet fully comprehended. It rouses in him something that has to do with forces not limited to the merely personal. The cross, the crescent, the pearl, the golden flower, are symbolic expressions of deeply buried truth. They awaken an energy which is connected with the idea embodied in them.

As we study the material of many dreams we see certain images which appear so frequently and whose meaning seems so general that unless there is a contradictory personal association (which means that in this case the symbol relates definitely to the dreamer's personal past) we are warranted in assuming them to be of archetypal origin. Water is a universal symbol of the unconscious; the vastness of the ocean suggests the vastness of the unconscious life. Its changing motion, its depth and the treasures which may be found far below its surface all make it a *natural* symbol of the unexplored depths within the self. Fish also may appear as the contents of the unconscious, something to be drawn up from its waters. The great fish, the whale, often appears as a force which can swallow up the conscious (the most familiar example of this is found in the myth of Jonah swallowed by the whale). The star in a dream may be the symbol of a guiding light, the wind a symbol of the breath of the spirit, the rose, of the center of the being and also of the power of growth within the human psyche.

There are, of course, times when it is impossible to know whether the symbol has appeared as a result of previous knowledge, or whether it has arisen from the collective unconscious. But there are also many dreams where an image appears of which the person has, and would have had, no previous knowledge; and from which, once its archetypal significance is made clear to him, he gets a connection with the energy which it contains. The spontaneous appearance of the same symbol in different races and cultures, and the spontaneous appearance of these great symbols in the psyche of a person who has no conscious knowledge of them, warrants an hypothesis of a collective unconscious. The fact that this hypothesis *works*, that the acceptance of it enables one to obtain valuable psychological results not otherwise obtainable, warrants our use of it, at least until we can replace it by a more adequate one.

The images of the collective unconscious, like those from the personal unconscious, reveal themselves in dream, daydream, moving phantasy, vision or drawing. As we study this material we see that there are certain typical figures which emerge. These vary in every individual, yet they have a sufficient similarity to permit the use of certain classifications which will help us to understand them.

In early life most of the energy goes to the development of ego-consciousness. As we shall see in more detail later, in this development the images which the child forms of its father and mother will play a leading role. Even after childhood, they will continue to play an important part, if they remain active agents in the unconscious. The examination of these images helps us to understand the elements which have entered into the building up of our own personal ego. This ego, the conscious personality, has to deal with outer experience. In the struggle to do this, it fashions for itself an image of a being who can meet the world, a being who can withstand the outer assaults and also gain for itself its own worldly desires. This image is called the Persona, the conscious face, the mask which is shown to the world. But there are other elements which are quite at variance with this Persona self, dark and dubious qualities lurking like shadows in the background of consciousness. These unrecognized elements of the personality are often embodied in unconscious material, in an image which is called the Shadow. Again, in a man's dreams, there appear figures of women which represent both his ideas about women and his own feminine attributes. This feminine image in the unconscious is called the Anima. And its counterpart, the masculine image in the unconscious of woman, is called the Animus. We gain more power of choice as we gain consciousness of these conflicting elements.

As soon as one attempts to give a precise definition of these images, one is confronted with the fact that they are vague, shifting, imprecise. An image rarely arises in sharply defined form, nor does a particular image appear only at a certain period of life. They are always changing, appearing, disappearing, returning in some new form as the conscious problems change. Yet as one studies the material of the unconscious one gains a certain familiarity with typical traits of the psyche, even though these traits appear in varying guises.

The chapters which make up the first part of this book are in no way to be confused with a description of analytical procedure, for no analysis moves from image to image, from one designated point to another. The concept of individuation (which may arise within the psyche through experience of a great idea or in dream or vision) may happen in early life or early in an analytical procedure. It is a concept, not a *fait accompli*. These chapters are merely definitions which are applicable to the actual case material in the later chapters. To see the inner drama in which these images play their part one must follow such a case as the one given from page 164 to page 220, where we see that the life of the image is not dependent upon our conscious decision or intellectual understanding.

An increased understanding of these images moving in the unconscious gives one a chance to reckon with them with greater clarity and have more understanding of our real motives and desires. It would be convenient if the images marched along in the order given, but unfortunately they do nothing of the sort. Nor is the concept and process of individuation one which has appeared in the world with the birth of modern psychology. Nothing in the process is new except the technique of approach, the attitude toward the reality of the inner experience. Though the designation "the unconscious" belongs to modern psychological terminology, the process by which one becomes aware of subliminal elements is not new; a willingness to examine the intrusive thought or the sudden disturbing emotion is not a quality which has newly developed through analytical psychology.

We all know people whom we meet and can never forget because they seem rooted in their own being; their words, their acts, all seem part of themselves. Whether they have arrived at this place through analysis or not is a matter of no consequence. It is the attitude which counts. Such people remind us of trees whose roots are deep in the earth, their life is a process of growth, their nature a maturing of some central germ, they are deeply themselves. They are also more than themselves because they are rooted in some universal form. We may find them in any walk of life, for their reality is not dependent upon outer circumstances but upon the fact that in some way they have always maintained their connection with themselves, and in the various experiences of life have accepted their own responsibility and have looked for the meaning behind each personal experience.

Perhaps we could best describe these people by saying that they do not accept life ready-made, as does the ordinary person Whether their thoughts are brilliant or simple, they are their own; whether their taste is crude or subtle it expresses something that they wish to express. Whatever they create in life, whether it be a philosophical theory, a work of art, or a human relation, it is their own creation, not something which they have taken over from outside. It is perhaps this creative quality in them which makes them stand apart. For the ordinary man accepts more than he creates. Yet this acceptance is often so unconscious a process that the thing which he makes appears to be his own choice, and his experiences seem to him to be unique and personal, though they may have become very far removed from any original creative source.

Man has always had an inclination to seek authority from without, to look for someone who will relieve him of responsibility for his own life. It may be in the security of a fixed creed, it may be in reliance upon a man whom he has made into an image of desired infallibility, that he hopes to find this absolute authority; for the archetypes are factors of life whether we accept them or not. Anyone seeing the effect of a symbol upon mass emotions (the flag, the swastika and the cross raised before a multitude) does not doubt its energizing value. But the energy is unconscious, undifferentiated. It is only when through an original experience one sees one's own relation to the symbol that it becomes an individual value and the energy which it contains is released and is available to the conscious.

The individual relation to the inner image is the subject of this book. It makes no attempt to cover the field of analytical psychology, but only to give special instances where the experience of the image has contributed to the growth and development of the individual. In each case, it is recorded exactly as it happened, except that in many instances much illuminating material has had to be omitted because of its personal nature. In the first half of the book an attempt is made to define certain typical images; the second part deals with illustrative material where the images are shown in their interplay, their constant reappearance, their varying forms.

II. THE APPEARANCE OF IMAGES

IN THE previous chapter a dream was cited as an illustration of the way in which images from the unconscious may help us to know what our motives in a given situation actually are. These images may appear in other ways, some of which will be discussed later, but they most often appear in dreams.

Everyone, at some time or other, dreams. This is a phenomenon so well known that no one questions that it is a normal one. When conscious attention is lessened the unconscious becomes activated. This ordinarily happens in sleep, for that is the time when we relinquish all conscious direction. Upon waking, the conscious springs again to control and the dream fades unless it has had such intensity as will carry over into the waking hours.

Many people believe that they do not dream. If, however, such people become interested in the unconscious, they "begin to dream," or, to speak more accurately, they begin to *remember* their dreams. The psychic activity which produces dreams is always going on, whether we are aware of it or not; for the activity of the unconscious is not dependent upon consciousness. It is a continuous process of our psychic life. Since the material of this book deals so largely with dream images, it seems almost necessary to say at once a few general words concerning dream analysis.

Dreams often have a trivial and grotesque character, and at first appear meaningless. But when we study them, they reveal themselves as fantastically portraying existing conditions. A few years ago a newspaper cartoon appeared which depicted an ancient spinster with ringlets and flounced petticoats riding a donkey; the beast is shying, terrified at the sight of a derby hat, and the old lady is in danger of being thrown. This picture would convey nothing but a comic situation to a foreigner unfamiliar with the

American political situation. The ordinary reader of the time knew, however, that the Democratic party had been thrown into consternation because Al Smith's hat, the famous brown derby, had been thrown into the presidential ring.

The dream is somewhat analogous to the cartoon. Just as we cannot understand a cartoon unless we know something of the situation it portrays, so, to understand the images that appear in dreams, we must learn their language, and how to translate and interpret them in the light of the conditions of the personal situations to which they relate. It is to the apparently trivial, easily ignored dreams that we must give our first attention, because they show us those forgotten elements in ourselves and in our outer situation with which we must reckon if we are to meet our personal life with understanding.

The particular truth which these personal dreams bring out is directly applicable to the dreamer himself. *An apparently grotesque and trivial dream may have a deep importance in showing what the dreamer's immediate difficulty actually is.* Sometimes it also gives a clue to the solution of the difficulty:

A young woman who had no belief in her own power of meeting the world had returned home after an unsuccessful attempt at independence. Though she felt a childish need for security, she resented her dependent position. Yet she was too distrustful of her abilities to make another attempt at living on her own.

She dreamed that she was back in her family's old summer estate where much of her childhood had been passed. This estate was on the coast, and in the dream she was standing in a familiar rocky cove. The rocks seemed more menacing than she had ever known them to be, the waves were dashing about her, the tide was rising. She must venture out upon the turbulent water. Boats were tossing about, some disappearing under the waves. Then she saw a curious little pink craft bobbing about, but not capsizing. A voice told her that this was the only boat which she could trust to take her safely, that she need not fear if she would embark in this. She looked closely and saw that it was a beetleware tooth mug.

The setting of this dream—the rocky coast, the stormy sea, the ships setting sail—was one which might have been related to the situation of any person who realized the necessity for taking up his independent life. But here it had a distinctly personal reference. The summer estate was associated in her mind with childhood pleasure and complete lack of responsibility; and also, at this time, with financial security. Nonetheless, the beetleware tooth mug was the only symbol which could not have been made to bear a general interpretation. It was peculiarly personal.

The young woman was asked if she had any association with this pink mug, and replied, "I have one in my own room." She was then asked why, of all the objects in her own room, should the dream choose this particular one. She was at first puzzled. Then she suddenly realized that this was the only thing in the room which she had bought with her own money.

Her own intuition now furnished the answer and she said, "It looks as though I would have to pay my own way." It was then suggested that money is often a symbol of one's own energy, one's psychic capital. In other words, if she was to take this voyage, set out on her own journey, find her own way, she must depend upon her own abilities, however small they might appear to her.

This young woman's conscious idea was that she had no resources within herself that she could trust. She underestimated her abilities because they were not talents, she distrusted her feelings and intuitions because she overvalued the intellect and was not intellectual. Her conscious mind was full of fear of life and of what would happen to her if she tried to be independent. So the apparently trivial symbol had an important meaning to her at this particular time. It said, "You can trust the thing that really belongs to you." The unconscious gave her a deeply needed assurance that her own resources could really be depended upon. Since she was consciously so full of fear and was so overdistrustful of herself she needed this compensatory picture from the unconscious; she needed to see the aspects of her situation that her fears had excluded from her conscious consideration.

For the dream has a compensatory and balancing quality. If the whole conscious attention is concentrated upon one aspect of a problem, the excluded and conflicting aspect becomes active in the unconscious, and the dream, portraying what is going on in the unconscious, reveals the other side which we need to remember in order to evaluate ourselves properly and to see the complete picture. It says, "This, too, is true." It is as though when the conscious is concentrated upon one aspect the unconscious said, "But this is the way things appear down here—you forget about this."

The dream, therefore, gives us a true picture, but often its truth is only comparative, the truth about one aspect which needs to be brought to our attention. Even when the dream startles us by its vivid, pertinent comment we cannot rely on this as the voice of infallible wisdom. We must connect it with our conscious attitude and our outer situation at the time. For we are full of contradictory elements: we can love and hate, fear and trust, desire and reject, and we must remember that both sides are present when we are in a tight place. Only by a comparison of the "affect" of the dream—that is, the degree of emotion aroused by it—with our own conscious attitude can we see that other aspect, and then choose for ourselves the side we will accept, always remembering the other side with which we must reckon. So the dream is continually reminding us of the part which our conscious is forgetting. It does not speak with any absolute authority; it simply gives a true picture of *a* situation which exists in the unconscious. It speaks truth; but not, as some persons believe, *the* truth. It shows the other side.

The interpretation of this dream was entirely dependent upon the dreamer's personal association with the tooth mug. Her own intuition furnished the association and verified its truth to her. Each detail of a dream is important, for each is related to some phase of the dreamer's situation. Dream symbols are not casual; and when a dream is carefully studied it will be seen how each detail helps, by its particular form, to clarify the picture, and can only be understood by considering its relation to the dreamer. This is why it is so dangerous to give a fixed interpretation to any symbol. It is only when the association "clicks" for the dreamer, when it carries an emotional conviction to him, that one can feel that the interpretation is the right one.

Even when the dream deals with symbols which ordinarily have a collective interpretation, we must consider the personal association. For when the personal association and the collective interpretation contradict each other, as they sometimes will, the personal association must always be given the priority. The following dream uses the image of a snake, a collective symbol which has appeared in hundreds of dreams to connote sexuality, earth wisdom, instinctual life. Its common interpretation in a dream is a sexual one, yet in the following dream the meaning was quite different and was discovered through personal associations:

"I heard the voices of people talking and laughing in the street. I looked out of the window and saw a conglomerate crowd of people, evidently having a very good time. I wanted to join them, but realized that I had on thin satin slippers, unsuitable for the street. I started to put on my street shoes but in one of them was a small green snake, curled up as though ready to strike. It seemed quite beautiful and I had no fear of it. I knew, however, that I must brush it out before I could put on the shoes, but as I tried to do this, its head began to flatten and there was an evil gleam in its eye. I then struck at it with the heel of my other shoe, but with each blow its head flattened slightly and it only became stronger and more venomous looking. Suddenly I grew terrified; I knew that I could never go into the street and mingle with the crowd unless I could kill that snake. I woke screaming."

She asked what the snake meant, and the obvious answer would have been that the snake was a sexual symbol and that the dream indicated an abnormal fear of sexuality. But since so often the obvious meaning is not the real one, it was suggested to her that the snake was hers and she should "look at it" and see if it could explain itself. That is, she should keep the dream image in her mind and see if spontaneous associations arose.

One day when she was trying to "look at it," that is, concentrating upon the dream image, a vivid association did arise. She saw the coat of arms which used to hang in the front hall of her family's home, and realized that this coat of arms had on it a snake exactly like the one in her dream. Then she remembered how, when she was a little girl, her mother had carefully chosen suitable playmates for her, and that when she was starting out to play her mother would sometimes point to the coat of arms and say, "Don't forget that you are a Vanderloon, and don't do anything a lady would be ashamed of." She had so faithfully kept this advice that it was no longer possible for her to see people as they really were. If she wished to describe a person, she described his family tree.

Now, at a time when she was beginning to long for a real life of her own, the unconscious presented this picture which said, "Your greatest peril is symbolized by your own coat of arms. Until you can overcome this sense of the importance of your ancestors, you cannot go down into the street and mingle with all kinds of people and meet the common experiences of life."

This woman was very much disturbed because she could not make friends easily. She felt she was not wanted. If she had been told, "You are a snob, you care much more about family position than personal worth," she would have denied it indignantly. But when her own dream of the snake was associated with the ancestral coat of arms and with her own childhood and had showed her how these attitudes had grown up in her without her knowledge, then she could not repudiate the meaning of this dream.

If the snake had been used as a collective symbol of sexuality in interpreting this dream, its special value to the dreamer would have been destroyed. Often the "obvious" interpretation is accepted because the dream seems so obscure that no other meaning can be found, but a subsequent dream may appear which throws a new light and reveals the real meaning of the symbol. It is, therefore, necessary to study many dreams so as to see the different factors at work. Though an occasional dream may be so vivid and clear that we can see its application to the existing situation in the dreamer's inner life, it is only by studying a series of dreams that we can understand the movement of the unconscious and the relation of the dream symbol to the personal or individual life of the dreamer. When the dream is studied in this way one can see an interplay between the conscious and the unconscious. For a personal dream must be interpreted in relation to the *conscious* life of the dreamer. As this conscious changes and different factors are "forgotten," these become active in the unconscious and reappear in dream. Contradictory aspects really exist in the unconscious, and dreams which mirror the unconscious may say first one thing and then another.

The following dreams came to a woman at a time when a better understanding of her relation to her husband was the paramount problem: One night she dreamed that her husband turned into a sinister man, waiting to steal her jewels. She was sure this dream was a picture of his real nature, and that it warned her not to return to him. On the next night came a dream that her little white dog had been lost and now came back, and that she received him with joy. This little dog had been given her by her husband, and had symbolized to her the instinctual bond between them. In this meaning the little dog had appeared in many previous dreams.

She woke with a sense that all was well; she would return home. But immediately the picture of the sinister man returned. She was thrown into great emotional confusion by these dreams, and felt that she could not trust her own unconscious. Yet it was very clearly showing something which she must at this time recognize; that both of these elements existed in the actual situation with her husband and, what was more important, that these two types of feeling existed within herself. She was naturally outgoing and warmly emotional, yet she would at times become a prey to doubt and distrust which she projected upon anyone with whom she had any strong relationship.

The dream said: "These contradictory feelings exist in you—they are the motive forces acting below the surface of your conscious thoughts and feelings. These dreams show also your intuitive perceptions of contradictory sides of your husband's nature. Try to remain conscious of these contradictions both in him and in yourself. Remember the situation is neither all good nor all bad, but a mixture of both. You must try and keep both these aspects in consciousness when you are making a decision that affects the relationship."

If a dream vividly portrays a side of the personality which the conscious wishes to ignore, and if the dreamer refuses to acknowledge it is a picture of something which exists within himself and for which he is responsible, then this side may reappear over and over in varying forms, until it has been accepted both intellectually and emotionally. A woman who had a very destructive side which frequently took possession of her at critical times was unable to see this element in herself as the cause of her many disasters. She was greatly interested in dreams as presenting an inner drama, but whenever her destructive side actually rose in real life, she felt the true cause of the resultant difficulty lay in other people or in a deep injustice in life itself. This destructive side appeared over and over—at least thirty times—in different forms in dreams, as a prowling beast suddenly loosed, as a furious man, as an insane woman. Still, she did not accept it as something within herself for which she and she alone was responsible. Then came the following dream:

"A huge, vicious horse, with his forelegs planted firmly, was blocking the doorway of a house I had to enter. It was on an empty village street, and I stood in the road, terrified, not knowing what to do. Whenever I moved toward him, he bared his teeth but otherwise remained immovable as a marble statue, barring my way to the house. Then the horse seemed about to step into the street and, frantic with terror, I ran to the house on the other side and banged on the door, demanding to be let in. When no one answered, I tried the handle and discovered that the door had been open all the time. The top of the door was of glass and through it I could see the horse coming. I slammed the door and locked it. When I looked through the glass again, I saw, close against it, not the horse but the brutalized face of a heavyweight boxer, whose ugly little eyes met mine threateningly. I shouted that if he tried to hurt me I would call the police and, though he did not move, I ran to the window and began to yell. The face outside the glass was shadowy, but all the more terrible for that."

At this time she was faced with an outer situation which put her under a really intense strain. Fed by fear, resentment, self-pity, the old destructive energy stirred and rose within her. Acting in blind anger, she did violence to a relationship, believing the fault was not hers. She was sure that her own outrageous behaviour was an inevitable response to the injustice of others. Then, on returning home, still in the grip of this force, she happened to see her face in the glass, and was terrified by its resemblance to the face of the boxer into whom the horse had turned. At last, she saw this evil thing as something which at times actually became herself and, in so doing, she was able to say, "This is a real part of me. I did this thing," and to accept her own responsibility.

In this woman's case, it seemed as though the unconscious with infinite patience had repeated this lesson over and over, trying with new images, new pictures, to show her the truth. To express this relationship between unconscious images and conscious life is not the same as asserting that the unconscious is purposeful and itself acts with consciousness. The unconscious simply paints the picture, this picture, that picture, as the sea may cast up treasures on any shore; what use we make of these things is entirely our own affair.

In each case the event, whether dream or outer happening, must be accepted as an experience. It is as true with dreams as with life events that the importance of the happening itself is secondary to the importance of what we do with it. The dream does indicate that something has happened in the unconscious, that an event has actually taken place. If we will accept this inner event, experience it, make it part of our consciously lived life, then it becomes a potent factor, it produces change; we go from there to a new grasp, a deeper reality.

So, in the evolution of a young man's dreams, the changes in his attitude toward sexuality were shown by the changes of the symbol appearing in his unconscious material. At the beginning of this series of dreams he had the attitude that sexuality was merely a physical act to be accepted for itself and not connected with feeling or responsibility. You "played fair," that is, made no pretenses. You did not involve a woman but were "completely frank," and took what came. This attitude protected him from any necessity for forming permanent relations. The unconscious, however, furnished a different picture:

He dreamed of a negro, apparently likable, smiling, inconsequential; then he became aware that this smiling figure carried a knife and was ready at any moment to stab him in the back.

This negro he felt to be the instinctual side of himself. In fact, the figure distinctly suggested his own external friendliness. The back often appears in dreams as the unconscious, the region we cannot see. It was from this region that the danger would come, because he was unconscious of what he was really doing, of the values he was destroying by his irresponsibility. The smiling, instinctual side had become a peril to him. He himself interpreted the knife as the threatening aspect of his sexuality.

He began to study the nature of this peril and his first reaction was that this instinctual side must be repressed because it was dangerous. But the instincts had something to say about that, and he found that the "repressed" sexuality had only taken on new activity and was constantly intruding into his thoughts and phantasies. It was quite evident he would have to find another way of dealing with it. Into his dreams were coming other images which dealt with his problems of feeling and masculine adaptation; and then came the following dream:

He found he was the owner of a snake which was friendly to the Chinese but terrifying to the Japanese. To him the Chinese were an introverted, reflective race who lived deeply in experience and had an inner connection with wisdom about human life. They also were a simple people deeply connected with the earth. The Japanese, on the other hand, represented to him extraverted activity, they were opportunists who seized upon the momentary advantage, whose thinking was specious and plausible, who were bent on getting what they wanted in the outside world.

It is always important to remember that it is *what an image means to the dreamer* that must be considered in the interpretation. We therefore are not so concerned with what the symbol actually means as with what it means to the dreamer. So this dream, interpreted by his own associations, showed him that though his sexuality in its "Japanese" aspect was a danger, it had another aspect, the "Chinese," a connection with real experience and inner value; and that it could be friendly in this form and accepted in connection with feeling and real life.

In the next dream he again saw a snake, this time gliding over the water. It had (quite surprisingly) long silky ears. When he waked he realized that these ears were those of his hound, who had always appeared in his dreams as an image of loyal feeling. Now in the dream image the snake began to partake of the nature of the hound. In this curious way the unconscious seemed to bring these two symbols together.

During this time—for the dreams were spaced over quite an interval—his feeling had undergone a considerable change and he had a very new attitude toward relationships, though there was still a good deal of conflict in his ideas about sexuality.

He dreamed that he again saw a snake with hound's ears, but this time it had a softly feathered breast, and he knew that he could pluck these feathers to make a warm coat for K, the young woman he had learned to love. Out of his sexuality something warm, tender and protective was growing. As he understood this dream, he perceived a change had taken place, that feeling and sexuality had come together. He became aware that his whole attitude had changed, that he no longer desired casual and irresponsible expressions of his sexuality. The violent conflict between conscious decision and unconscious desire had ceased.

In these dreams the snake appeared as a collective image. That is, it was used as a symbol taking on one of the meanings in which it has appeared in dream and myth throughout countless ages. Though one can never insist upon the collective aspect of a particular dream, sometimes the collective images appear so graphically that there is no mistaking their meaning.

A woman of a very gentle Victorian type, who felt sexuality to be a concession to the strange law of procreation, acceptable only as a marital duty, dreamed:

"I came into the living room. In front of the fireplace was a snake seated in a rocking chair, with a bonnet on its head. The bonnet strings were tied in a bow beneath what would have been the snake's chin—if the snake had had a chin—giving it a chaste, matronly look. I said to myself, 'I suppose as long as it sits in the rocking chair and keeps its bonnet on, it can do no harm in the house.'"

This dream was told with the utmost naïveté, and with no realization of the way in which this absurd image satirized her own limitations.

In another person's dream this same symbol appeared in its true collective—that is, its supra-personal—form. It was shown as a force greater than the individual, a force inherent in each one of us:

"I was in a great cave where I was about to build a fire. It seemed like a place which I had taken over as my own. Suddenly I became aware of a great snake watching me from the dark recesses of the cave. I felt quite indignant at his presence and went up close to him and said, 'This is my cave and I must ask you to get out.' He looked straight in my eyes and said, 'I was here a long time before you came, and I shall be here a long time after you are gone. You had better learn to live with me.'"

This particular dreamer had a delightful little theory that one could sublimate all one's instincts; that life was a purely personal affair which each one decided for himself. But the serpent brings to his attention the fact that he is part of a life greater than the personal, and that it is wise to make friends with one's instincts because they are rooted in universal soil. They belong to a great collective life in which we must continue to share. This snake, quite clearly, was an inhabitant of a world quite different from that of the little green snake in the shoe. He did not owe his origin to a merely personal situation—that is, he did not derive his existence from a prejudice connected with a family coat of arms, or from any situation personal to the dreamer, but from a universal instinct. He was a collective symbol, an archetypal snake.

Such symbols may appear to any of us at any time—we have most of us had extraordinarily beautiful or terrifying dreams which seemed unrelated to ordinary life and which remained in our mind for days or years, perhaps even lingered on from childhood memories. But when we become interested in our dreams, especially when we study them analytically, we see that they generally move in series, so that really to understand them we must study their relation to each other. They are not always as clear and vivid as the ones quoted, but they all have a meaning and they relate to a process which is going on continually in our inner life. In an analysis the early dreams usually deal with these personal problems. It is as though one had to meet the small personal difficulties, clear away the petty entanglements, before one could perceive the greater, the more impersonal aspects of life.

Even small, personal dreams frequently have a double aspect. They not only show the difficulty but also suggest a way out. As in the first dream cited, that of the beetleware tooth mug, both the difficulty and the solution are indicated. Yet the situations are very personal and the way out has to do with a more efficient adaptation to every day life.

There must come a time, however, when the important thing is not to uncover all these early difficulties, but to see our relation to a life which is greater than our own personal problems. It is at this time that dreams often take on a larger, more universal aspect. It is this quality of universality that marks the distinction between the dreams which arise from the superficial layers of the personal unconscious, and those which come from the deeper collective layers. The personal dream deals with the imagery of the personal emotional complex, that is, the overemphasized affect which destroys our sense of proportion. The collective dream deals with the image of racial experience—the archetype.

Archetypal dreams may appear incidentally in the early reductive stages of an analysis, but when the investigation of the personal material has resolved the emotionally toned complex, a change takes place in the material of the dream. The archetypal dream is more frequent, and brings with it a sense of liberation and a conviction that through inner experience one can turn away from the past toward the future. The archetypal dream in such cases is often followed by a personal dream, which indicates what we ourselves can do to make the new way possible.

The following dreams may give some idea of this process; they were the dreams of a homosexual man who felt that he needed help not because of his homosexuality but because of a neurotic physical symptom which separated him from a normal life. The homosexuality started when he was a very small boy. He was the weakest child of a sturdy family. He was an intensely lonely boy, always trying to get a relation with some man who would be a father to him. Deep in his unconscious was a conviction that he was really not a man himself and never could be one; and his search for a man to whom he could attach himself made all his images of love turn away from women and toward men.

Then, as he grew older, shame and a feeling for the necessity of great secrecy overwhelmed him. He tried to push his emotions down into the unconscious, not realizing that there they would only gain strength and take on more and more infantile and regressive forms, and finally become stronger than he was himself.

Up to this time, over a period of months, the dream associations had always returned to his early childish memories and the variations of his homosexual phantasies. And yet they had indicated in these variations a change in attitude toward sexuality. He was beginning to understand more clearly how these phantasies had come into being and was trying not to repress them but to deal with them. The following dream was the culmination of a long series:

"X came to me and said, 'Show me the statues of Y and Z which you have in your room.' I went into the room to get them but they both were gone, and in their place was an image of the Mother and the Child."

X was a former physician for whom he had a deep feeling, but also a strong homosexual attraction. Y and Z were men whom he knew as homosexuals. They were all connected with his personal experiences. But now these images were gone and in their place were universal images, ones which have been spiritual symbols in every religion.

His immediate desire was to reduce these images back to the personal level, to become a child and to force the analyst into the role of loving mother. But these were not images from his personal life, they were supra-personal and to experience them he had himself to go beyond the merely personal.

The next night he dreamed that he saw a mother and a father with a little crippled boy; then father and mother were gone and the dreamer was on a bench in the park. He became aware that the little crippled boy was seated on the bench by his side. The child seemed neglected and pitiful. He smiled at the boy, who at first drew away, but then came near him and leaned against his shoulder. He had a feeling of fondness and responsibility for the child; that he must "give the kid a break," and look after him himself.

He woke with a feeling of strength that was quite irrational but none the less real. Something had happened in his inner life. The experience of the dream was more vital than any he had had in actual life. There was a sense of freedom from the old compelling images; something new had been born. It was symbolized by this child. The image of the Child with the Divine Mother and that of the neglected cripple were curiously one.

He now realized that he had misinterpreted the other dream. It was intended to portray the birth of a new value, which is the meaning of the eternal child (the Savior). Through the acceptance of this new value, he could follow the way indicated in the second dream. The child is within himself, it is the image of a new attitude. It is crippled, as this spiritual side of himself always has been crippled. But its positive power is shown from his own emotional experience, the sense of strength and energy that came to him on awakening. This energy came from the birth within himself of a concept which is old and universal.

Frequently a dream which uses one of the great impersonal images, such as the mother and child, or the medicine man, or the prophet, or one of the mythological heroes, marks for the dreamer a real transition. The dreams begin to deal with new life, new attitudes. They are prophetic, not in the way that was accepted in antiquity as foretelling outer events which will happen, but prophetic in showing what is about to develop within the psyche. Dreams of this sort will be discussed in later chapters in other connections. They are more readily understood when one is familiar with those images whose influence is felt in all our lives, whether or not we perceive them in the material of the unconscious, and which appear in the experience of most normal persons who give any attention to the unconscious.

Before turning to a discussion of one variety of them, the parental images, it may be well to repeat that the images of the unconscious may appear in waking phantasy, as well as in dreams; they may present themselves as visions; they may seek representation in drawings or paintings. Such manifestations will be discussed later in the book in connection with certain special instances where most of the material came in one of these forms.

III. PARENTAL IMAGES

THE ORDINARY person who begins to study his dreams is usually surprised to discover how much they have to do with his relation to his parents. He may have left home years before, both his parents may be dead, and he may rarely recall them to mind. Nevertheless their influence persists in his unconscious.

A man whose father had been dead for many years and who prided himself on his complete independence brought this to an analyst as his first dream:

"I am going to get my automobile which I have left in a shed near an amusement park. I find it and start to drive out. Suddenly I know that it is not mine though it looks exactly like it. I go to search for my own. I find it down in the cellar. There is only one exit—a long spiral staircase. I must get it up this. Then I know someone is helping me. I wake."

The cellar which he saw in the dream was the actual cellar of his childhood home. It was the place where, as a very small boy, he had gone to do as he pleased, to work out his own small inventions. They were secrets from his father. When he was only eight he had moved from this house, started in a school approved by his father, put away childish things, begun to be a man. But being a man had meant taking over his father's ideals—those of a self-righteous, idealistic, dominating father, ruling under the guise of serving the world. He followed this father pattern faithfully, trying to become like the paternal image, though unconsciously always rebelling.

Then he "threw off the yoke." He went a way very different from the prescribed paternal one. He violently advocated iconoclastic, modern movements which were anathema in the family home. He embraced one "ism" after another and became the missionary apostle of the new creed, each time following, he supposed, his own convictions. Yet nothing lasted.

The dream showed that what he supposed to be his own automobile, his way of getting about, his way of life, seemed to be his but was not; that to find a way of life which was really his own, he had to go back to the place where, as a child, he had followed his own inclinations without regard for his father's ideas. In some irrational way (represented by the spiral staircase), which would take a long time, he had to bring his own way of life up into the daylight of the conscious world.

In this dream no image of the father appeared. The automobile left in the shed was not recognized as his father's. But his association with the cellar showed that whenever he came up from the cellar he entered a world which his father ruled.

Another man's dream, which also was the first to come after analytical work had begun, presented actual, though vague, parental images. He was a man who had no conscious sense of being dominated by his father or family. After all, he had not lived at home for more than twenty years:

"I was alone in a dark shadowy forest seated by a very small fire. Suddenly a great owl dropped from a tree and beat out the fire with his wings. Then he started off in the forest, half flying, half fluttering near the ground. I followed him. He led me to an opening in the side of a hill. We entered, and I found myself in a subterranean cave. The owl disappeared, and I had a candle in my hand. In the dim light I saw the cave was full of images. At first I felt, rather than saw, that they were images of my own family. As I came up to the first one and lifted up the candle, I found that I was looking at the face of my grandmother. I was filled with fear but continued to look, and slowly the image dissolved before my eyes. Then I woke, but the feeling of the dream was so strong that I still retained the knowledge that I must look at each one of those figures until it, too, should dissolve."

The dreamer associated the owl with the bird of Minerva, the goddess of wisdom. He saw it also as the bird who can see best at night, hence as representing a wisdom connected with the time of sleep and of dreaming. The candle as a light made by man was to him a symbol of consciousness. In the dream the owl takes him to the cave where he will find the images, forgotten but still existing, but he must himself turn the light of consciousness upon them.

The light falls first upon the grandmother. Hence conscious consideration must be given to her. Although he spoke of her with tolerant amusement, thinking of her as of someone long since dead and gone, it soon appeared that she had been a dominant figure in the household. She had treated her daughter, the dreamer's mother, as though she were still a child. She had been the deeply religious member of the family; she was forever "making her peace with God." Hence God had seemed to him a being to be propitiated. His childish fears, he recalled, were all confused with this concept of a stern, exacting deity; God and the devil to him had been two almost equally unpleasant characters. Sometimes his grandmother had seemed to him like a witch who knew all the dark secrets connected with these two personages.

After this came recollections of nursery magic rites by which he had tried to keep evil away at night, formulas in a language which he had invented, ways of getting into bed backward, arrangements of furniture, and many others. All these magic rites were connected with a sense of guilt, a need of propitiating unknown powers, and were closely associated with the image of his grandmother.

It was now possible for him to understand why in the dream he had to examine this image of the grandmother, for the discussion of his early fears brought to light the fact that they were still alive in him, and that he still had little superstitious habits which were really expressions of that same primitive fear persisting in his unconscious. Although he had supposed himself to be wholly rational in his attitude toward religion, it now appeared that much which was irrational remained, and that his emotions were in many ways determined by these infantile superstitions.

The image most closely connected with that of the grandmother was naturally that of the mother. She had been a woman constantly beset by fears. Although he had loved her, he had perceived—with that strange intuition which children have—these fears of his mother's and had been made afraid by them. Hence he had unconsciously tried to separate himself from her. Because of this separation, he never saw a whole side of her—an imaginative, irrational, artistic side—which had done a great deal for him as it was, but which would have done far more if he had not been so much cut off from her. He had tried to get what she could not give him by imagining a mother who was an image of security, and by daydreams of what she would be if he could find her. But, of course, he never could find her.

As he talked of this phantasy figure, it became apparent that even as an adult he was still looking for her. He might, therefore, be said to have three mother images, sometimes separate, sometimes merged: a dark image of power held by the grandmother; the phantasy mother, an image of understanding love; and the actual mother, less real than either of the others, and yet never to be dismissed because she held for him values which he only vaguely intuited.

Each of these images affected his life, and from the separation between them came consequences which were no less real. As long as he was unaware of these images and of their power he could not see an actual woman as combining attractive and unattractive qualities. He saw each one as a dangerous witch or as an understanding mother or as an irrational, artistic, attractive creature. Therefore he could establish no real relation with any woman.

When he discussed the image of his father he saw the part which his mother had played in building it up through her constant references to the father's authority. Apparently unassertive herself, she had made use of this image as a proxy to convey her own wishes. ("I shall have to tell your father"—"What will your father say?"—a not uncommon practice with mothers when they want to have their own way.) He remembered how throughout his childhood his mother had always spoken of his father's verdicts as final, and this had helped to create an image of a figure of authority whose judgments must always be relied upon.

He spoke of his father's anger, too, but when it came to actual memories he could recall only two occasions on which this had broken out with any violence. But these two had so impressed him that they had become part of his image of the father. Actually, the father had been a mild man who was generally dominated by the other adults of the household. But it was the image, not the actual father, which had governed him and was still governing him.

When he left home he immediately looked for some other man who could embody this image. He found a man who fortunately appreciated his very real talent, and under the influence of this surrogate father he developed this side of himself successfully. But he was still excessively deferential to the opinions of this man and to those of other older men. He was unable to assume responsibility for his own life, to be his own final authority. Now he saw that he was, on the one hand, dominated by an image of the father projected upon some other man—that is, by an image ruling from without—and on the other hand he was affected from within by the qualities of the actual father which were also his own. These qualities gave gentleness to his feeling but were still weaknesses in his development and independence as a man.

Through discussions of the images of the grandmother, of the mother and of the father, it gradually became apparent that only by bringing the light of consciousness to them could they be dissolved, could he end the dominance over his life which they had exerted.

By no means all of these associations, by no means all of these inferences arose directly out of a discussion of this first dream. Some of them came only after some time and after other dreams had been considered. But this first dream clearly indicated the importance of consciously investigating the parental images.

It should, moreover, be apparent from this dream that parental images are not always images of the actual parent. This man's image of his father was made up in part out of suggestions received from the mother. Into it entered also elements found in the unconscious of most people, elements which may be better presented in connection with another dream, this time that of a woman.

This dream came, not at the beginning of an analysis, but some time later, when the dreamer, a young woman, who had had great difficulties with her dominating, possessive mother, seemed to have solved this problem. Apparently her resentment of the mother, a deeply buried bitterness, had been brought to consciousness, and she had been able to understand their essential differences. After the beginning of her analysis, the girl had left home to take up her own life. With this freedom came a great access of new energy.

Yet after a time she realized that her new-found power was waning. She again became beset by fears and anxieties. What could be the trouble? She had done the thing she knew must be done, and yet the trick was not turned. She began to doubt both her own ability and the rightness of what she had done. Then came this dream:

"I was on the shore of a great sea. In front of me was the house of a witch-woman. A tall totem pole rose on one side of the door and behind this the witch-woman was concealed. It was the day of the sacrifice and I was compelled to bring four children to be slain in front of that terrible door. I struggled against this doom but knew that there was no escape. The sacrifice was inevitably demanded. Then the witch-woman stepped from behind the door—great, terrible, like no one that I had ever seen, yet, in some strange intuitive way, I knew that she was my mother."

She was confused and terrified. Had her mother such fearful, unrecognized power over her? Was this power still unbroken? If this were true then, indeed, her situation of dependence would seem inevitable.

This dream, however, had a completely new quality. The strange land, the illimitable sea, the figure of more than human potency, the sense of doom and mystery, all these indicated that here was something more far-reaching than she had encountered before. But why, she was asked, had this figure chosen this especial setting? What was meant by the totem and the typically Alaskan scene?

A small Alaskan totem lay on the analyst's table, where it had been for months. Because of it, the girl had connected the analyst with Alaska. But why should this figure, which was at once a terrible witch and the mother, appear in a setting which suggested the analyst, for whom the girl had felt no fear? She had, on the contrary, shown gratitude and affection. Yet, at the question, "Why is the figure on the Alaskan coast and standing behind the totem?" a look of terror spread over her face. She showed the same hatred and resentment that she had at times showed when she talked of her mother. What she saw was not the analyst but the witch-woman. Her fear was not a fear of the analyst, nor was it a fear of her mother; it was a fear of something in her own unconscious.

This something, an image of a terror-inspiring mother, the Terrible Mother, is a collective image, one that has appeared to thousands of people over thousands of years. No mother wholly wishes her child to leave her; no mother wholly lacks the desire that her child shall remain a child. Some mothers become identified with this desire and fight every effort of the child to become an adult.

On the other hand, there is in every child the wish to remain a child, the wish to avoid the difficulties and pains of adult life. This desire is projected upon the mother, so that the young person believes that the mother is holding him or her back, when actually the force is not that of the mother, but something within the psyche. It is this inner force which is the more potent. It will hold a child to a mother who is quite ready to set it free; it will make the child believe that not only the mother but other adults are holding it back. It is this, much more than anything in the mother, which is personified by the image of the Terrible Mother.

There is a time in the life of everyone when this figure becomes most menacing, the time when we must take over the authority for our own life and have the courage to choose our own way. This girl had assumed that her difficulties had been caused by her mother. Now she had to see that the problem was her own, that she had assumed an outer independence without sufficient inner preparation. Hence in her dream she had seen this archetypal image, a figure which did not belong to her any more than to her analyst or to anyone else who reaches this step in universal experience.

Yet in the detail of her dream a special symbolism had been chosen by which the witch-woman was surrounded. Why had this figure, in coming to her, chosen the totem pole as its place of mystery, its enshadowing retreat? Why should it be the Alaskan coast, and what did the totem mean to her?

Throughout her analysis it had seemed to this girl that it was her mother's authority and her own economic dependence which had rendered her helpless. Then slowly she had begun to perceive that her own fear, her habits of conventionality, her dread of criticism, all held her in bondage. She saw that even with the problem of economic independence solved, she did not dare break the mysterious bond that held her to the maternal authority. There lay in her a sense of guilt in following her own path, an indecision, all of which she attributed to fear of the actual mother. During analysis she had slowly substituted for this dark mother image, another figure, that of the mother who understood and helped. This she had projected upon the analyst, and through it had been able to come to some degree of freedom, so much so that she had announced that she was "free of her mother." But now the dream showed that the dark power was still there. When, through the association of the totem, she connected the witch-woman with the analyst, a new fear arose. Was the analyst really a dark and sinister person? Was she, too, seeking to enslave her? After a moment, the terror vanished, her fear seemed to have gone, and the analyst was again the trusted mother-surrogate, the helper. All could be well once more.

She now wanted to explain the connection between the analyst and the totem as a mere coincidence. She knew the totem to be the ancestral god, a sort of sacred family tree showing the tribal intermarriages, the clan animals. These associations, which suggested her own family, were, she thought, surely enough, without pursuing that malign feeling so suddenly projected onto the analyst. Had this plausible way out been accepted, she would again have related the problem to her own personal mother relation, and to the conventional bonds prescribed by her personal code. To all practical intents, she would have been back where she started, with the same old problem.

But the fact remained that, despite her warm feeling for the analyst, this girl had seen her as the witch-woman. In her unconscious there was some connection between the analyst and the danger represented by the witch-woman. Since, in the course of her analytical work, she had projected the image of the loving, understanding mother upon the analyst, the fact that she had connected her with the witch-woman showed that there was something to be feared, even in a mother of this sort. If the unconscious could have spoken in words instead of in images, it might have said:

"You are in danger. You may fall a victim to the Terrible Mother when you least expect it. A loving mother is also a peril.

You may be bound to her by the need of approval, by the desire for the security of affection, and so you may still remain a child. She may demand the sacrifice of your growing individual values, the children you saw in the dream. If you are not careful you are in danger of only changing mother images. You may become a happy child instead of a frightened one, but you will still remain a child."

The dream, therefore, by placing the dread image in surroundings where the dreamer would have expected to find only the image of security, brought her to a new understanding of her problem. By its strange and ancient form, it showed her that hers was not a peril which was a merely personal one, but a universal life experience. Her danger, like that of countless others, lay within herself.

This dream, by presenting what could be clearly seen as an archetypal image, showed a fact which underlies nearly all dreams having to do with the relation of parent and child. The image of the father in the unconscious of the man who dreamed of the cave originated in part from the collective image of the father as the patriarch, the image of absolute authority. Even where, as in some of the dreams presently to be discussed, there seems a close connection between the dream image and the actual parent, the image is not merely that of the parent. Its power comes in large part from its collective origin. It was of great assistance to this girl to realize that her difficulty was a universal one; it is of great assistance to anyone to know that his problem is not that of a peculiar, neurotic individual who has been wrecked by a deadly parent, but that it is shared, to a greater or less degree, by any young person who has reached the time when he must become adult.

Becoming adult is not by any means the mere result of increasing age. Nor does a person always become adult in all sides of his nature at once. A man may seem thoroughly mature in his relation to the world and yet in some one respect remain a child. At forty he may still, in his unconscious, be dominated by a parental image from which he has never freed himself. The man who dreamed of the cave, for example, was still caught in a childish emotional pattern. He was only happy when working under the authority of some other man, and he could not assume the responsibilities involved in marriage. Nevertheless he occupied a very important position in the professional world, and in most respects his life was wholly normal.

This situation can be illustrated again by the case of a man who had a brilliant father whose god was the intellect. This father had impressed upon his son the idea that it was through rational scientific thought alone that a real man functioned, that the rest was "concession to the lower centers." The son's relation with his father was the deepest thing in his early life, and since thought was the only way of making contact with the father, it became to him the only basis of relationship. But as he went out into the world of boys, others did not see things as he saw them, and he became very lonely.

The lonelier he became, the more he tried to reach people through his mind. In college he worshipped an instructor who could tell him how to think better, because he found in the instructor something corresponding to his father. When he tried to find emotional security in a woman, he chose a hard, brilliant woman whose thinking he admired. She, of course, could not help him. Such women never can because they have lost connection with their own feeling. They have little sympathy with anything in a man which is not mature.

Suddenly this man developed a really serious neurosis. He became unable to trust the thinking upon which he had always depended. His undeveloped, childish, emotional side took control and interfered with his thoughts. At this point he sought help from an analyst. He was still, however, wholly unaware of what the trouble really was. He expected the analyst to restore his confidence in his old intellectual attitude. Then came this dream:

"I am in a medieval castle ruled over by a tyrant. A strange masculine figure of terror and suspicion points the way to a secret chamber. I am then told that this is the torture chamber, where the sons of the house are tied to huge antlers and slowly starved to death in sight of food."

An association between these antlers and those that had hung in the family dining room immediately rose in his mind. This astonished him, because the family table had always been well supplied with food. Obviously the starvation of the dream was not a physical starvation. After this interpretation was suggested, he recalled the actual torture of meals, when the children were ridiculed if their remarks were "not intelligent" and where any childish emotions were strictly repressed because of the fear of the father. Association after association showed that he had, from his earliest childhood, been chained to a way of functioning which was not his own. The antlers represented to him trophies of the hunt in which beautiful animals were slain. It began to appear that his father had slain his own simple instinctual side and had, as a matter of fact, been very far from a complete and well-balanced person. Having idealized his father, he had assumed that, in imitating the father, he had followed the right way. Actually this had been far from true, and the attitude toward life which the father had maintained had been one producing disastrous consequences for the son. Only by freeing himself from the unseen chains imposed by the father, only by letting the instincts live, could he find his own way of life and regain any inner security.

Even where the father is truly to be admired and the ideal image corresponds as much as may be to reality, and where the relation has been one of great value, the parental image has still to be dealt with, unless at adolescence the normal break has taken place. A young man who had a most admirable father dreamed that he was fighting his father for the possession of a wallet containing something of great value. Money here, as it often does, represented energy. Much of his energy had, without his knowing it, been controlled by the father's ideas and feelings. He had to make that energy his own so that he could, so to speak, pay his own way in the world.

Where the childish emotional attitude toward the father still exists in the unconscious, the father image rules, whether it be through love or hate. For the negative attitude, which is the result of hatred, is no more independent than is the positive attitude of admiration. It is only when one chooses in accordance with one's own nature, and not in order to deny or please the father, that one is free. For the overcoming of the father means accepting both the virtues and the faults of one's inheritance and early environment as something now one's own, and dealing with them as such, assuming toward them an adult responsibility and authority.

PARENTAL IMAGES

The father image in its combination of personal and collective aspects is essentially the image of authority, and until the final authority for one's own life is found within the self, one is still a child ruled by an image.

The image of the father is of deep importance to the daughter also; for it may speak in her opinions of man and in her choice of work, so that her relation both to her own masculine side and to real men can be ruled by this image unless the unconscious bond has been broken, when the child's need for the father no longer exists. This problem is discussed in detail later, in the chapter on the Animus. If the attitude toward the father has been one of hostility, whether open or buried, then the daughter may be unconsciously hostile to any man. An overloving attitude, on the other hand, toward a protecting father may cause a woman to seek the father in other men. In that case she takes no adult responsibility in a relationship. Things "happen" to her. Men who are not ideal creatures "disappoint" her. It is not uncommon for such women to dream that they have gone to bed with a lover only to find the father sleeping there.

It would be possible to cite any number of dreams illustrating the dominance exercised by parental images over the lives of grown children. Countless men and women have dreamed, for instance, of finding themselves in a car driven by the father or the mother. It will be enough to give, as one example, a dream which came to the man whose dream of the car and the cellar appears at the beginning of this chapter. Since the time when the first dream appeared, he had done some analytical work and now supposed that he was ready to rely on his own authority and to accept what life brought him. Then he dreamed:

"I am going on a journey by sea. It is to be a great adventure. But I find that my father has bought me my ticket and that my mother is taking me to the boat in her car."

At the moment he thought of analysis as he had thought of the "isms" he had previously embraced, as something which would enable him better to serve humanity. The philanthropic aims of his father still determined the direction he was to take; his mother's ideals of what a man should be still guided him. Hence in the dream the father chose the destination by buying the ticket, the mother carried him in her car. A journey thus directed would be no great adventure. He still saw the analytical process in terms which he had taken over from his parents. Until he could see it otherwise, as a way of finding his own unique place and finding within himself an ultimate authority for his own choices, he would remain the guided and directed child. If he continued on this sort of journey in the service of humanity he would probably be a great nuisance to himself and to such portions of humanity as were unable to escape his services.

Dreams frequently show us negative elements within the psyche because we wish to repress them from our consciousness, and therefore they reappear in the material of the unconscious. After reading such a series of dreams as those given in this chapter, the reader might easily wonder if in modern psychology the parental relation was considered the root of all evil. Psychology does not question the positive value which a child obtains from early security in a right parental relation, nor how much is built into adult life through such early influences. But an inevitable problem occurs at adolescence when there is in every young person a natural conflict between the desire for adult independence and the desire for childish security. And every parent faces another aspect of this problem; for the attitude of authority—no matter how loving or understanding—must give way to an acceptance of the child's growing independence.

It must be remembered that in this chapter we are for the most part discussing the early, so-called "reductive" aspects of the exploration of the personal unconscious. We are therefore concerned with the projections and identifications which still cause confusion and which prevent a person from seeing himself as he is and recognizing the problem of consciousness as his own. These emotional confusions belong to the less-developed side of the self and therefore are frequently projected upon the image of the parent or of one on whom the parental image is placed. That is why the parental image so frequently appears in its negative aspect during early phases of analysis. But just as the negative aspects of the parental relation may be repressed and appear in dreams, so we may be unmindful of, or forget, or consider "outgrown," the very positive and continuing values which have been derived from this relation. In this case the dream image will present these values.

A woman who had been forced by circumstances to take up a professional life had gradually allowed her own personal life to become neglected. She dreamed that she was in her library, which was also her favorite sitting room. The room now seemed to her cold and formal. She said, "This room needs living things." Then a man turned on the lights which were brilliant and hard and she saw an alcove in which were glowing plants. But the man was moving from plant to plant nipping the buds with his fingers. She realized that the shades which were on the lamps were ones which he had given her and that by turning on the lights so shaded he gained power over the living plants. She said, "I must change the lighting in this room." Then she saw before her a box which she opened. In it were transparent shades of luminous green shaped like the buds of flowers. She recognized them as ones which her mother had always used and which, though they had been left to her, she had now discarded. If the lights fell through these shades instead of the garish ones now in use she knew the room would be all right and the flowers could grow unmolested.

The details of this dream are clear. The library represented her professional life and the man, whom she knew in real life, and who, in the dream, determined the quality of its lighting, was a writer who was brilliant and successful but whose ruthlessness often injured his friendships. He represented the professional, masculine side of herself which cast a hard, brilliant light upon her room of life.

As she woke, memories of her mother came vividly to mind. She remembered the old library in her early home—a room which was also a family gathering place. This room recalled long talks in which her mother's understanding had helped her to meet various situations that had come to her during adolescence and early womanhood. It was from these hours and from the influence that her mother's own life had had upon her own unconscious attitudes that she had formed her concept of feminine values—a concept once hers but now temporarily disregarded. Her mother had lived deeply and had accepted both the personal and impersonal aspects of a woman's life.

This dream reconnected her with that mother image in its

symbolic aspects — that is, as embodying the feminine elements which she had first understood through the actual relation and which she must now reconnect with in her own unconscious. She did not have to abandon her library (her professional adaptation) but only cast another light upon it — and to admit into it new life. Her first association with the living buds was with "flowers of feeling "which grew with their own life-energy if the atmosphere was right. Through the reconnection with the mother image her own feeling would again live.

In using the symbol of the light the dream showed that the problem was an inner one; the mother, long since dead, was not in the dream represented by a surrogate mother — a woman from whom the dreamer must learn as a child learns from a mother — but as an atmosphere, an inner attitude; the problem was the dreamer's own.

The examination of the parental images is one important step in the process of integration by which one separates oneself from old identifications and discovers the elements that belong to one's own personality. These elements are not newly created within ourselves at birth; they derive from the ancestral stream. No one is born a new being. He bears in his psyche the imprint of past generations. He is a combination of ancestral units from which a new being must be fused, yet he also bears within him an essential germ, a potential of a unique individual value. The discovery of this unique essence and its development is the quest of consciousness.

IV. THE EGO

When the unconscious power of the parental images is broken, man, psychologically speaking, emerges from the nursery. A new energy is released. It is an energy arising from a contact with the elements of his own nature, from a new connection between his conscious willing and something essentially his which heretofore has been unconscious within him. Thus, unconscious energy is released for use in his conscious life, and a step is made in the integration of his own center of consciousness — a process which must be repeated over and over as life proceeds and the personality develops.

It is only when a person can recognize the elements within himself that he can estimate the assets and liabilities with which he must reckon in carrying on the business of life. When he knows about these factors he can begin to direct them and can start on a road to freedom. Until this happens he is like a man taking over a business enterprise with no knowledge of its assets or liabilities. In this process of understanding the strength and weakness of one's own personality, a new center is gradually formed, a center of consciousness which is known as the ego.

It is not possible to continue with a discussion of the images which move in the unconscious without examining this conscious entity, this ego, which is developing through contact with the outer world and through the influence of the inner forces. It is therefore necessary to make a rudimentary definition of what we mean by this center of consciousness, and to suggest the way in which it becomes integrated so that more and more it can direct conscious choice and can make a successful adaptation to life.

The ego is the "I" of whom we are aware in our waking life of activity; it is also the "I" in most of our dreams. It is the one who experiences the outer world and also the one who perceives the inner images. Again, it is an active agent in the creation of the images of the *personal* unconscious through the combination of perception and emotional reaction, and is in turn re-created by them through their unconscious influence on future choices. It is acted upon by our social milieu and also by the factors of the collective unconscious. It draws to itself certain assimilable contents—assimilable, that is, to itself at any given moment—both from the outer world and from the world within.

Just as our sensory vision is limited and we can see only a little at a time, so is our consciousness limited and very little can be held in consciousness by the ego at any moment. Yet through memory one can establish a continuity. Memory, in this sense, is not to be confused with factual memory, it is not confined to the remembering of actual experiences; it includes the reanimation of those experiences through the recalling of the emotions connected with them. It also implies a continuity of thought processes, which makes a connection between the individual experience and the ego that has developed out of the original unconsciousness of infancy.

At first, ego-consciousness has little or no continuity. It is like a flickering light that comes and goes. A real sense of an existing conscious personality may be very slow in developing; it involves memory of acts and experiences, and the power to relate them to each other and to oneself. As ego-consciousness develops, events or emotions of significance are no longer merely experienced and forgotten. They become part of the stream of memory.

Memory, as the reanimation of experience, carries with it a certain critical quality; it enables the ego, through the comparison of experiences, to establish its relationship to events and its responsibility toward them. The ego, therefore, directs (or should direct) conscious choice. It experiences, selects, weighs, evaluates. It develops through each consciously accepted experience. To establish its continuity is a primal necessity.

By many people this continuity is never attained; life just happens to them. It all *seems* to come from the outside. They fall into one situation and out of that into another, often a similar one. They are victims of circumstances, or they are varying personalities reacting differently to each change of circumstance or to each change of mood in accordance with the fragment of personality that assumes temporary control. Therefore, they never really experience their life; they never ask, "Why did this come to me? What does it mean? What is its value or its peril? What in me made it take this form? What is its connection with my particular life? What, in short, is the *me* who has this experience, and what is my connection with this event that has happened?"

For the ego must always reckon with those other elements of the psyche, the parts that move in the unconscious, elements which suddenly take possession of a person through a mood or an unpremeditated act contrary to conscious volition. The distinction between the ego and other elements in the psyche may begin early. Whenever the child can distinguish between himself and the outer circumstances of his life—whenever he can say, "*I* hurt myself," not "it is bad, *it* hurt me;" whenever he can say, "*I* think this;" whenever he can control a sudden emotion so that a conscious being inside himself directs the affect; or when he can consider himself responsible for the emotion he has failed to control, the ego develops.

This process of separating the ego from the affect continues throughout life. For the forces contained in these unconscious affects are full of dynamic and creative power; unless there is a directing ego one cannot admit them to consciousness without being overpowered by them—becoming temporarily the affect, not the ego. That is to say, when one is swept away by anger, one temporarily *becomes that anger*. It is the anger that acts, that assumes charge of the conscious ego. When the anger has passed the ego is often dismayed at what the anger, the affect, has done. Or a person "in love" may seem like one possessed by a primitive passion—it is the emotion which is controlling the ego, not the ego which is consciously accepting the reality of the emotion and directing it into constructive channels which will bring a valuable relation out of the emotional intensity. The problem of consciousness, therefore, is more and more to differentiate the ego from the affect.

When the affect takes on an autonomous character—that is, when it has gained such power that it can assume control—and is no longer under the direction of a central ego, it is almost like another personality. The ego then is not integrated, but split — first one ruler or autonomous complex, then another, takes over authority. In this way, affects that should properly be in the service of the ego may assume lives of their own. In children, these often appears as "imaginary companions;" in pathological cases as split-off parts of the personality with equal powers of control, so that the ego-direction seems to reside first in one, then another, of those split-off personalities. In ordinary persons they appear as compulsive emotions, prejudices, preconceived ideas, suspicions, irrational certainties. They may clothe themselves as images that appear in dreams or move in phantasy as "people" with a life of their own, able to help or hinder the ego in finding its own way of life. Sometimes these images are personifications of autonomous complexes; sometimes they represent lost parts of the personality which, left behind in the pressure of adaptation to the demands of life, seek a re-entrance into ego-consciousness.

A woman who had become separated from her feminine feeling through a concentration upon a consciously accepted idea of duty and responsibility, dreamed:

"I enter my living room and see a pile of disorderly rubbish which I feel has been left there by my husband. A feeling of angry desperation comes over me. How can I *make* him clean it up? How can I *make* him behave differently? While I am wondering, a quiet black woman enters. She is called Lucy. She looks at me with an amused and tolerant smile, as a nurse might look at an unreasonable child. She very swiftly clears up the rubbish and goes out still smiling."

The dreamer became conscious of Lucy as a woman having instinctive feeling. She learned to talk to her — that is, to draw into consciousness the meaning of this dream image, so that her imaginary conversations were discussions of values re-estimated by the neglected side, her feeling. These conversations gave her a feeling of integration, a sense of renewed contact with a lost side of herself. In her girlhood she had been over gentle, too yielding, overconscious of the needs of others. In her attempts to meet the increasing responsibility adequately, she had called upon another side of herself, a capable, assertive side, which had gradually taken over the central position until this feeling element of herself which had functioned in the past had been lost. Now, through understanding of the dream image, she regained a necessary connection with that side, and discovered that "Lucy" was able to do things that in her one-sided adaptation she had found impossible.

Many such personalities may appear. Sometimes four or five distinct figures will be constellated, or come to consciousness, and can be made to tell of the role they play in the drama of the life of the individual. This is no mysterious magic. To talk with oneself is a well-known procedure. This is merely an objectification of the conflicting ideas and emotions in the form of images, a process of activating the unconscious through attention and concentration. It is no more mysterious than the case of Margaret, given at length in the chapter on Imaginary Companions in a previous volume.* Here the "good" side of the self became personified as Anna, and the bad as Dophy in the Kiki house. Through asking the advice of these two, and considering with an increasingly impersonal attitude the relative merits of their counsel and of their actions, choices were made, desirable factors integrated in the ego, and undesirable ones recognized and increasingly controlled.

The ego which became integrated through this process in the case of Margaret was one which she herself developed through consciously choosing between these two companions. They personified moving and creative processes set free within the self and voluntarily related to a growing ego-consciousness. They had, therefore, an entirely different effect from that of a conscious conformity with outside advice, however good this advice might be. It is through a similar process continued in adulthood by means of a connection with dreams and fantasy that the ego can choose a way of integration that does not deny the unconscious.

Through these different processes—the control of the affect and the integration of lost sides of the personality—the center becomes strengthened and gradually one begins to find the way in which the ego can function without being drawn into conflict with inner forces at variance with conscious desire. To do this one must become increasingly able to discover which ideals and choices are one's own, and which have been accepted as axiomatic

* *The Inner World of Childhood*—pp. 183-196.

truths, swallowed whole but never assimilated and exerting a secret influence. For the ego is conscious and visible, that is, its actions are visible to ourselves and to the world, but the forces acting upon it and depriving it of energy are often unconscious and invisible.

The problem of the developing ego is to meet with increasing power the reality demands of the experiences of life. These demands may come from without through the necessary contact with the outer world, or from within through the necessity of understanding and assimilating the events occurring within the self. But in whichever world the ego is functioning it must find some normal approach, some way of apprehending reality, and must be able to make acceptable and conscious use of experience.

Each man must find his way of establishing himself in life; must contrive a coin with which to pay his own way. The demands of normal living and ordinary responsibility must be met. His first way of doing this is properly determined by his own natural approach to life. Man has different approaches to life, different ways of apprehending reality. He may function most spontaneously through his thinking, his feeling, his sensation or his intuition.

This brings us to a discussion of one of the deep and fundamental concepts of Jungian philosophy*—the concept of psychological types and functions, which involves a study of normal variations in individual reactions to life. Such a concept can be given only in briefest outline, but it is essential at this point for the reader to have at least a glimpse of the basic structure underlying the living form.

Sensation tells you that a thing *is*. It gives the immediate reality—the *now*—it informs you of the existence of the object which impinges upon the senses at the present moment. By it we are aware that something is here in our immediate inner or outer environment.

Thinking gives a name, a concept. It tells you *what* a thing is. It is a process of apperception by which you become aware of the nature of the thing with which you are dealing.

Feeling gives you a sense of values. It tells you whether a

* *Psychological Types*—Carl G. Jung.

thing is agreeable or disagreeable. It decides upon its acceptance or rejection by determining what is its value to you.

Intuition deals with the potential, the thing which will develop. It is the function which has to do with the element of *time*. It is not concerned with what *is*, but with what is *going to be* or *has been*. It is the "hunch" by which men estimate the possibilities of a given situation.

All four of these functions exist in everybody, but the particular function which is the natural approach is normally the one which is more consciously used, and therefore, through use, one becomes more skillful in its handling. In other words, it is more under control of ego consciousness: it can be directed in accordance with the will or conscious intention. We should like to think that we had all these functions under control. But our ego, busy with conscious living, usually represses the functions that interfere with its chosen expression. The repressed functions, however, do not cease to act because we cease to direct them. We find them acting of themselves.

Two of the functions, thinking and feeling, are rational—controlled by judgment and proceeding in accordance with logical steps. Feeling is often considered to be irrational, because it is confused with mood and emotion, but feeling, in the sense of a differentiated and conscious function, is controlled by judgment, and a definite sense of the values contained in human situations. So a person of differentiated feeling has his own standards by which he proceeds in the weighing and judging of any situation. It is the mood and emotion which are the unconscious side of feeling, the raw material out of which feeling is made. These act irrationally, but no more irrationally than does unconscious thinking. For unconscious thinking is governed by uncontrolled opinions and obsessive thoughts, and these can rise up out of the unconscious with as overwhelming an irrationality as any mood or emotion. Yet thinking is commonly accepted as a rational function, although, like feeling, it is only rational in its differentiated form.

Intuition and sensation, on the other hand, are essentially irrational in their differentiated form. They do not proceed by logical steps, but their conclusions seem to come of themselves without the intervention of the intermediary processes. Intuition suddenly finds itself at the end of the road, but has no idea of how it got there; whereas sensation finds itself sitting firmly upon an established fact, without any concern as to the implications of that fact or its relation to past and future—it simply *is* a fact.

Though all these functions are present in each individual, they cannot all be conscious at the same time. Feeling and thinking are very upsetting to each other; and sensation and intuition are quarrelsome bedfellows. In fact, one or another may exist almost entirely in the unconscious. Of the functions acting in consciousness, one plays a superior role and another acts as auxiliary. If the superior function is rational, the assisting function is irrational, or vice versa. So we speak of a man who *thinks* intuitively, or of one whose thinking is assisted by his sensation. Or, if intuition is the first function to act in any given situation, it is assisted by either feeling or thinking. But the two rational functions stand at opposite poles from each other, as do the two irrational; for thinking would exclude feeling, because feeling values pull it back to earth, and feeling fears the cold, calculating, logical quality of thinking, because it has a merciless way of disregarding the value of a situation in which feeling is involved.

So, also, sensation and intuition view each other with suspicion; for sensation, keenly aware of the values of the immediate situation, is comfortably settled among facts, and possibilities of change disturb this security; whereas intuition, darting into the future, searching out the possibilities, feels imprisoned when enclosed by factual reality. If, through a concentration upon a single function, a successful adaptation is made, then the ego becomes closely identified with one function. A too-successful adaptation, produced by the overvaluation of one's superior function, limits development: in such a situation one behaves as though this superior function could dispose of all sides of the question. The thinker rationalizes—thinks things out of existence—the feeling type smothers them in warmth or freezes them out. The intuitive drives out existing realities with the image of past or future. The sensation type shuts the lid on everything which he cannot objectify in the immediate moment, and fears change because it would destroy his existing security. Hence the absolutism of the superior function really leads to unconsciousness of all other sides of life.

The way in which these functions are used varies in accordance with a deep temperamental difference. To some it is natural to go out to meet the outer experience; to others to withdraw into the subjective aspects. Or one might express the difference in another way. It would seem that in some individuals the ego ascribes greater reality to the images arising from within, and we call such individuals "introverts." Others ascribe the greater reality to images presented from without, and they are termed "extraverts." One has a right to speak of these typical reactions as innate in the temperament, because one sees them even in a little child.

To one child, the new experience, the new person, the object which offers a new interest, are things to be seized upon eagerly. To another child, the new and strange is viewed guardedly—one must withdraw from it, ponder it, fit it into the inner pattern. The introvert seeks to connect the world with his own inner life and admits only such aspects as have a subjective importance. The extravert seems to connect his life with the outer world, and by the way he plays his part in that outer life, he judges his success or failure. And this congenital difference must be respected, for a denial of the inner reality produces as great a conflict as the denial of the reality of the actual outer circumstances of one's life. Only here again, the ego may, by an overemphasis of the existing value, make that value master instead of servant.

The dream and the phantasy which follow show the result of pushing either of these adaptations to the extreme. The first is a dream of an overextraverted woman:

"I had cut myself up and was passing myself round on a large and handsome platter. At first there seemed nothing unusual about it, but suddenly I became terrified and tried to pull away the platter and escape, but I could not move or speak. Then a monstrous woman, I think a negress, appeared and began throwing the people away. She was quite dreadful but I was not afraid of her and felt she might help me. Then I woke, saying, 'I must blow my nose.'"

The first part of the dream needs no interpretation, for it so plainly illustrates what the dreamer had been doing. She was a woman of extraverted feeling type, and had followed so many extraverted activities and met so many situations with proper feeling that she had passed herself round in very small pieces indeed. Resentment that people had taken these pieces and walked off with them had stirred something deep inside her. A realization that she had established nothing permanent began to grow within her. The negress seems to her dreadful and yet she appears to be the one who can save the situation. She must let her own sense of reality, so repressed, assume control, for she has lost all connection with what she is really doing in relation to her whole life, not just to each situation. Then she cries out, "I must blow my nose." She thinks of the nose as smelling out things. It is the instinctual intuition. She says she often has thought of situations as "smelling badly"—unsavory. She has always assumed that this was not a nice feeling-attitude to take and she must not think of such a thing. It would not create a good atmosphere.

Normally her intuition was her auxiliary function, and should have been used to help guide her feeling, to serve as a check. She had, however, "stopped it up" and not allowed it to function, for it sensed the undesirable potential which might interfere with the pleasant attitude. Now her dream, in this rather infantile fashion, tells her she must blow her nose. That is, she had to give her intuition a clear way to function and it would help her not to be led into all sorts of places—not to use her feeling indiscriminately wherever the outer situation demanded it, and where often it was a violation of her simple, instinctual, feeling self.

The danger of the extravert is that he will become lost in multitudinous happenings none of which will be accepted, understood and assimilated, so that he has no real center to which he can relate each experience and so make it part of his development. On the other hand, though the introvert has a deep need for contact with his own inner realities, this need also becomes a danger, because it may be used as a retreat from life.

A small boy developed sullen moods; he failed at school; he would not adapt to the community interests of the home. When pressed, he often gave way to violent fits of temper. There were three boys, and as he was the middle one he always shared a room with one of his brothers, who were alike in boisterous temperament, whereas he was the only one who desired quiet. One day he explained a phantasy which he had built up for himself:

"I have my land. It is an island in the middle of a lake-river. The bank of the lake is very winding and there are towns on it, but the boats have to zigzag back and forth to get to them and everywhere they pass my island they see high rocks, so they cannot land. There is only one way to get there. Back of two towns and between them there is a wood. It is very dark and mysterious. There are big rocks there, and they all look alike but one of them lifts up and back of it is a door, and back of the door is a tunnel, and you can go through that tunnel and under the lake and come out in the middle of the island where the trees are thick around a little quiet place. That's where I go to think. (Then scornfully), *They* don't know about it. *They* don't know who I am." This phantasy had become a retreat from every proper demand of outer life. In working this out he came to some realization of the times when he ought to leave the island, a rudimentary understanding of the balance of adaptation and inner withdrawal.

In this course of his explanation of his inner phantasy, he had drawn a picture of the island, the curving bank of the lake and the course of the boats. This map really was in accord with the old eastern drawings of the inner center of the psyche. His deep distrust made him cut the center off from all communication, because he had found no one who valued his desire for withdrawal into himself.

The extreme extravert is carried along by the ceaseless stream of self-created activity until the personality becomes lost, dispersed in its own creations. To the extravert the images from the inner world are unrealities if they intrude upon his established reality. When the extravert is told to follow through a dream or phantasy association there will often come across his face an expression of caution, distrust, or even alarm. He will ask timidly if that does not lead to a morbid introspection? There is a popular confusion between introspection and introversion, which are thought to be much the same thing. Whereas introspection is a morbid dealing with material already conscious, and has no creative power, introversion is a turning to the unconscious to connect with creative energy.

The attitude toward experience is, in the two types, totally different. To the extreme extravert multitudinous happenings are the breath of life; yet he may experience in himself little or nothing. The introvert shuns the actual experience and withdraws to contemplation. He may have cataclysmic happenings in his inner world, images of doubt, fear and the like to encounter. Out of apparently trivial happenings he may create a whole world of important events. It may seem to him he has lived deeply through his inner experiences, yet he may not be able to translate his experience into terms of outer reality. In such a case he may stand apart from the life of others, scornful yet envious.

For both the extravert and the introvert there exists a mysterious region, which he fears; the introvert finds that in the outer world, the extravert within.

Through these channels, then, the ego functions; by the use of these tools it carves out its form of life. Yet it cannot finally be described in terms of this or that function or type reaction. Such concepts are very valuable, but if they are too rigidly applied they are apt to diminish, rather than to increase, our understanding of ourselves and of others. The whole question is a very intricate one. It is so easy to dismiss a person of an alien type by saying, "Of course, he is an extravert," or "Oh, well, you are an introvert," and then feel that we have, with scornful charity, put him in his place. Psychological terms, superficially used, may easily descend into a mere jargon which appears to offer an easy explanation, but which explains nothing.

A description and definition of types, such as the one in the preceding pages, necessitates dealing with the "typical;" that is, the extreme example. In reality, both reactions, introversion and extraversion, are present in every one of us, but one or the other is more natural, more spontaneous. Often the flow of interest between the inner and the outer experiences is so balanced that it is difficult to perceive which is the predominant attitude, or often life has forced upon a man an adaptation not fundamentally his own, so that it is difficult to know to which type he really belongs. But the understanding that these fundamental differences exist can make us more alive to our own needs and dangers and more willing to admit that there may be valid reasons why other people have reactions which differ from ours but which are no less valid.

In the realm of the functions this is also true. We can see there are other approaches to life than ours. Our own difficulties depend upon our own weakness, while the problem of another person may be completely the opposite of ours. The thing which is so easy for us may be the most difficult for him. To one person it is easy to love; to another it is easy to think. The problem differs, but to each it involves increase of consciousness, balance of personality.

And behind type and function lies the undefinable essence. There is an entity that defies definition. The ways in which the elements of personality may be fused are innumerable, and even when one is acting in accordance with one's type, and through one's superior function, one may still be denying essential elements of the self. One may be separated from the energy of the unconscious, because back of the ego stands some dominating idea or concept which is at variance with one's unique value. In such a case choices appear to be one's own, yet they lead nowhere so far as establishing an inner unity is concerned; for some element which would connect one with one's individual destiny has been disregarded. The short analysis given in Chapter X illustrates this, as do the two dreams given on pp. 36 to 47 in the previous chapter.

In this latter case, the man dreamed that the new journey which he had assumed to be his own, was really under the direction of his father and mother. Here the dreamer was not denying either his type or his superior function. He was a feeling-intuitive, an extraverted type. Though the tools which were being used were his own, their use was being directed by parental traits of which he was unconscious. That is, they were not in the service of his ego; his individual activity was not expressing itself; he was doing the work of somebody else. Nor, however various his experiences, could he hope to find his ego until he found something bigger; until he had found where his ego belonged in life. For the ego can assume control only through a continuous widening and deepening of the area of consciousness, which more and more makes one see what is one's own, and what are the unconscious influences. It is through such a process of the increase of consciousness that the continuity of the ego is established.

This establishment of the ego is an absolutely necessary step in the process of integration, but it has to do primarily with conscious adaptation, for the ego is the center of consciousness, not the center of the psyche, which includes both the conscious and the unconscious.

V. THE PERSONA

SINCE THE aim of the ego is one of conscious adaptation, it is naturally concerned with its appearance in the world, and with the activities which will give it what it wants. When a thing works—be it a smile or a protest—it is registered as having a value in relation to the environment. As the ego develops the ability to obtain its outer desires it learns to put on a "good face," one which seems to attract the kind of attention which is desirable. At times this face is like a mask assumed in order to play a social role. This mask worn for the outer world has been called the Persona, a name used for the masks worn by actors in ancient times.

The Persona stands between the ego and the external environment. It is a result of the process of adaptation to life in the world. In forming the Persona the ego consciously takes account of desired goals, of wished for achievements. Unconsciously, it forms the Persona through identification with persons embodying its ideals and through acceptance of standards esteemed by its surroundings. But this process is dangerous as well as necessary. One may forget that the Persona is merely something built up by the ego for its own special purposes. Then one identifies with it and loses sight of other things, of the unconscious factors which must be reckoned with if one is really to be an individual. A man may easily be a good college professor, or lawyer, or clergyman, but forget he is a human being. Since the Persona is engrossed with its appearance in the world, it registers the reaction of the persons by whom it is surrounded, noting what is *considered* respectable, worthy and desirable in the chosen circle in which it moves. Or, when the ego decides upon an imaginary goal and eliminates all knowledge of the factors within the self which are not concerned with this ambition, the building of a Persona which will express this before the world becomes the absorbing aim. This Persona image with which one identifies may gradually become one's idea of oneself, and this image, so clear to the ego, is also believed to be what is seen by others.

Sometimes a dream will reveal the real nature of the Persona, perhaps through an actual image which may caricature it, perhaps through a revelation of the way it really appears when looked at from the outside, as the world looks at it:

"I am in a great assembly. In the center of the room is a circular space surrounded by a low green hedge with a little gateway. In this space is a table where a man is seated, writing the names of the people who enter. I see myself walking rather majestically through the crowd, and as I reach the gate I proudly give my name in a loud voice—'Head of Fifty-seven Committees.'"

One hardly needs the associations of this dream in order to see the dreamer, clothed in a garment of respectability by her own efficient good works, beholding her own image as it walks through the ordinary crowd—the image of herself as she believes the world sees her.

This dreamer was a woman who had made an extremely successful adaptation to the demands that society had made upon her, and she felt only resentment that she had received so little personal love. She was, therefore, quite astonished when the dream showed how too-successful the adaptation had been, so successful that the name which she gave to be written in the book of life belonged only to the adaptation instead of to the individual. It was not her adaptation that was at fault but her lack of inner reality. She herself had become the garment; she was unaware of anything in herself not represented by it.

Yet the conscious ego must have a garment of suitability, an image in which to clothe itself in order to meet the world and to play a proper role in the drama of life, a mask, a Persona suited to this role. So each man assumes his Persona, or personal image, which (ideally) meets the outer demand as adequately as possible and decently covers over the things which do not belong to social life. And it is right that man should wear such a garment and should play his chosen role, provided he does not believe the role is the man. One can no more show to a casual and ultimately disgusted world all one's moods and immature hopes or despairs (or even one's intimate deeper experiences) than one can go about naked, without in either case encountering very unpleasant reactions on the part of other people.

The following is the dream of a man who had found society strangely unsympathetic toward his self-revelations and his gaucheries: "I am in a room where many people are gathered. I notice they all avoid the center, glancing there perhaps, but turning away. I look to see what they are avoiding and see a huge, unformed sort of creature of most unattractive appearance. It is waving its head about with an evident attempt at communication. It has thin, wrinkled skin and you can see its whole insides palpitating. It is a turtle that has come out without its shell. As I wake I think, 'How indecent of it.'"

In real life, the dreamer, conscious only of his naked helplessness when among people, cannot see why the exposures of his "sensitive soul" (frequently no more attractive than would be an exposure of his own intestinal workings) should not be treated with tenderness. He has never troubled to cover himself over decently when he goes out into the world. His own irrational feeling of the dream was, the turtle had no business to make such a spectacle of himself, why didn't he wear his shell? His own disgust showed him far more clearly the reactions of others to his Persona-less ego than hours of painstaking argument. Dreams must be interpreted often in relation to their affect—here the disgust the turtle roused in him. The dreamer felt quite sure that the turtle had really chosen to leave his shell at home, that it was, in fact, a case of indecent exposure.

Here, then, are the two equally unpleasant extremes; the one resulting from an overvaluation, the other from an undervaluation of the Persona.

As soon as ego-consciousness begins, this Persona image also begins to take form. The child soon learns what is acceptable, what will bring approval and reward or else involve him in unpleasant consequences. A little girl in one of Jean Ingelow's almost forgotten novels, when asked, "Would you rather sing psalms or have a gingerbread nut?" replied, "Oh, sing psalms. Angels sing psalms," knowing full well that she would receive two gingerbread nuts as a reward for her infant piety. This child was building up a Persona acceptable to the attitude of her environment. On the other hand, a more independent child of eight, who was being urged toward the same Persona type of "goodness," remarked to me, "But why should I be an unselfish little girl just so Johnny can be a bigger pig than he is already?" This child was resisting a world which she instinctively felt had nothing to do with reality, which would impose upon her the mask of a good little girl. With such a child, though an acceptable social Persona might be slow in developing, it would conform to the sense of real values contained in a given situation rather than to intuitive diplomacy—an appropriate covering, not a garb of concealment.

The following example illustrates how a Persona which caused much confusion in adult life was accepted unconsciously in early childhood:

A woman of charming manners and much outer graciousness came to an analysis because she found the demands of life too hard. Even in analytical hours it seemed impossible to break through the conventional social shell which she presented. Something outwardly acceptable was always offered. One had, however, a sense of other things of very different character lurking in the background. Resentments, bitterness, jealousies came crowding up. One thing was noticeable in these resentments, that many of them seemed roused by the ordinary experiences of life—the sacrifices necessary at the coming of children, the difficulties of a small income, everyday demands. Why should she feel that life should have set her apart from these common struggles?

As we went back through childhood memories we found that she had identified herself with the phantasy figure of a princess. She had been brought up in a small village where her family had been the wealthiest and most important. At school she had been treated differently from the other children. The princess could do no wrong. Gradually this idea became the reality; in her ego adaptation she *was* the princess. This adaptation worked as long as the environment was unbroken. But when she married and moved to a larger town she did not expect to take the small place that her own limited qualifications gave her. She still expected to be the princess, whereas to others she was only an ordinary woman of no special abilities, and her husband a man of minor position. Simple people were unacceptable to her as equals; she expected life itself to stand aside to arrange a new setting of superior privilege. She finally developed a neurosis in order to return to her place of importance.

This Persona which had been assumed in childhood had become so much herself that it was almost impossible for her to see herself as part of common humanity and, as such, subject to any of the human experiences. The Persona is a consciously chosen portion of the psyche with which one is in danger of identifying until gradually the other parts of the self are dropped from consciousness. So this princess image moved, smiled, was gracious, courteous, gently condescending, all with a consciousness of the charm and beauty of this image mirroring forth the ego. The resentments, the selfishness, the emotions which might destroy this image were invisible to her. The childhood phantasy of the princess had become her Persona, and the other sides of her nature —which might have become conscious and broken the image— were finding their life in neuroses. For when the inner reality is at variance with this Persona adaptation, then the image must sooner or later stand aside and the inner reality must find its outlet either in neurosis or contradictory protest.

Here one sees clearly not only how the conscious ego had chosen the role that gave satisfaction, but also how the outer circumstances, the suggestions of adults unconsciously accepted, the whole ideal imposed by surroundings, had played their part in the building up of the Persona image. The ego had not only accepted but welcomed all the influences that had gone to the building up of this Persona, and so it had become identified with the Persona image.

Sometimes there is a very real desire to live out one's own reality, but the pressure of environment may be too great. The inner force is not strong enough to withstand the insistence of the social demand; the accepted outer form does not correspond to the inner reality. And yet the inner reality will not die. So there is a continual conflict and neither side is ever really accepted. Then there is only bitterness and defeat.

Even when the person has achieved an apparently successful adaptation, inner reality may still be alive and the effort of this reality demand may produce an image which will show the existing condition. This conflict was shown in the visual image which came to a man who had molded his life into conformity with outer demands, but was struggling to find the reality that had been buried. One day in imagination he saw a man tearing a mask from his face. The mask had little clawlike hands—like clinging tentacles—which had sunk deep into the flesh, and underneath was a shriveled thing that seemed hardly human. This man carried his chosen role and had played his part successfully, but he had forgotten that a role is a collective expression of what society decides is success, and not all of life; that in following it one may lose connection with the manifestations of things deeper than the temporary system of adaptation. One cannot become identified with a momentary, transitory, perhaps more or less incidental role, however much that role meets the outer demand of the time. When one's own inner values are sacrificed to the demands of circumstance, and outer expectations, the Persona may have a satisfactory appearance, but the man himself may feel that he is imprisoned in it.

A man who in childhood had tried to meet the ambitious expectations of his parents in his education and career, and later those of his wife and family (who saw his value in terms of success in his profession and position in the community), dreamed that he came to his hour of analysis and, as he sat in the room, felt a sense of great peace. Looking down, he saw that he was completely naked.

The feeling of peace which this gave him was a right one, for one must be able to strip oneself of all self-deception, to see oneself naked to one's own eyes before one can come to terms with the elements of oneself and know who one really is. So the hour of analysis was a place of understanding and revaluation in which he might rightly appear "naked and unashamed." Then the Persona worn before the world would cease to be a concealment of inner reality and would become a fitting garment voluntarily assumed.

The Persona, in other words, is the mediator between the naked ego and the outer world, just as clothing is the mediator between the naked body and society. But one should not be sewed into one's Persona any more than one should be sewed into one's clothes. This can happen even when the ego image is one expressing real value.

A man whose intellectual ability had put him in a place of authority and leadership, yet who had accepted this idea of himself so completely that he felt called upon to give instruction even on the most informal occasions, had this dream:

"I saw people dancing to very gay music. Suddenly a gong sounded, there was a great silence, and out on the platform in front of the musicians stepped a very large and important dodo."

The dream had no meaning to him, for the Persona image which his conscious ego perceived was totally different from the image presented by the unconscious. But to anyone familiar both with him and with dreams, it would be impossible ever to see him again except as a dodo. To have even suggested that the dream might have an inner connection would have been disastrous to any friendly harmony; for these people of impregnable Personas are very sensitive and must keep the world at arm's length lest someone coming too near might tear aside the garment and reveal an inner emptiness. In such an event, the person retires to rebuild the Persona (the dodo will smooth his own ruffled feathers) but, ever after, views with distrust and suspicion the one who has so blasphemed. It was right that in his professional life this man should assume the role of instructor, but when he continued this role in places where ordinary feeling and interest in daily human life was demanded, his authority became pomposity and his lack of human interests made him appear as absurd as the dodo. Worn in the proper place, his garb would have made him seem not a dodo, but a very dignified and handsome bird; for one may have Personas to fit the varying roles that one is called upon to play quite as properly as one may have clothes to suit different occasions.

The extravert slips more easily into these varying Persona roles than does the introvert, and this without hypocrisy, because the outer situation arouses the reaction. An extravert may appear in a bewildering number of Persona garments—the same man may be the medical authority, the charming host, the warm friend, even perhaps the mountebank or the tragedian. By showing the various sides evoked by circumstances to which he responds, he is being not hypocritical but natural. The introvert, however, feels strangely ill-at-ease in the Persona garb unless it fits his inner mood or concept. He finds great difficulty in meeting an outer situation which is at variance with his inner feeling. His Persona often gives the appearance of having been borrowed from another and of fitting most uncomfortably.

A danger arises for both types when there is such concentration upon the Persona that one becomes oblivious of everything which it conceals—in fact assumes that anything which is not found out is nonexistent. An apparently absurd but actual occurrence illustrates this point. A woman came to an old country doctor. She had been attacked, robbed of a small sum, and her two front teeth had been knocked out. The old man tried to comfort her and said, "Think, my child, of what might have happened to you," to which she tearfully replied, "But, doctor, your front teeth show so much more than your honor." This woman's attitude is really no more ludicrous than that of people who remain undisturbed by their meannesses, or weaknesses, or petty selfishness, or even their uncomfortable potentials of greater reality, provided nothing affects their position in the world in which they live.

Relationships formed upon a Persona basis are endangered the moment either person involved becomes aware of a reality beyond the image. For example, a marriage between two such images gave every appearance of desirability. The husband was a successful businessman, holding a position of great respectability in the community. He provided a perfect setting in which moved the image of the good wife and mother—"the ideal of womanhood." When she had intimations of things that might be wrong with their life, she kept them to herself and continued her role of the understanding wife. The husband moved about in his garment of respectability, but occasionally took little side excursions into places where this garment did not fit. These excursions he promptly forgot, and his charming wife never appeared to see them. Then something happened. The wife found herself emotionally involved with a very real man. She had supposed such an event could not happen to a good woman, but it had happened to her, and something hitherto unknown in her rose to meet it. The Persona image was broken. This, of course, threw a tremendous problem on the husband. He had never had to carry the burden of relationship, because his wife had never been to him a real woman. One does not have to come to terms with a saint on a pedestal, she can be worshipped and forgotten. She is also a sort of glorified hat rack—one can hang up one's own halo while one goes into little corners where a halo might shed inconvenient light or become recognizably tarnished. Then one can retrieve the halo as soon as one re-enters that chamber of sanctity where "the real self" is supposed to be. Now, with the saint off the pedestal, busy with real living, it looked very much as though he would have to get rid of his halo altogether.

There is a naive assumption that it is only the thing that is inconvenient and upsetting that has very great importance. Now here was a situation upsetting in the extreme; it threatened the "sanctity of the home," because it had reality and also might easily be found out. The wife was not willing to break off her relationship as casually as her husband had been accustomed to discard his mistresses. He came to analysis to see what could be done to bring the woman to her senses, and found that he himself was suddenly compelled to think furiously. Was he or was he not a centralized person who had control over his own acts? If not, he too had a problem of which he had been conveniently unconscious.

The Winnebago Indians have an old saga of Trickster, the Undifferentiated Man. He carries his genitals in a little box on his back and can send his own membrum virile off on excursions of its own. In one episode Trickster takes a nap by the side of a stream, while the "little man" crosses the river and finds an Indian maiden on the other bank. The episode over, and the member restored to the box, Trickster wakes and goes on his way as before. This fable is a perfect picture of the sexuality of a conventional morality which condones the thing which is casual and unrelated. The conscious side sleeps while the unconscious goes its way to the other side of the stream and has "its little adventure."

This modern man had been as unconcerned as Trickster until now, when he was suddenly asked that inconvenient question, "Is your sexuality something for which you are responsible, or is it not?" In the society of men, his sexuality became at times quite his own, an evidence of his virility, but at other times it was only the thing in the box about which he did not have to worry. The wife had, through the experience of a mutually shared reality, become conscious of the unreality of the Persona which she had been forced to assume during her marriage and which, until now, she had accepted as a beautiful self. She was not this combination of virgin of the spirit and holy mother, in which she had been encased by the man's invention and her own conception of womanhood. She was a very real flesh and blood woman, undeveloped in many ways, with passion and rebellion heaped up in her unconscious, until finally they had found an outlet unacceptable to the Persona.

So through this experience they both had to realize that these Personas who had been walking about reacting to accepted patterns, respectable and admirable, were not individuals at all but only shells. And when these were broken they came face to face with each other.

The Persona which is formed upon an accepted collective pattern may make use of either a collective social ideal or one based upon an ideal of the collective unconscious. If the identification is with an inner ideal, this is likely to be an archetypal image and the garment a pseudo-spiritual one. This "impersonal" Persona can be the result of a failure to make an adaptation to ordinary human relationships.

A woman who in childhood was repulsed by her mother made her first relations with sick animals which she tenderly nursed, and then substituted tenderness toward human frailties and saw herself always ministering to needs. This ministration extended to her sexuality and she saw herself as Cybele, the great moon goddess, the goddess of the cult of love. Whenever she gave herself to a man, it was always with the idea of helping and ministering to him, so that she moved about the world as a sort of prostitute with halo, so conscious of her halo that people accepted it, and were inclined to think of her as a saint. She dreamed this dream:

"I saw a great moon rising from the waters of the ocean. I felt myself to be its priestess. But greatly to my bewilderment, I found that it was only a great paper balloon."

Balloons are easily punctured, and so, at the first touch of reality, was her own image of herself. The moon which she served was only a paper balloon.

When such an identification with an image of the collective unconscious has been made, an ego inflation may take place, and this ego, clothed in the archetypal Persona may be utterly unmindful of the reality-demands of human life. A youth identified with the image of the archetype of wisdom could not see why he should be expected to meet the demands of daily life or consider the trivial needs of others. He dreamed:

"I have been given three great eggs. They are huge, like the eggs of some mythological or prehistoric bird. I feel them to be a great honor and a great responsibility. I entrust two of them to old professors, and the other I carry carefully to my own room where I can watch over it till it hatches. I keep it carefully at an even temperature, warmly covered. I am so anxious about it that I can hardly bear to leave it to go to my classes. I hurry back and spend every possible minute watching it. It seems an interminable time before it hatches, and I am filled with anxiety over it. At last the shell breaks; an enormous bird steps out. At first I am greatly excited, but suddenly an appalling thought comes to me. I look at it in hopeless perplexity and I say to myself, 'What on earth am I going to do with this damn thing now that I *have* got it?'"

In spite of his certainty of greatness this youth had been aware of some misgivings. Was he losing something other young people had? Yet he clung to his hero identification; all would be justified in the great "by and by." In the dream he becomes one of the three wise men who are to hatch these great, mysterious birds; he is the director, and delegates responsibility to the other two. He is, so to speak, head of this hierarchy of wisdom. The great egg fills him with excitement, and a sense of enormous values to be born. The egg hatches and suddenly he realizes that the bird has no place in real life. It is a monstrous absurdity.

The following dream also illustrates how the Persona may be formed through identification with the collective unconscious. The dreamer was a young woman who found herself irresistibly drawn to a man who seemed to be an extraordinarily spiritual person. He had identified with the intuitions of beauty and holiness which had come to him, and moved about the world clad in a garment of spiritual beauty. He accepted this woman as a sort of vestal votary and she fell easily into the role assigned to her. But in spite of all his charm she had intuitions of dangerous insincerities in his nature. Actual facts had been brought to her which proved his extreme unreliability, yet she could not seem to escape the power which he had over her. While in this confusion and struggling blindly to extricate herself, she had the following dream:

"We were in a strange country and in the service of a young prince, the pretender. We were hidden in a dark, low room like a serf's cottage. A man's hand was thrust in the window, giving me a package containing a mask. This I knew I must wear if I would find the prince and go with him. Then we rode out into the night through a strange dark land, down a steep mountainside with great yawning chasms. At the bottom a green valley opened out, the sky was blue, the sunlight dazzling. A voice said, 'And so they came to their fair land.' I knew I should find the prince here. But suddenly I also knew that I must take off the mask, even though without it I might lose this land. I lifted my hands to my face. Immediately, I was in a simple homelike room. X stood before me. He was dressed all in gray. I saw him as the prince. I tore off the mask. Slowly he changed and stood as I had often seen him in his own familiar clothes. There was a sound in the room like that of a wind harp. It was both beautiful and sinister, and again the voice spoke, 'Behold, he is hollow, and the wind blows through him.'"

The strange setting of this dream lifts it away from ordinary life and shows that it belongs back in the greater past. We therefore feel at once that we have to do with the collective unconscious. The voice which speaks at the end shows clearly why the young woman had not been able to have any feeling of trust or security in the relationship, for the man was really lost in the collective unconscious. He had identified with these figures that had come to him. He thought of himself as lifted above ordinary humanity, and he did the thing that possessed him at the moment without any discrimination as to its reality value, or as to whether it was really good or evil. She herself had a close connection with this unreal world (unreal because of the confusion of images), hence his magic charm for her. It is her own mask of unreality which makes her a participant. When she lifts her hands to take the mask from her face, the problem becomes clarified, and the voice which she has stifled within herself can now tell her that this image which has held her by its fascination is hollow, and that the charm of the music is made by the wind of the collective that blows through. It was a vivid intuition of reality, for the man had lived so long in the chosen image that his real self had dwindled and shriveled away and only the Persona image remained.

If all the inner life has been sacrificed to the building of a Persona image, there comes a time when one seems almost to have been encased in a magnet or shell which draws everything from the center to the periphery, so that one is hollowed out within and individuality is lost in the image. Whether the identification be with the social collective or the collective unconscious, the person so identified sees himself only as this very special desirable image, but others who can look at him clearly see, peering out from behind the Persona, another image, the image of the Shadow.

VI. THE SHADOW

The foregoing chapter cites the instance of a woman identified with a Persona image built upon her early fantasy of a princess self. It was as the princess, gracious, charming, condescending, that she still saw herself. But others were often aware of another being, whose presence was expressed through resentments, jealousies, false assumptions, manifestations of a side of the personality very different from that which she consciously presented to the world, a dark side which may be termed the shadow side, or, more briefly, the Shadow.

When this Shadow took part in a situation, the other people involved reacted quite naturally to it, that is, they turned away from it; but the woman herself, oblivious of all but her Persona, saw in their reactions unkindness and lack of appreciation. Unaware that the cause for these reactions was within herself, she attributed them to the dark sides of other people, and her life became increasingly unhappy until she was the prey of obsessive fears, doubts and distrust of life. It was only when she was forced by her neurosis to face the increasing difficulties of her reality-situation that she sought help. Then her attention was turned toward the unconscious, and she began to see, in the form of images, forces within herself that had been acting destructively.

These images took the shape of women who were distinctly of inferior quality. Examining them, she became aware of the activities of a side of her life which she had excluded from consciousness.

She had plenty of feeling, only it had become negative because it was continually thwarted; she had strong instincts but they must not appear in connection with an ordinary person, such as she had discovered her husband to be; she had a good, normal, selfish desire to enjoy life, but this, too, was unacceptable to her

Persona. And so all these qualities, so necessary to her life as a woman, had been pushed down into the unconscious and had become part of the shadow side. And this side was behaving as primitive woman would have behaved when thwarted—it was furtive, resentful, and destructive.

First of all, then, she had to see the Shadow in its destructive form as a part of herself, not as the evil side of other people. So the acceptance of her Shadow was the first step toward freeing herself from identification with her own Persona and from projecting the Shadow upon others. Once she had realized this, she could see that her Shadow held values which, if consciously accepted, would make her life much more enjoyable and desirable. For the Shadow is not just a lurking evil; it is an inferior personality which does not fit into the cultural and accepted idea. It frequently knows more about our essential needs than does the Persona. There was, therefore, no way in which she could become real except by acknowledging the Shadow, for so much of her reality was there.

The more we attempt to live in the Persona the greater will be the Shadow's strength. But we all have a Shadow, whether we are identified with the Persona or whether we are not, and it always appears in our dreams as an inferior human being, of the same sex as the dreamer's. The personal Shadow takes its nature from our own personality, just as a silhouette cast upon a screen takes form from the one who casts it. It stands in direct relation to one's own conscious adaptation and is as personal as the ego. But, unless we accept it and become aware of its activities, it moves in the obscurity of the unconscious. Having become aware of it, we can increasingly anticipate what it will do.

Merely to admit, in general terms, that one has a Shadow is not enough; we must see the part it plays in specific acts. It is easy to say, "I know I have a selfish side"; it is harder but much more important to say, "This particular act which I did was petty and selfish, and when a situation conflicts with my desires, I generally react in a selfish way." It is also easy to evade the petty, personal aspects of the Shadow by dramatizing it, by seeing the uncontrolled mood as that of the melancholy Hamlet, a tragic hero; by seeing petty business dishonesty as the cleverness of a wily Machiavelli; by seeing trivial sexual vagaries as the lures of a great courtesan. This kind of evasion gives the Shadow a remoteness which is very comforting.

Dealing with the Shadow in ordinary life is difficult enough, but a catastrophe that shatters the Persona may give the Shadow a sudden and dangerous power. A man of very real talent, who had achieved a remarkable worldly success, but at the expense of every side of himself but one (his professional adaptation), met with catastrophe. He found his outer life in ruins and he became distrustful even of his own special ability; so distrustful that he had no faith in his power to re-establish himself. Then came this dream:

"I am in my favorite restaurant and have before me a bottle of my special wine; but a whining man comes up to me and thrusts into my face his thumb, which is bound up in a dirty rag. He will not go away, but keeps sniveling and complaining. At last I turn to the proprietor and say, 'Unless you get rid of this fellow I cannot drink my wine in peace. He is only a whining impostor; I do not think his thumb is even hurt.'"

He saw here an aspect of the Shadow, his own self-pity that would not let him enjoy even his normal pleasures, but intruded with a demand for sympathy for injuries that were not even real. It was this self-pitying impostor who now dogged him, preventing him from understanding the mistakes that had contributed to his failure, the weak spots in his wall of defense where disaster could creep in. Confident in his own powers, he had been naive as a child in his business arrangements, trusting in places where intuition would have told him to be careful, oversure of his ability to pile success on success.

When he found himself confronted by failure, he lost his confidence in the powers which were really his. For when one loses faith in one's own integrated ego value, one becomes as impotent as one's own inferior function; this impotence enhances the mysterious power of the Shadow; and the ego seems to shrink in proportion to the increasing stature of the image that threatens.

His own self-pity stood between himself and life; for as long as he felt himself to be the victim of injustice, he could not see where he himself had been to blame, or understand the possibility of using his values in a new situation without repeating the same mistakes. He had, therefore, first of all to realize that these mistakes came from a disregard of everything not actually connected with what he had thought worth while. He had been too intent on his ego adaptation to be mindful of the values of human relations. He had been too one-track in his thinking to perceive the various factors to be considered in professional life. These things had not been worth bothering about. The first Shadow dream opened his eyes to a side of himself living in the unconscious. If he could, by examining his mistakes, see the value of what he had once disregarded in the outer world, he could see the necessity for developing the disregarded sides of his inner self. The catastrophe would then open the way to a broader and more understanding life. And through his encounter with the Shadow, he would gain a greater consciousness.

He saw in this dream what he was actually doing. Therefore, if after this actual experience he should again attempt to project the dark side upon others or upon life, it would be the Shadow, not his conscious self, who would feed upon this experience and grow strong, while the ego would become more disintegrated.

An experience of this sort is always used by some part of the self, the conscious or the unconscious. For the personal Shadow is the negative side of the ego-consciousness. It turns toward the dark unknown, even as the Persona faces the outer world. It is an image that derives its power from its ability to darken and confuse our ego choices. *It contains also the strength of the dark forces needed for our life.* It holds the negative intuition. This man, seeing the Shadow at work, traced its influence in the other sides of his life, and by watching the Shadow qualities in himself made a reintegration which included sides of life heretofore shut away by the autocracy of his early ego choice.

Sometimes the Shadow may appear in a dream as a tempter, even though the context of the dream warns against the danger of accepting its temptation. The dream in its inner meaning often confirms the real knowledge and decision of the conscious, but also, perhaps, will present a picture of the strength of the underemphasized element in the unconscious and of the choice to be made. Then the problem is whether the person is strongly enough integrated to withstand the Shadow when its power falls upon him.

A young woman had perceived in herself elements which might act destructively in a desired situation, and consciously she had chosen to wait quietly and to let the potentials which the situation contained develop slowly through understanding. Even from early childhood, her problem had been to reckon with a Shadow side of herself that snatched and grabbed, and that suddenly swept her into situations before she had made a conscious decision. She dreamed:

"I am going down a mountain road; a woman in a car asks me to come her way, which is straight down the mountainside, a precipice. She tells me that her way is the quick way. I tell her the dangers are too great, that it is the wrong road, that I must go down a long winding one."

Then the actual situation, which she had decided must not be accepted at present, arose to confront her in real life. She seized upon it, thus disregarding the clear warning of the conscious and the unconscious. She snatched at what she wanted.

At first, she felt only an intoxication of achievement, for when one acquiesces in the triumph of the Shadow, one experiences that sense of elation which follows any victory. The dark side has obtained its desire and has triumphed over the conscious sense of rightness and the warning of the unconscious. In that false elation one feels a false sense of rightness, but those who stand outside see that the victory is in the hands of the Shadow. For example, this young woman found that she had in her haste left behind many things that she now needed in this new situation into which she had plunged so suddenly; and she had to toil back along the winding way to get them, and not only herself but others had to pay for her victory. She had to see all that she had not wished to remember when the Shadow had spoken. That was a long and difficult process, for the way back is often longer than the way down, and the Shadow is a heavy burden as one climbs back to consciousness.

Sometimes the Shadow appears in short, graphic dreams, stating succinctly its existing relation to the Persona or to the ego. A woman who had taken a deep dislike to a fellow worker, because she distrusted her colleague's egotism and her methods of gaining her ends, was beginning a piece of work which she considered important. She dreamed that she was starting on a journey and found this woman, whom she disliked, sharing her berth as a bedfellow, to whom she must give attention. Hitherto, she had seen her Persona adaptation as her very real value, but the dream showed who was really the bedfellow of this blameless Persona. That is, the woman was an image of the dreamer's Shadow, her inseparable companion.

Even good deeds may be used by the Shadow if one is unaware of the motive behind them. A man who was really philanthropic and whose conscious attention was focused upon good deeds, but whose generosity rarely lacked publicity, dreamed that he was in bed. By the bed he saw a shadowy figure. It was Y, a boy whom he had despised at school for his underhand and ungenerous ways. He knew that he had to rouse himself and throw out this intruder, but to his horror the figure grew larger and larger, and he felt as though he himself were shrinking. He cried, "Help, Peter," and woke.

Peter was a straightforward, affectionate brother whom he had greatly admired in his youth, but whom he now undervalued. He needed the help of Peter because he had substituted a magnificent semblance of generosity for real human feeling. Even his good deeds had fed the Shadow, because the hidden motive of ego pride robbed them of their human values. For the Shadow is like a prowling jackal ready to seize anything left outside the light. Secret motives, if they contradict the good deed which embodies them, have this Shadow life and seem to give off a strange atmosphere, so that people have a distrust even when they can find no conscious reason for criticism. They feel the presence of the undesired, unseen Shadow.

Sometimes when one feels that the obstacles of life, even when faced with courage, are insurmountable, one may discover that part of the difficulty is caused by the unsuspected activity of the Shadow. Such activity was disclosed by the following dream:

"I was talking with a woman who was having great trouble with her husband and I was trying to help her with her problem. In despair, she said, 'It is just like being up against a stone wall.' I answered, 'Be careful that you are not yourself the stone wall.'"

The dreamer was very lonely. She was full of negative attitudes toward people. The ones whom she knew best she found dull; or, with that oversensitivity which negative feeling produces, she was sure that she was not wanted because she was herself too dull. Most of her energy was given to her creative work; she was, so to speak, wedded to it. She saw her problem solely in terms of her creative ability and its professional success. She felt that if she could achieve that kind of success, she would be accepted by people who were really worth while. Now the dream says, "It is not this work with which you battle, which is the stone wall. It is the negative side of your feeling which needs attention. It is the Shadow which blocks your way." For anything that is in obscurity—that is, outside the light of consciousness—is in the power of the Shadow. Here her own neglected feminine values, ossified by the Shadow, were like a stone wall shutting her from life.

But even to see the Shadow clearly is not enough. One must be prepared to accept it, understand it, and take responsibility for it. A woman had the following dream:

"I was walking down the road with Y. We met a woman of the lower class standing by the roadside. She seemed in great perplexity. Y began to censure her for some fault that she had committed. Another man standing by joined in this. I said, 'Why do you treat her this way? After all, her faults are no greater than any of ours. It is because you think her of an inferior station that you treat her so. We should befriend her.'"

Y was a man of extraverted sensation. He dealt with the factual aspects of a situation. In the dream he represented a hard, factual side of herself which censured the Shadow side but made no attempt to understand its nature. In the dream she says that one must see one's own Shadow with the same tolerant understanding that one tries to use toward others. It lives in an inferior situation but is not to be despised on that account. For these inferior sides have energy that may be redirected.

The becoming conscious of the Shadow and the discovery of what potential it may contain gives one a greater understanding of reality. An awareness of the Shadow limits its power. The Shadow is not lost, it is met and dealt with, it is "assimilated"; that is, its energy is placed at the disposal of the conscious.

When, as often happens, one continues to regard the Shadow as unimportant, there may come a moment of sudden realization that, somewhere, something dark and cruel has really been at work. For instance, a man dreamed that he had before him a tablet covered with clear, careful writing. Suddenly, a creature, half man, half beast, rose from the floor beneath and with a huge paw wiped out all that had been inscribed.

This dream graphically depicts the ability of the Shadow temporarily to wipe out all that the conscious mind has laboriously created. It is connected with a supra-personal force, a shadow from the collective unconscious, which man does well to fear. It is through the door that the disregarded personal Shadow leaves open that this supra-personal force enters. For instance, to remain unconscious of one's resentment and to repress and deny the flood of emotion which would find an outlet in anger, may let the dynamic energy sweep in as a flood of hate that may bring terror to the one who experiences it.

A somewhat similar result of ignoring the personal Shadow is graphically illustrated by the dream of another man. At the time, he was involved in a situation which called for more conscious responsibility and frankness than he was willing to give. A relationship in which he had looked for unalloyed happiness developed unexpected difficulties. He had intuitions of the unpleasant elements at work. The more he tried to ignore these, the more his energies seemed to go from him. Doubt and distrust crept in, and he put the blame for this upon others. He feared to face the situation frankly, desiring to hold to his infantile phantasy of perfection.

Then he tried to dismiss his intuitions as disloyal. He tried to reason things out consciously and to argue to himself that it was all unimportant, but he only became confused as to what faults were real and what were projections. He thrust the problem down out of consciousness. But though his attempt was to repress only the negative side, he lost all spontaneity of feeling. Then the dynamic energy of the unconscious seemed to go from him—not only had his feeling gone out, but the creative quality which had been present in his work was no longer at his disposal. At this point, the unconscious came to his aid by painting a dream picture:

"I am on a ship which has become stranded in a strange waste land. I know that we have submerged this country in order to drown out the inhabitants, whom we feared. But now we are attacked by a greater enemy; we are prisoners. Then I realize that if we had not drowned out the inhabitants we might have got help from them, whereas now we are delivered over, helpless, to some unseen but omnipotent tyrant from whom there is no escape."

His own interpretation was, "I have been trying to pretend that all sorts of things which I knew intuitively were wrong in this business either were better not talked about or else were the fault of others involved and that, therefore, I could do nothing about them and had best ignore them. But this has left me high and dry, delivered over to the enemy who, in some strange way, has drained me of my energy both in feeling and in power to work. I feel absolutely unable to get back any enthusiasm for life."

Here, the Shadow elements which he tried to drown were the negative, distrustful elements in himself which were roused when he was faced with the responsibilities involved in the working out of a difficult reality. In becoming unconscious of these, in letting the waters of the unconscious cover them, he projected the whole thing upon other people involved and felt it all was due to the influence of *their* shadows. He feared to test out the truth of his doubts lest he should discover the situation to have no value for himself and he would lose even the illusion of happiness. He would not frankly face the disaster which might result from acknowledging the truth. First he projected all the difficulties upon others, and then he tried to repress these projections as being disloyal. He refused to become aware of the inner voices which were contradicting his conscious decision. So the whole problem was pushed back into the unconscious, where it acted like an ever-increasing magnetic force continually drawing down his energy.

In the end, it made the unconscious assume the proportions of a great inundation which drowned all his spontaneous energy and finally left him helpless, delivered over to one of those greater shadows of the collective unconscious which in the dream appeared as the inescapable tyrant. For, whenever he had pushed down any of his fears, he had really been feeding the Shadow until it had grown to proportions too great for his personal ego-consciousness to meet. It had taken from him the dynamic and creative elements of the unconscious which before fed his creative life.

For if one ignores the personal Shadow, one may be delivered over to the greater enemy. In such a typical human situation as this, for example, a failure to meet the problem may leave one at the mercy of the archetype—here the unseen invincible tyrant. If the archetype succeeds in swallowing the ego, the individual values are disintegrated and one becomes possessed by the unconscious and bereft of energy.

This man was acting in accordance with a generally accepted social standard, that the negative and disturbing aspects of a situation should be passed over in well-bred silence; that unpleasant things are best left out of a discussion; that resentments and anger should be hidden; in fact, that all the realities of the situation should be concealed if they interfere with harmonious adjustment. But realities dwindle when one fears anything which might disturb surface calm, whether these realities are in the outer situation or the inner. Then the difficulties may be projected. The devil is at work in the other fellow. The shadows of others fall across the path and they must be avoided. The outer life narrows, the inner life becomes more shallow. But down below, the Shadow has a good supper.

When we have had the courage to look upon the personal Shadow, we have taken a step forward in our integration. But there are greater shadows moving in the depths. These move in a world beyond our control, and they may determine the destiny of a man, or a nation, when one is unconscious of them. If one is dominated by an archetype, the ego is dissolved, one loses one's personal identity.

The danger of the Shadow is the danger of being drawn into unconsciousness, into that obscurity where man can no longer perceive things as they are, or himself as he is. As Desdemona says, "Something hath puddled his clear spirit. . . . And in such cases, men's natures wrangle with inferior things, though great ones are their object." Through this unconsciousness, a man stands in danger of the disintegration of the center of consciousness which he has built up. If on the personal level it is perilous to try to escape by giving no attention to the personal Shadow forms, it is even more perilous to try to be oblivious of the nature of the greater ones of the collective unconscious. Not only may one be taken unawares by their power, and the ego be disintegrated, but one may, through neglect of them, become like a tree without roots or a being of two-dimensional existence. For one is cut off from the irrational creative force, from a renewal of energy which arises from the experience of those images.

No experience deeply affects the whole nature of man except his own original, individual experience. To explore for oneself a strange land is dangerous, for one may encounter forces which are destructive as well as creative. The Lord walketh upon the wings of the wind; so too does the god of fear walk upon the wind of the night. The fire of the spirit both quickens and consumes, but he who would escape danger also escapes the possibility of the renewal of life. To turn from these greater images is doubly dangerous. It may put one in peril of being sucked back into the unconscious through fear or identification, or it may limit the whole personality through limiting life to conscious rational concepts.

VII. THE ANIMA

It is possible to discuss the ego, the Persona, the Shadow, without stressing the difference between masculine and feminine psychology. There are, however, figures in the unconscious of men which are so distinct from those in the unconscious of women that they cannot be considered without reference to certain fundamental differences in masculine and feminine psychology. In every man's unconscious is a feminine figure which profoundly affects his life.

The pattern of a man's *conscious* life is, as we have already said, determined by his ego, his conscious personality. It is a man's first business to find his goal, his chosen work, to concentrate upon it in order to make his place in the world of men. In finding his goal, he relates himself to the essential masculine principle, the Logos. Logos means literally "word" ("In the beginning was the word"), i.e., that which creates by understanding, by definition, by differentiation. By finding the word, the name, for something one separates it from other things, gives it independent existence, makes possible a logical relation between it and other things.

The Logos principle is, therefore, that which gives form, that which brings order out of the chaotic elements of life. It is to the working out of the chosen form that masculine energy is bent. The youth may at first be concerned with his physical masculinity, with strength, with virility. Later his conscious energy is directed into a chosen channel, into his profession or his work, into a definite pattern.

In his concentration upon his masculine choices, he is apt to ignore certain elements in his psyche which he considers feminine, and so thrusts out of consciousness one of the images that still exert great power over him, the image of woman. For the little boy, this is embodied in the mother. His growing masculinity is ashamed of the undeveloped feminine elements in his psyche, and yet he is aware of them; they have to find a place in his life, so he shows them to the one person whom he can rely upon to accept them, the mother. It is her ability to understand which determines his first idea of woman. As he grows older he may break from the actual mother and feel that he has also overthrown her image, but it may be still active, perhaps even dominant in his unconscious. If this is so, "woman" and mother are synonymous terms in his submerged emotional life, and he sees "mother" clothed in various bodies, so that though in outer form these women differ, inwardly they are to him the same, and he expects them to react in accordance with the nature of the image.

More commonly, however, a new image of woman is gradually taking form, one which may derive some of its characteristics from the mother but which, for the most part, comes from other sources and which has an existence quite apart from the image of the mother.

This image within a man's psyche is derived in part from experiences with actual girls and women, in part from his father's ideas about them, from his mother's remarks about them, from schoolboy phrases, from the accepted ideas of the particular environment. But deeper than all these lie the racial images of woman, the archetypes, the sense of woman as the Harlot, the Virgin, the Mother, the Witch, the Vampire, the Temptress, the Spiritual Guide. Hence, in his actual experience with a girl or a woman, he does not see her as she actually is, but as a being whose nature is partly her own and partly that of the image which she arouses in him. This image can best be described as a complex of objective experience, of racial ideas about women, and of the undeveloped feminine elements within himself.

This complex image is called the Anima, a Latin word meaning "soul" or "breath of life"—that which animates. It is this inner woman whom the man, preoccupied with his conscious masculine life, ignores, but it is this woman with whom he must reckon, the woman within himself, the woman side of his own nature.

The image of the woman is usually quite hidden from his conscious perceptions. He cannot see her real nature nor understand her activities. Yet that woman within the self is the one who will rule him without his knowledge, who will work upon him a magic against which he seems powerless. She appears in his irrational moods, his undeveloped feelings, and may even, in extreme instances, make him behave like an hysterical woman. Hence the misery which his unconscious, unadapted, and irrational moods and feelings may cause him. They are something contrary to his conscious nature, beyond his understanding or his control. He therefore prefers to consider them as the work of an outsider. The feminine side of life, relatedness, feeling, irrational and intuitive feeling-reaction, is not that with which he is consciously familiar. But all these qualities are embryonic within him. They belong to the woman image moving in his own unconscious.

But if these elements, these demands of the inner woman, are disregarded, they go their own way in the unconscious and live as undeveloped, infantile, womanish traits. In this case, man seeks woman not for an evolved relationship, but so that she may carry and live out his own unlived feminine side. For deep down in the unconscious is a purposefulness toward the completion and fulfillment of the self. If this is not consciously met, then there is an obsessive demand to complete life through another. The inner image is projected upon someone who can impersonate these needed qualities; and so the man of strong masculinity, aggressiveness, who is outwardly ruthless, will often fall into the power of a very feminine woman who, rightly or wrongly, represents to him "the loving woman." Or a man too gentle, too unassertive, will be fascinated by the dark power of a woman of force, either tempestuous emotional power or an overmasculine development. Xanthippe is the unacknowledged side of a too-gentle feeling; as the child wife, the angel woman, is the complement of the overagressive, brutalized, or undeveloped emotion.

The too-infantile feeling cannot accept the Anima, but continually seeks the Eternal Mother, the first embodiment of the woman image. As long as this condition exists, the Anima as a subjective value cannot really appear.

A man still under the domination of the mother image dreamed:

"I was climbing a mountain when I came to a great cliff. In the side I saw a tunnel through which the path lay. It seemed as I approached it to be utterly dark, but then I saw a little light from the other end. After that I saw standing by the entrance a woman clothed in a black garment, which hung in heavy, rigid folds. Her face was covered, and her head seemed almost enclosed in a heavy square block of the dark mantle, so heavy that it might have been black marble, like a tombstone. She stood directly in the opening of the tunnel. I woke in terror, and as I woke it seemed as though I had dreamed the same dream many years before."

The imagery of this dream is strikingly clear. The mother, long dead, is enclosed in black marble like a tombstone; yet the tombstone is alive and terrifying, because she bars the way to the tunnel. The tunnel is a well-known rebirth symbol, the way out from the womb to life. Here the dead mother stands, blocking the way to his rebirth. He thinks of her as the actual mother, but she is the archaic figure rising from a region deeper than any personal experience. This dream came as the culmination of a series of dreams in which had appeared figures of dark, sinister women; it was the revealing dream, for it showed that the mother image had dominated all his ideas of women. The Anima could take no form except the one dictated by the mother.

The appearance of the Anima is shown in this second dream, when the power of the mother image has been really broken:

"I was in a very beautiful garden looking for a flower. A gracious woman came toward me. We walked together down the path. I saw a beautiful white blossom, and knew that it was the flower I was seeking. She said, 'It is yours, you may pick it. It is the rose that grows only in Palestine.' Then my mother came up to me and said, 'I, too, have that flower in my garden.' But I said, 'No, mother, the flower that grew in your garden was not one that grew in Palestine.'"

In this dream, he distinguishes clearly between the Anima who offers him the living symbol—the flower that grew in the land of the Messiah, of the new life—and the mother image whose garden had nothing to do with this new value. With this dream, the real Anima appeared. The mother was no longer Anima. The world began to be peopled by living women not mother images, and his own moods and reactions were seen as elements within the self.

Or, if the man has never been freed from the authority of

the father—that is, from the dominance of an image of masculine authority—the Anima also remains under the role of that image: A man who was struggling to throw off the domination of an overconscious, over-rational adaptation dreamed that he had found his Anima, but she was feeding a machine in a factory and wearing long flannel underdrawers; also she was completely under the domination of her father. She was very beautiful and he loved her passionately, but realized his problem was to rescue her from the situation which held her. The father image still held authority over the material of his unconscious and reduced his impulses to rational conformity with accepted values. They therefore were kept feeding the well-regulated machine of life, while Victorian attitudes, consciously denied but continually appearing in unconscious material, might be the flannel of which the enveloping garments were formed. Although he believed himself to be ready to follow whatever might arise within himself, the dream showed what his own overemphasized, over-rationalized masculinity (in the dream appearing as the father) had done to the Anima.

The Anima is not a single image having only one aspect. It can take many shapes which the man, if he still confuses his subjective moods with objective reality, may project either in succession upon one woman, or upon several women more or less simultaneously. The women he meets will be good or bad, angels or devils, in accordance with the aspects of the Anima which appear in connection with them. So, too, a man, very much swayed by the Anima, may be unable to see any one woman in her totality; he may see her merely as the embodiment of a single trait. This dream is an example:

"I was in a large hall. My wife came up to me. She seemed very pale, insipid, anemic. She claimed me, but I pushed her aside. Then X appeared, dark, in deep blue, both passionate and compassionate, and I accepted her. I looked out of the window. There on the church steeple, Y was sitting."

The woman pushed aside was the image of the woman to be loved—that is, of the feeling which he did not want to be bothered with, his own feeling which he must give to a woman; X was the image of the woman who could give love, the embodiment of a romantic idea of intense passion—that is, the Divine Harlot; Y, the image on the steeple, was the image of the Spiritual Guide, who seemed now to be in a somewhat precarious position.

Or, again, a man may project his varying moods upon a single woman, who will change at the dictates of the Anima. In one instance, a woman who was a trusted friend and not connected with immediate feeling demand appeared in successive dreams. First she appeared in the dreamer's bedroom as a dark, violent witch, who "more or less raped me." Later she appeared in the dreamer's bedroom dressed in blue, and gently quieted his fears. These two dreams occurred within the space of a few days, when the dreamer was completely at the mercy of his moods—so much so that his friend had been made to bear, in rapid succession, the image of the Vampire Woman and the image of the Spiritual Guide.

If some special quality which a man needs to complete himself an an individual is buried so deep in his own unconscious that he cannot get at it, or if he represses it, then some woman possessing this quality may seem to him almost to possess his soul, and he feels he must in turn possess this woman because, so to speak, she *has* his soul. He says "This is my woman." He thinks he feels the magic power of love. But he is really under the intense necessity of completing himself. He looks then for an embodiment of his own inner image. The power of the projection is so great that the woman on whom he places it will exert a compulsive fascination, she will "bewitch" him, she will cast a spell over him, and the intensity of this spell is only increased by his repression of the trait within himself. There are so many irrational possibilities closed to him by his "duty" to his profession, his responsibilities to life and to society. He fears the stirring of potentials that might lure him away from these. Secretly, he wishes to break the chains that hold him to the accepted routine. Then the most "unsuitable" woman embodying all those secret desires may appear. She is the Witch Woman, La Belle Dame Sans Merci, She-Who-Must Be-Obeyed, the "Eternal Feminine." Or he may be irresistibly attracted to the woman who is herself unconscious and unaware of the demands of her own being, who shapes herself in conformity to man's ideal of her rather than to her own reality, and lends herself to the task of carrying his unconscious and becoming the image of his desire. Until he can accept the problem of the Anima as part of his own inner drama, he is at the mercy of the projected Anima.

At times the Anima is not projected upon a woman but lived out in an unconscious way through an identification with the woman side of the self. A man may be lost in his unconscious feminine side, living in phantasy or in womanish moods and emotions. Such a man will be effeminate, overgentle, submissive. He cannot come to terms with the world of men and, as a timid child fears a forceful and aggressive mother, so he fears life with its demands for courage and action. Since this is an unconscious process, it is subject to all the irrational variations of the unconscious, and such a man is much at the mercy of his moods —elation and despondency sweep over him, he is spilling over with sentimental feeling or filled with distrust and suspicion. He thinks he is longing to love and be loved, but really he is looking for someone to relieve him of the task of growing into manhood and finding his own goal.

Frequently, an identification with the Anima will give the masculine image an obsessive power, for the man then seeks his own masculinity and looks for it in another man. Sometimes the image is projected upon a man of inferior quality, who possesses a certain crude form of masculinity which is clearly recognized as inferior and yet which exerts a completely irrational power, because *to the unconscious* it represents a picture of the masculine vigor and aggressiveness needed if the Anima identification is to be broken.

Or the life of the Anima may represent to him the reality. His irrational life may appear as the greatest value. A man thus Anima-identified dreamed the following dream:

"I am on a hillside. It is bare and lifeless. The sky is luminous but is of the pale green that one sees in sunsets when it has suddenly grown cold. Ahead of me is a cross. When I come up to it, I see it is made of pale green stones, like aquamarines. I feel a sense of exaltation. Then I see seated at the foot of the cross a very beautiful woman. She has golden hair and very blue eyes. I start to undress her, in order to have intercourse with her. She lets me, but watches with a strange smile. Then as I take off her garments, I see that she has the genitals of a man. Suddenly I feel a sense of bitter defeat. I wake trembling."

This whole dream has an unreality. The sky of pale green—a sky "grown cold"—the cross of aquamarines matching the sky, form an unreal aesthetic concept entirely disconnected from the real symbol of the cross. Here he finds a woman whose golden-haired, blue-eyed beauty suggests the Angel Woman, the spiritual Anima, one who, he believes, will give him a life experience. But when her woman garments are taken from her, he sees that she is not a woman but a sort of monster.

From his early childhood the images of his unconscious had fascinated this man more than had the outside world. The masculine world of action held no attraction for him, and so he constantly retreated to this world of images, until his dreams had become his life and his life a dream. Thus, the Anima had usurped the energy of his masculinity; she had stolen his virility.

In yet another manifestation, the Anima, as the intuitive perception of beauty, may lead a man to artistic achievement. Yet even in this form she may be a danger, for the man may be so occupied with putting into form the revelations which he has received through her that, though he gives to the world the results, he himself has no personal life. It is a matter of history that the artist has often destroyed his own personal relations in order to bring to fruition his relation to the Anima. For the Anima, in this impersonal, introverted aspect, is a mistress who frequently exacts the sacrifice of the human side. The man of genius gives to the world so great a value that the sacrifice is accepted, even demanded, by society, even though his personal life is the loser. To develop both sides appears a task too great for his strength.

This same possession by the Anima may take place in the life of a very ordinary human being. In this case, the personal life is sacrificed for undeveloped phantasy, and the outer world is lost for a mere dream. A young man dreamed of a beautiful woman who called him to follow up a mountain path. Her laughter sounded "like the rippling of brooks." In the dream, he stands uncertain as to whether or not he should follow. This figure reappeared in his waking hours. At last, in active phantasy, he followed the figure and then felt an impulse to paint a picture. It was of a man following a woman over a path of luminous snow to heights inaccessible to a human being. Behind them the path drops away, in front is a precipice. He saw these heights bathed in ineffable light which he could not paint. Then something appeared in the picture. It was like a mirage far below, a vision of a village with small houses with smoke curling up from their roofs. As he looked at this, it became as vivid as any reality experience could be. The village became activated. He saw people eating and drinking and dancing. He longed to cast himself over the precipice and felt he had followed the woman into a place of death.

This man had not established his life as a man. He had not married, he had never taken over the responsibility of a permanent relation with any woman, but had followed his Anima projections until, in each, he had become "disillusioned." He had not accepted permanent responsibility in his profession. His problem was to break his identification with the Anima so that he might meet the experiences of his life in the world and find in living woman something necessary for these experiences. He needed the ego integration which could come only by attention to the demands of masculine responsibility, by an exercise of the conscious will, and by an attention to the reality problems of his daily life. He was too near to the world of the unconscious. Until he had paid his debt to the social collective and earned his place in life, the voice of the unconscious held for him a present danger, but as his later development proved, it also held for him a future promise.

Just as a man may be utterly under the spell of his feminine side, so, too, an overmasculine man may completely ignore or repress all the feminine elements in his unconscious. He is ashamed, not only of feeling as being womanish, but of all his irrational desires and intuitions. His repressed and undeveloped Anima, however, will make unpredictable intrusions into his rational life. At such times he behaves in a childish and even a violent way. He becomes unreasonable and undependable. Just as a child turns to his mother, so he is apt to turn for understanding to a woman whose attitude is expressed by some such phrase as "men are just children at heart." This attitude is scarcely helpful—in the first place because he will bitterly resent it as soon as his Anima permits him to return to rational life; and in the second place because he is in the grip of unconscious forces too great to be susceptible to such facile understanding.

It is difficult to describe the Anima without giving an impression that she is a personification of feeling—a limitation which is quite unwarranted. She is the voice of the irrational, of the unconscious psychic forces that are so apt to be ignored, but which, if released, would give a renewal of energy and life. She is the temptation and lure of the unexplored; and she is also the dark force that speaks in suspicion and doubt.

And so, upon a man who is able to preserve an overmasculine adaptation from such irrational and childish outbursts as the ones described above, she may act in quite another way. She may act secretly, secretively; she may undermine his rational concepts. There will be moments when he will feel suddenly hesitant or uncertain; as though a foreign voice were speaking inside himself. In such moments, he might almost be saying of some outside person—"What is this woman talking about?" So, in his concentration upon a work to which he has given his energy, he may hear her speak like an insinuating woman, "Do you really imagine this has any value?" A sense of futility seems to creep in. He has done what he has set out to do, but, somehow or other, he is unsatisfied. Something is lacking.

A man in this situation dreamed the following dream:

"I stood before a Greek temple. I had a sense of having come a long way and yet the temple was familiar to me. About me stood trees which were not real trees but columns of marble in straight rows. I started up the steps to the temple and saw a woman lying upon them—blood was trickling from her mouth, descending the steps, and at the bottom separating into four streams. Suddenly I was filled with horror. I had killed her. I went to her and took her up. I carried her to a river that ran at a little distance, but the river was ice. I dipped my hands in the blood and it became an icy crystal. I plunged this into my forehead. Then the dream changed and I stood at the edge of the wood, which was now a forest of green trees, full of flickering light and shadow. The woman was gone, but in her place was a child, a little girl. She smiled at me, beckoned to me, and vanished into the forest. As I started to follow her, I woke."

This man had with conscious determination excluded everything which did not serve his desired end. Though his life was supposedly creative, his work conformed to a pattern more and more dictated by his ego. His human relations were not allowed to interfere with or to distract him. Even the images of the unconscious were not permitted to speak unless they too contributed to the concept of his message to the world, and at times his message seemed flat and strangely remote. He lived with "the good and beautiful." He raised a temple of classic beauty to the Anima. Yet it is here that he has killed her—the temple has become the place of her death. He feels now a horror at this thing which he has done. He takes her to the river, which in his association relates to flowing life, but this river too has become ice. He plunges his hands in her warm blood, but at his touch it too is frozen. Then a strange irrational thing happens. He uses this now lifeless frozen energy as a weapon with which he achieves the sacrifice of his chosen idea of life. He plunges this icy weapon into his forehead, slaying his abstract thought. With this sacrifice the scene changes. The dead Anima vanishes, and in her place is a living child, a little girl, a new aspect of the Anima, which will lead him away from the classic temple into the forest of light and shadow, a place of mystery and life, a place where he can no longer decide what is or is not to be admitted.

When the second half of life has been reached and the man has achieved his conscious connection with the world and his ego integration as a man, there is danger that he will limit life to the possibilities which his conscious adaptation accepts. It is at this time that his need of understanding the Anima is most imperative, for without her his life becomes limited and rigid, or else a doubt of all his attained values may assail him. Then curious dreams may appear. Frequently, the dream image is of a woman, diseased or spiritually repulsive, whom the dreamer attempts to evade or even to kill. Or, it may be a child who needs his attention. One man dreamed that a woman, young but haggard and of repulsive aspect, dogged his footsteps. He turns and asks, "What is the matter with you?" She replies, "Syphilis." This man, finding his emotional life dull, was looking for renewal through small erotic adventures.

A man dreams that he is going to his office, when he sees barring his way a woman whose face is nearly eaten away by leprosy. She is asking alms. Suddenly, he feels a violent fear and hatred. He seizes her by the throat to strangle her, he gets her down, she grows weaker and seems to be dying. Suddenly he realizes that her hands (though lying inert on the pavement) are really about his own throat. He wakes with a feeling of horror.

Both these men had achieved worldly success, both were respected members of society, with a professional position earned by real devotion to their calling. Both were married and had for many years fitted excellently into patterns of good husbands and fathers. "Nothing was wrong." Yet one had turned to petty erotic adventures and was trying to find love and new excitement in them. The other had depersonalized his feelings and had rationalized his thinking. His intellect functioned with clarity in the chosen field, his feelings served his Persona—his professional adaptation—excellently well. His intuitions were limited to the problems presented by the interests of the intellect. His horizon narrowed without his realizing what was happening. More and more he dismissed as irrelevant or absurd the intrusions of the unconscious, either into his own life or into the lives of others. Now the neglected Anima makes a last demand for attention. And, when he turns upon her and attempts to kill her, it is really she who is strangling his life.

The role which the Anima, if accepted, can play in a man's life, is suggested by the following dream:

"I was going to my first analytical hour. I knew I must take the subway. I came to the entrance. There stood a strange woman. She said, 'It will be useless for you to go unless you take me with you.' I said, 'Who are you?' And she answered, 'I am the midnight woman.' I felt strangely affected by this, then."

In this answer is given, with solemn clarity, the statement of the dreamer's problem. It is as though the dream said, "It is useless for you to go this way unless you realize that your first concern is with the woman within yourself, the Anima. You have believed it was your wife or your mother, or your mistress who was responsible for your emotional difficulties and failures, that the demands which they made upon you kept you from following those voices that would lead you to success. It is easier to put the blame on them. They are real women, you may see them by day, but 'I am the midnight woman.' "

This midnight woman recalls "the hour of the living midnight," that is, the time when the power of the unconscious is at its greatest height. It is also the moment when night turns again toward day, the hour of the awakening, the hour of new birth. "When the dark is at rest the light begins to move." As in the old fairy tales and legends, it is also the time when the witches and demons walk abroad, the hour of ghosts and shadows. This woman who must go with him on his journey is the midnight woman, the spirit moving in the depth of his unconscious. In the dream she combines the attributes of an ordinary woman and the Woman of Mystery. She stands at the top of the subway steps and says he must take her with him. The subway is a means of transportation which he will never use in real life, although his need is to economize both time and money. He prefers taxis because the subway is "crowded with common people," "one is pushed and jostled," it is "sordid." Yet in his dream this is the way he must travel to reach the place of the real exploration of his unconscious, and, as a matter of fact, that *was* his way, for before he could come to any deeper knowledge he had to go through all the sordid paths of the unconscious background of his daily life—a life, indeed, crowded with detail which he preferred to ignore. In this, his Anima must accompany him, for he could not get anything from the journey without her.

In this first part of the inner adventure, she appeared in all his personal material. He tried at first to see her only in projected form. The problems of his life were Anima problems, but to him they were caused by the women who surrounded him and carried the image; it was these women who must be changed, or, if they would not change, they must be got rid of—put out of his life—and better ones found to take their place. So he was continually seeking for the Anima and continually rejecting her, never realizing that it was *she*, moving in the troubled waters of his unconscious, who was confusing him, bewildering him, filling him with ecstasies or despairs, leading him into crooked bypaths or suddenly transporting him to dizzy heights. But all the time he was trying to see her simply as a factor in his personal unconscious —to reduce her merely to an element in his own small personal life. This superficial layer had indeed to be examined, and this journey through the subway was the reductive phase of his analysis in which he had to see his moods and emotional difficulties as affects within himself, something which could not be projected nor identified with, but for which he must become responsible. On this journey the Anima must accompany him, but the place to which they are journeying lies beyond the personal unconscious. It is in this unknown country that the Anima has her real life. If he would really know her, he must follow her as Dante followed Beatrice (his Anima) through the dark mysterious regions of the collective unconscious—the midnight of the soul— and find the stirring of the new light.

Once a man can see that the Anima is not merely an element in his personal life, not just a problem of relationship between himself and this or that woman, he can begin to understand why she has acted upon him with such illogical yet irresistible power. He can begin to understand her duality; that she is not only the feminine side of his individual self but also the expression of a timeless life force.

One no longer speaks of the song of the siren, yet her voice is heard in that irresistible impulse to follow the unknown possibility embodied, perhaps, in a woman whom the reason would reject as unsuitable, or in an aspiration which is contrary to the ordered pattern of life. This siren voice, no less potent, but no longer projected into myth, can be understood today as an irrational factor within the self. The Anima, like the siren or the water sprite, still promises a man the kingdom at the bottom of the sea. But, also, she offers him a renewal of life through luring him from inertia, which is always ready to overpower him and to make him settle into the old, the safe, the small, the secure. But it is not only as this temptress that she appears, for she is also an embodiment of that deep, instinctual wisdom which is close to nature—a wisdom about life which is only to be found in a certain feminine quality, often spoken of as earth wisdom, a quality which has its roots deep in the collective unconscious. She leads him to a greater understanding of life as it really is, and of his own unconscious processes.

The Anima is perilous because real life is always perilous, yet through challenging a man to leave his rational security, she becomes—if the challenge is accepted—the one who reveals the secrets of the soul, the animating spirit. For spirit is a combination of the Eros and Logos principles; and this a man finds only through the acceptance of the feminine principle in his unconscious, which completes his masculine consciousness.

VIII. THE ANIMUS

As a woman becomes more and more aware of the images moving in her unconscious, masculine figures appearing in dream and phantasy become more and more related to her own inner life. That is, they are seen not as figures of adolescent daydream, nor as portrayals of actual men whom she has met or may meet, but as elements of her own psyche that she must reckon with if she is to understand and develop her feminine nature. The central principle of life which woman serves is Eros, the principle of relatedness and receptivity; the principle of love, not simply in its instinctual biological aspect but in its deeper meaning. It is this principle which leads woman to understand and nurture all potentials of life, both personal and impersonal. This principle also gives to woman a deep instinctual contact with what may be called earth wisdom, an intuitive perception of truths relating to human experience, truths which seem to rise to her consciousness without the process of logical thought. This wisdom is like the matrix—the mother lode containing the precious ore.

It is through her connection with Eros that woman finds her own center as woman, yet she must also find a way to relate herself to the Logos principle—that is, she must develop the embryonic masculine side of her own psyche—so that she may increasingly bring about an harmonious balance between the opposing elements within herself, a union of her masculine and feminine qualities.

It is necessary, therefore, to study the real nature of the masculine image—the Animus—which appears in women's dreams and which often speaks with the voice of authority, the Jehovah voice. It is only through studying this image that she can see where the final authority for her life is invested—whether she is ruled by an unconscious masculine image or whether, as a conscious woman, she directs her own life, and under that direction develops the values of her masculine side. It may make this clearer to cite the experience of a woman in whom the image of authority was so completely hidden from the conscious as to be undetected for years.

She was an energetic, forceful woman, who was once described as being "as good a business man as any," and she found herself in that truly feminine predicament of being in love with a man. But she could not accept the happiness of this new-found relation because of doubts which assailed her. She was always vaguely mistrustful of the man. Up to now most of her energy had been given to her professional struggles. In childhood she had been petted and spoiled by her father, but just as she was entering adolescence she discovered that he had for years been disloyal to her mother, not only in his life with women, but in money matters. When the storm broke, she turned violently against him and as violently espoused her mother's cause. There was a period of bitterness and hate between them. Then he "went out of her life" (or so she believed), first through her mother's divorce, after which time she never saw him—then by his death, which occurred soon after.

She started work far too early in order to carry the financial burden of the home, and became absorbed in making a success. Even her mother's death, which occurred a few years later, did not alter this adaptation. Instead, she put all the energy released from relationship into her profession. This apparently succeeded beautifully until the unexpected intrusion of the man who roused her hitherto dormant feeling. On one side she desired the relation, on the other she resented it. While in this state of uncertainty she dreamed the following dream:

"I am going to meet my lover. He is in a castle on a high hill. I go up the hill, and as I approach the castle the drawbridge drops of itself. I enter the castle garden but he is not there. I go through dim corridors until I come to a council chamber full of men and see my lover among them. Then a solemn voice says, 'Behold, these are all the men of the world.' As I look, their faces slowly change until every man, even my lover, has the face of my father."

Her own interpretation was, "I heard this voice as clearly as though a living person had spoken. It was a revelation of truth. I knew it told me that all men were alike and that I could trust no man. If I married, I would only repeat the tragic experience of my mother. I have never heard a clearer voice."

She had indeed heard a voice, but she had not tried to ascertain *whose* voice was speaking, nor what forces had given the speaker his authority. Here was the father, long since dead, stamping his own image upon the face of every living man. Her hatred of men, first aroused by her experience with her father, dominated her feeling life, so that her idea about the father became her idea about all men. She was living under the power of this idea of man, derived from her father image. Whenever a real man came along, she clapped it over him and he disappeared as though under a gigantic snuffer. She therefore moved about in a world peopled with personifications of her ruling idea. She had broken from the actual father, but his image still ruled and with greater power, because it had become invisible. Hatred and scorn of man, quite as much as love for the mother, had prompted her ambition. She had tried to be what her father had refused to be, the man of the house, and had taken over his unlived life.

In so doing, she had allied herself with the masculine element which is in the unconscious of every woman. She had pretended to be a woman, while unconsciously adopting the attitudes of man. A primitive medicine man would have said to her, "Woman, you are possessed by the ghost of a man." On the one hand she became a man, and on the other she tried to assert her superiority to men. This had undermined her feeling judgments. It made it impossible for her to be really a woman, especially in any relationship with a man. In marriage, she would always be struggling for supremacy, just as she had always struggled for it in business. To accept the real meaning of this dream, she would have to relinquish much that had become dear to her, and to listen to the woman voice within herself. This voice would have said, "See how your hatred and bitterness toward your father have permeated your attitude toward all men, until, under the dominance of an opinionated idea, you have remade them all in his image. The voice which you have heard speaks truth, but it is the truth about yourself. It is the voice of your own unrecognized negativity, which has usurped control of your feelings and ideas."

Though in this dream the one who speaks does not appear, yet she distinctly recognizes the voice as masculine. It is, in fact, the voice of the Animus stating with dogmatic finality that by this simple experience with her father she can judge all men. But it is important to realize that the one who spoke was a complex being, derived partly from the father image and partly from the misused masculine attributes in her own psyche. For the image of the Animus, like that of the Anima, is built up from within and from without; from without, by any man who influences a woman's life—father, brother, lover, friend, teacher—or from the ideas about men which she may receive from other people, from the mother's attitude, the opinions of women friends, or through stimulation by or identification with the Animus of another woman; from within, by connection with the embryonic masculinity in her psyche, and with the archetypal images in the collective unconscious.

This complex Animus appears as an entity which takes on varying forms, and which uses the libido to express the masculine side of the woman's psyche. And as in her life experience she is biologically and physically and spiritually developed and completed by her right relation to a man, so in her individual development she is psychologically completed by her right relation to this Animus, this masculine principle within herself.

That the Animus appears so often in dream or phantasy as something destructive is not due to its being a negative part of the psyche, but because any factor ruling from the unconscious takes on a negative aspect. In the dream quoted, this aspect was especially in evidence because of the unusually negative experience of the actual relation to the father and of the influence it exerted over her own masculine side. Since this woman had naturally much force and energy, the dominating idea had all this at its disposal. And since this idea was furnished by the negative image in the unconscious, she became the typical Animus-ridden woman, that is, the woman possessed by the idea instead of herself possessing it.

Had the relation to the father been a positive one, it would still have been used by the Animus, if it was unconscious and dominating, for all men would be judged by the authority of the father image and would stand or fall in accordance with their similarity to it. She might have looked to find a man to relive for her the relation which the father had given her and to voice the truth for her. So the unconscious man would still dominate her. For when the "idea" is preconceived and unconscious, it takes on the character of mere opinion. It loses those qualities of differentiation and discrimination which are attributes of directed thought. As unconscious feeling is emotional and undependable, so unconscious thinking is opinionated and generalized. The woman dominated by the Animus tries to fit everything into an arbitrary pattern, thus limiting the potentials of life, instead of nurturing them. The masculine qualities which the dreamer had used in her professional life were real and valuable; it was only the preconceived idea behind them which made them destructive to her life as a woman.

The most obvious form of Animus identification manifests itself, as we have already said, in opinions. An Animus-ridden woman argues, not in order to discover truth, but in order to overcome her adversary. She passionately defends her opinions (the children of her Animus) in the same intensely personal way that a biological woman fights for her children, not because she has considered the merits of the case, but because they are hers. For the negative Animus would rather be right in an argument than in a human relation; and argues for the sake of domination, not for the discovery of truth. So, in herself and others, the Animus-ridden woman destroys the potentials of creative thought.

The opinionated woman may use her opinions to build up a satisfaction with her own limitations. She then takes refuge in generalities. She judges the opportunities that life gives her in accordance with those generalities, and so feels superior in refusing life unless it comes to her in a preconceived and static form. Also, in her generalized opinions about other people, she judges all acts in accordance with her code, not in their relation to the inner motive and the life values of a given situation. And so, while she may live adequately enough within the limits which the Animus prescribes, the chances of evolved thinking or feeling are rather slim.

While woman was content, as many women still are, to place the Animus image upon an actual man, to give over the responsibility for her thinking and doing and position in life to the authority of a man, she appeared to get on, provided she could find a satisfactory man to carry the Animus image. With certain women this worked very well, but, like the old recipe for hare soup, "first catch your hare," it was sometimes not easy of achievement; and this hunt for the hare made woman overvalue certain feminine lures and undervalue certain real feminine qualities.

In the image which the woman projects, there is a blending of actual experience and of certain ideas which come partly from the collective social attitudes and partly from certain images within herself. For the image of the Hero, the Scholar, the Spiritual Guide, the Man of Authority, she can find certain personifications in the world of men. Which image she projects is determined by her age and her temperament. The adolescent girl is likely to project the image of the Hero upon the physically powerful man. The overfeminine woman is likely to place this Animus projection upon a man whose accomplishments and deeds attract her—some man who has achieved success in the world of men. Or a woman who does not want to develop her own thinking may project her Animus image upon a man of intellectual attainments.

When the woman is trying to make one of these Animus projections upon a man, she is almost turning him into an archetypal image. An individual man cannot reproduce an archetype. He may have traits which suggest it, but the more individual he is, the less "typical" he is. If a man is made to carry an Animus projection, to be what he is not, he will have a sense of constriction; he will try to throw the projection off, as if it were a net hampering his every movement.

These projections represent an unconscious attempt to live out through another an unlived side of the self. They must in no way be confused with the conscious relation which a woman may make to the man himself and not to a projected image.

There is perhaps no safeguard against the intrusion of the Animus except a life of actual relationships; he cannot be kept at bay by any theory. No discussion of love will save the woman from her Animus. She must actually love real people and relate herself to them. Only when she is related to people humanly can she safely relate herself to truth abstractly.

Every woman is faced with a real Animus problem, the drawing up into consciousness of the Animus side of herself. Her activities may be ruled not by herself but by the unconscious, and therefore inferior, man in her own psyche. Her thinking and her actions are then limited by the ideas which the Animus propounds, though she is not in the least aware of what he has been **doing** to her.

A young girl who had assumed that she had solved the whole Animus problem by leaving home and by espousing theoretically the new ideas of freedom and social reform, dreamed:

"I am coming down Park Avenue in a taxi. As I try to get out and join the crowd, a man steps up and brands me on the forehead. He tells me I cannot be received here. I protest, but he says I can never recover from the branding. He will listen to nothing that I say. I go home and look in the glass and find imprinted on my flesh in the middle of my forehead a picture of the Virgin Mary standing in the pose of the Statue of Liberty."

Apparently this image upon her forehead concerned only her feminine side. But the dream shows that it is the Animus who has branded it there. The forehead is the seat of thinking, and it is an absolute thought which he has imposed upon her. He permits her to stand in the pose of liberty, but it is not a figure of liberty who has taken the pose. The figure is that of the Virgin Mary. To her this figure represented not merely a physical virgin, but one who was altogether immaculate—that is, unsullied by life. It was this figure with whom she identified and which cut her off from all experiences which might involve human frailty in any form. So her theory of life, her pose, was liberated, but her real self was branded by the old idea, a preconceived idea, an opinion of what woman should be which shut her away from a real woman's life.

The negative Animus may not only limit a woman's freedom, but may destroy her connection with her own personal values. When this Animus reaction has become so habitual as to seem part of life, a reality that does not admit of question, a dream may reveal the Animus, catch him in the act, and make clear that it is *he* who is dominating the situation.

A young girl was convinced of her inability to achieve anything of value or even to complete anything she started. Interest and energy dwindled at the first discouragement and doubt took control. She had discussed the Animus with intellectual understanding, but had never felt any emotional connection with his reality. He was an excellent intellectual concept that had nothing to do with her own limitations. The following dream came as a revealing experience of an actual entity, a being within herself:

"I go into my garden. It is early morning. I feel a sense of things stirring, coming to life. Green shoots are sprouting from the earth, little creatures are waking. Then I see a great, monstrous man. Slowly he moves about the garden, stepping deliberately on all these newly living things. I feel a sense of despair. The garden now encloses me like a prison and soon there will be no life there except this monstrous figure."

Until this dream showed her the real nature of her problem she had believed herself to be an inferior person. Now she saw that it was this idea, imposed upon her in childhood, which continually destroyed her living values. Freed from the domination of this idea, she could cultivate her own garden. Further dreams showed her that her sense of inferiority was not directed merely at herself personally, but at women in general; she had fallen into that confusion where dissimilarity is seen as inequality. In setting free her potentials of life, she realized that not only could she develop her own values as a woman, but that she could make use of those masculine qualities of differentiation and discrimination which are inherent in the feminine psyche.

In the case of this young woman the Animus had appeared almost like a great inertia, which, acting through her sense of inferiority, overpowered any urge toward life. But he may also take on an aggressive form, where he gives a false appearance of achievement and works through a sense of superiority, an inflation of the ego. A young girl in this predicament, dreamed the following dream:

"I was walking along a road in the country with several other people when we came to an old house which was falling down. One small part was inhabited but the rest was deserted. We went in and found a room with a large double bed on which we lay down. We heard steps coming, and a large, bent man came in. His arms hung down like those of an ape, and he came toward us, but no one moved. I was farthest away from him, but he walked around the bed to where I was. Then it seemed I was eating bread and butter, and every time I took a bite the man took a bite of me, and I felt a sharp pain. After several bites, I woke up."

This dream showed what was really happening inside herself. There was an appalling disproportion between her feminine side and her unconscious masculinity, here appearing as a great deformed ape-man. While she was apparently feeding herself, this ape-man was really devouring her. In actual life, she seized everything that came her way as food for the ego; and though she did it with the apparent innocence of a child eating bread and butter, her unawareness of what she was really doing to her woman side and to others made her an easy prey to the Animus.

A woman of a thinking type develops the masculine qualities readily; her danger is that she may sacrifice to them her human side and use them to inflate her ego. For the Animus, like the Anima, when he rules from the unconscious, has no regard for the personal life. And just as a man may follow his Anima into a world of phantasy where he accepts the creative potential to the destruction of his own differentiated thinking, so a woman may follow her Animus into a world of differentiated thought where she becomes unmindful of her feminine values. Such a woman must remain very conscious of the ruling principle of her life, otherwise this clear thinking, so valuable to her impersonal professional life, may become a ruthless and destructive element in her personal relations, and she will no longer discriminate between the personal and the abstract—she will trample on human frailty as readily as upon an untruth. It is, therefore, only by giving a very real importance to her life as a woman that she can free her thinking to operate in its own sphere.

A woman of brilliant thinking, who had once used it in a competitive and ambitious way but who had freed herself from the dominations of the Animus, dreamed that as she started on a journey an old man placed a two-edged sword in her hands; and as she woke she felt that she could use this sword without wounding others or herself. She felt both gratitude and humility. The sword to her was the sword of truth, the weapon of clear thinking which before had been in the hands of the unconscious and which now could be placed in her hands because she would no longer use it in ways destructive to life.

This dream might lead to a possible misunderstanding. Thinking is not necessarily a product of the Animus. It may be a woman's superior function. Although the Animus often manifests itself as opinionated thinking, its activities are not limited to any one function. Whatever a woman's superior function may be, whether it be thinking, feeling, intuition, or sensation, the Animus may be destructive of that function if it does not serve the conscious woman but the masculine side in the unconscious. The dream does, however, make clear the fact that the Animus has great positive values, that much of woman's creative power may come from him. As long as the proper relation to the Animus is maintained, its energy is available for life.

Yet even the freedom apparently given in this dream is a limited freedom; for if a woman is confronted with a crucial choice between her personal life and the life of abstract thought, between the Eros and the Logos principles, she must, if she is to continue to develop as an individual, choose the former. Otherwise her thinking has become the opponent of her feminine life, and there is every chance that her feminine qualities, in their turn, will sooner or later rise from the unconscious to distort her thinking. The problem becomes that of dividing her energy properly between the demands of her relationships and the demands of the Animus. Until she can consciously face this, and become able to discriminate between the varying values of these demands, consciously deciding, when new situations arise, the amount of energy which can rightfully be given to each, the demands of the Animus may disintegrate her life, instead of completing and energizing it.

The dreams which follow illustrate the development of this consciousness in a woman faced with this problem. These dreams did not follow one another in direct sequence. They indicated definite stages in a series which continued over many months.

"I am in a house with many rooms with L.K. We enter a bedroom. He slams a sliding door, without looking. It catches a sweet-faced woman, whom I know to be the housekeeper, right in the middle of her back, hurting her badly. I run out to her to comfort her. I apologize, saying I did not see her, and I take all the blame upon myself, shielding him.

"We enter the room and L.K. sits beside the bed, his head on my lap. His expression is abstracted, intense, listening. I also hear the music from the left side of the room he so concentratedly listens to, but I see a panel open in the wall on the right and doll-like puppets dancing and acting. I try to show him these, but he does not look. He is too intent on the music he hears and will not see what I would show him."

L.K., who in this dream represents her creative Animus, was in real life a man who followed his art without consciousness or thought of the existing reality of other people. In the dream she follows the Animus when he enters, intent only upon his own desires. On the way he ruthlessly injures the woman who represents feeling. The dreamer deplores this. But in real life, when she was possessed by the creative Animus, she was oblivious to the demands of feeling, and would suddenly become aware of injuries that she had inflicted quite unconsciously. Now, in her awareness of this reality, she sees how disconnected the Animus is from herself as a woman. He is intent only on the far-distant music—music which represents the magic of the unconscious, music which carries one away from the conscious world. Then suddenly the walls open and the puppets appear, but still the Animus remains unconscious. She only is able to see them. It was as though she, as a woman, had seen the real situation of persons who are in the control of the unconscious, how they become like puppets manipulated by invisible forces. So when she became possessed by the Animus, she too behaved like a puppet, and was afterward amazed at the damage which she had done to her personal life.

Several months later, after she had been trying to get a conscious understanding of the values of the Animus and of the way in which she could direct her creative activities, there came this dream:

"I see an assembly of people. A woman comes forward and strips as though for combat. I know that she has promised to wrestle with any man who accepts the challenge, and to marry the one who can overcome her. I suddenly realize that at any moment her strength may go from her and then she may be overpowered by the first comer. Then a young and wonderful man steps forward and says, 'Do not forget that whichever one among you prevails over her will have me to reckon with. Before he can win her, he must be able to overcome me.'"

Here are shown two aspects of the Animus—the undifferentiated masculinity which can overpower her in any moment of weakness, and the strength of her consciously developed powers of discrimination which will protect her from the assaults of her own unconscious.

In her third dream: "I am riding horseback through a wood. A horde of dark-faced people appear and I have a fear of their capturing me. But from among them rides a beautiful young man, and asks me to follow him. We come out on a hilltop, overlooking a wonderful country. He asks me to come away to this land with him. But I answer 'No, I cannot choose for myself alone and leave my children.' Then a realization comes to me, that I do not have to choose with such finality. And I say 'But I can be with you for part of every year.'"

Thus, when the creative Animus again appears, she decides what part of her energy can be given to him without doing violence to her life as a woman. In this decision she uses the discriminating appraisal of values which she has gained through understanding the Animus as he appeared in the second dream. In the dream the balance has been properly struck between the Eros and the Logos principles.

In most of these instances the Animus has appeared in relation to a woman's life in the external world, but there is a function of the Animus which is even more valuable. This is as interpreter of the images of the unconscious, a form of spiritual Animus who not only connects woman with primordial concepts but also gives her a power of appraising them and relating them to life. By turning upon these concepts the light of conscious discrimination he keeps her from accepting any voice that may speak from her unconscious as though it were the voice of God; and thus her perception of spiritual truth becomes clarified.

The spiritual Animus frequently appears in dreams as priest of the ancient mysteries, or as a sage, or he may come as a bird, —a messenger. He is the bearer of spiritual values. He gives her a connection with the ever-living spiritual symbols, a connection which comes from her own inner experience rather than one invested in the authority of a man. It is through this function of the Animus that she learns to evaluate the unconscious in the light of consciousness, and finds her own individual connection with life, which is deeper than the merely personal.

Through this she not only establishes a deep connection with her own irrational, creative side, but is able to examine those thought images which sometimes appear to come unbidden from unknown sources; to find their connection with her daily life. In this way, the spiritual or introverted Animus acts as a bridge or mediator between the ego and the unconscious. In this function, he establishes a balance between her inner and outer life, so that his activities in the outer world are related to her central self and are judged by life values rather than momentary ambition.

Never before has it been so necessary for this Animus principle to be used and understood by woman. The change in our cultural life, which has set woman free from all sorts of tasks which she formerly had to perform, has put at her disposal an amount of psychical energy which, if not consciously used, will fall back into the unconscious and there act in negative and infantile regressive forms. The woman of today cannot dismiss her Animus problem even if she desires to do so. She cannot return to the status of the old-fashioned woman. But though she must abandon many of the forms of activity once considered feminine, she must find, and become even more closely connected with, the deep feminine principle which has remained unaltered through many changing cultures throughout the ages. It is the discovery of this connection which gives woman her safety in the use of her masculine side.

IX. THE SELF

IN THE foregoing chapters we have touched upon a few of the many images which move in the inner world. Any attempt to cover the whole field would lead us into as many volumes as there are human beings. Then, too, every attempt to classify appears also to limit, for we are trying to define the undefinable; but through considering the images we gain some understanding of the sources of our life energy and of how our outer act is the outgrowth of our inner life.

For example, through a study of the Anima and Animus as they reveal themselves in our dreams and as we relate them to our acts, we see the workings of two great principles of life—the Logos and the Eros. This is true of all images; back of the act we see the image, back of the image we begin to see the life force that it embodies.

First our ego discovers the meaning of images. Their influence is negative if we try to remain ignorant of them or to separate ourselves from them; it is positive if we accept our true relation to them. As the attention is turned more and more to the inner world, forces become manifest that are far greater than those limited to our merely conscious life. Then we discern that the ego is not the center of *life*, but only of consciousness; that there is something beyond this, another center, an unattainable self which is the center of the psyche—of the known and the unknown.

It is as though, in attaining ego-consciousness, we become born psychologically, we come forth from the womb of the unconscious, but in the discovery of the self we become twice born and enter a larger world; we are born again.

There are many manifestations of this eternal principle of rebirth, for each new stage of development is born from the death of the old. This chapter can only suggest how the self, "smaller than the small yet greater than the great," becomes liberated and continually recreated. In order to trace some of these steps we may return to the consideration of the ego.

Through the separation of our ego from the state of original unconsciousness, we differentiate and recombine the ancestral elements, and through an integration of our own personal values reach a place of security in the external world, a place where we can pay our own way and earn a right to our own experience. In early years, we quite rightly assume this development of the ego to be the important task; for otherwise we remain back in the stream of unconscious life—thinking as our ancestors thought or accepting the affect that overwhelms us as though it were the central reality. But this necessary emphasis of the conscious may be carried to an extreme where we lose all connection with the unconscious, are severed from our inner roots, and no longer receive proper nourishment. If this happens, an inevitable sterility ensues.

To some persons who reach this point, life seems limited, meaningless; others find that the elements of the psyche, repressed and denied, have, in their forgotten life in the unconscious, gained strength from that deeper stream of dynamic life, and appear as shadow forces that bring about confusion or even collapse. In such an event, conscious life loses its meaning. There is danger of a diminution of the personality which has been achieved with such struggle. A man has reached his consciously desired goal, and suddenly he finds himself bored. A woman has successfully carried her children to a place where they are independent of her, and does not know where to turn next. This situation, with its endless variations, does not necessarily arise at middle age; it may come earlier or later. But if all of the energy has gone to the task of adapting to the outer world and to attaining conscious goals, this sterility must come.

In our day, more than ever before, conscious achievement demands a necessary one-sidedness which involves a concentration upon the single thing which we can do most successfully. This frequently necessitates the development of the superior function— whether it be thinking, feeling, sensation or intuition—for it is the tool most available to the ego. But too-great concentration may finally reduce the man to the status of the tool, that is, the superior function may itself become the master. Then life becomes limited, static—there is no new energy arising from within. In such a situation the natural attempt is to develop further the function which heretofore has served one. It is the only tool available to consciousness, but it no longer works. The thinker, assailed by emotional doubts and confusions, cannot think his way out, for he has become identified with his thinking. It can tell him nothing about these strange irrational intrusions, except that they should not be there and yet are. The intuitive can find no comfort in the realities which enclose him; the present has built a wall which shuts out the future, and he has lived in the future. Feeling cannot discover a way to meet the obtrusive thoughts that chill the warm enveloping atmosphere it has created, nor can the man whose sense of reality has given him a fine factual security meet the irrational intrusions of dark possibilities. The old adaptation can no longer serve to meet the new conditions.

In the chapter on the Anima are given examples of dreams of men who have made a successful ego-adaptation through their concentration upon the superior function. In these dreams the neglected inferior function appears as a menacing force, in one case infecting the psyche, in the other threatening to destroy the conscious life. In the dream of the Anima figure who lay dead in the Greek temple, we saw how, through the irrational act of sacrificing the superior function, a renewal of life comes from the apparently dead inferior function. That is, the dead Anima is transformed into the child who will lead the dreamer into a land of living trees.

These dreams show what happens when, in a successful ego-adaptation, the inferior function is completely neglected and how it is possible to reconnect with its energy. It may be, however, that through force of circumstance or through a misdirected idea, the ego will seize upon a function which is not the superior one. Through conscious concentration upon the desired goal, it may develop this function and achieve, at least temporarily, a successful adaptation. But here again, the neglected function will threaten the security which has been achieved at such expense. Therefore, in each case, it is the neglected function which causes the difficulty and which at the same time possesses the energy necessary for its solution. For example, in the chapter on Parental Images is given the dream of a man who had lived in false worship of his thinking function. All the first months of his analysis had been marked by scorn of the emotional, the childish (or womanish) attributes of feeling. Feeling was to him a "function of the lower centers" and his sexuality "a concession to the brute within." When, in the human and personal side of the analytical hours, something healing took place, he struggled to rationalize it out of existence. But then there broke into the rational thinking world an experience quite unbidden. He found himself emotionally involved with a woman whom he had always considered "silly" in her overemphasis upon love and feeling. Quite contrary to his conscious intention, he found himself caught in the reality of this situation, which his thinking assured him was "absurd." His desire was to climb back into the safety of his former superiority, for he was a little child in this new world and he despised childish things. Yet a new attitude of a more simple acquiescence had begun to take shape and was struggling for life. Then in the time of conflict came the following dream:

"I am seated among some bookshelves of yellow paper books, vaguely reminiscent of father's library, and I am in a cellar. I hear 'Little People,' that is, doll-like boys and girls with flaxen hair just like Mollie's, running around outside the bookshelves. I mention the fact, rather excitedly and gladly, to father, but he is annoyed. Suddenly the stacks of paper books rise high above me, and at the same time the crowd of gay little people seem to be becoming merrier and merrier beyond the books. Sections of the books are taken away by them. I call to father about them excitedly. To my excitement and delight, the walls of books collapse and I am playing with the little people. Then I am in a field with them and very happy to be there. Suddenly I know that the time has come for them to leave me. Then there passes before me an array of older people, each as distinct a personality as the figures in the procession of the painting, 'The Dance of Death.' But only one figure can I remember now, an old woman in a limousine, a person I had seen in church on Sunday and didn't like. Then individual nonentities grasp my hand. I note them ruefully, even as I mix with them, so sorry that I must, since I feel above them."

These children whose voices he heard calling him from without were his liberated feelings that could move freely in an atmosphere of living sunlight. It is they, these childish feelings, who can free him from his prison of intellectuality where, in a cellar walled by false sunlight of yellow books, he still sits with the father image. When he accepts them he finds himself playing like another child in the meadows.

In the dream, he notices that those children have hair the same color as that of the woman whom he has begun to love. These newly awakened children of his own inner life partake of her nature and energy.

Then the children vanish and he sees the other side—a dreary procession of older people "distinct as the Dance of Death." The old woman in the limousine he connects with an old woman he has seen in church, an incarnation of financial and religious safety which he had thought would bring security. The other figures he recalled later as men, all old and formal intellectual attitudes with which he had once wished to fraternize. These pass and he finds himself reliving an experience all too usual in his daily life—nonentities grasp his hand. That is, he has retreated once more to his sterile superiority of thinking where he can feel above most of the people whom he meets and so reduce them to "nonentities."

From the dream came a realization that if he would find life he must get back to the children. He must accept the *reality* of the situation in which he found himself. That is to say, the real fact that, whether or not they were acceptable to his thinking, his emotions were alive and real. He actually was "in love" despite his previous assumption that he was above such things. The existing situation was a reality to be reckoned with. Through his denial of his feeling, his intuition (normally his auxiliary function) had taken on a negative quality. It could no longer serve him, but only accentuated his fears. Through the acceptance of the existing situation, his reality sense could serve as a bridge over, and help him back to the function he had despised—his feeling. This did not mean only the joy and sunlight. It meant also the very real inadequacies in himself—emotional weakness, instability, cruelties, and childish reactions which were all part of his undeveloped feeling.

Up to this time his thinking had held a cruel dominance over his life, all the more cruel because its power came from identification with the father. This had prevented him from finding security even in his ego-adaptation. Now, through accepting his love for a living woman and acknowledging that it was real and important to him, he found a renewal of life through the despised element within himself. He sacrificed his arrogant ego assumption to the greater demands of the psyche. In so doing, he also released his intuition from the bondage of negativity, so that not only could he accept the love relation with the woman carrying the Anima image, but also use it in connection with the creative Anima moving in the images of the unconscious. No theoretical understanding could have saved him here; there were many times when he would gladly have taken refuge in that, but only by *living* his experience could he understand both the weakness of his feeling and its saving potential for him. Such an analytical experience is a reliving of the undying concept of the Savior—namely, that it is the despised and rejected element that brings salvation.

Psychologically speaking, the Savior is here the neglected and inferior function, which consciousness has rejected and which lives in the unconscious, growing in strength through contact with the primeval images. Those very elements which seem so destructive now possess the energy once held by consciousness, yet since their form of energy is unacceptable to the ego the desire is to continue to despise and repress them and to reinforce the strength of the ruling function. To leave the security of the known and to accept those unknown elements is an act of heroism, for there is no guarantee of safety. For as one turns to the inner world there seems only confusion. Yet it is in that inner world that the redeemer must be found. To do this one must sacrifice the achieved value, a sacrifice that is like a voluntary death; "Give up all thou hast—then thou shalt receive."

This is no theoretical step, but an actual living and dangerous experience. The sacrifice of the function that has been developed and trusted, even though it be not the naturally superior one, involves a supreme struggle. The thinking type of man attributes to feeling the quality of his own unconscious feeling, confuses it with infantile emotion, with hysterical, womanish reactions. The introverted thinker is especially separated from any differentiated feeling. He may even so project his feeling into objects that they assume a fetishlike magic and his daily life becomes dependent upon outer trivialities. The wife and children of such a man know the penalty of permitting these despised feelings to disturb the calm tyranny of thought, for they must carry the burden of the magic rites, the petty impositions demanded by thought for its undisturbed functioning. The burden of human feeling is projected upon them. They must be considerate, understanding, devoted. Thought must be free to soar, and feeling must be coddled and bottle-fed by others, lest it should break like an *enfant terrible* into the quiet realm of thought. So to the thinker feeling is a nuisance, except as it is exacted from other people. And the more that emotional confusion breaks upon him, the greater is his demand that others shall bear the burden. It is only when he can see that he must find salvation within himself, in taking responsibility for the archaic and irrational feeling elements in his own unconscious, that he can find the god within, the new value arising from the darkness.

The feeling type, on the other hand, undervalues thinking, to him it is cold, cruel. By bringing abstract truth to bear upon personal situations, by insisting upon differentiation, it upsets established and comfortable feeling situations. It makes one examine into the real sources of feelings and actions which have seemed wholly suitable and pleasant. But this type may also have to accept his inferior function.

To the intuitive there is nothing more disconcerting than facts. Present existing reality, the *now*, is to him a prison from which he must escape in order to find life in the pursuit of the potential. He therefore pushes aside the value of the present to pursue the future, or even to struggle to bring to life a potential once perceived in a now dead past. The words of the White Queen in *Alice Through the Looking Glass*, "Jam yesterday and jam tomorrow, but never jam today," describe the intuitive lost in his own intuition. But a situation may arise in which he finds himself caught. Ugly facts rise up to confront him, his intuition has led him into a trap. He is face to face perhaps with an actual deed which stands between himself and the desired possibility. Then suddenly he perceives that what he does now, in this moment of the present in which he lives, determines what is to be.

To one intuitive, at such a time of perception, a figure came in a dream and spoke these words: "It is life itself that you are creating and life is a thing of each moment. It is immediate, it is here. It is only of the immediate that the future is born; and if you destroy the present, you destroy also the potential of the future."

To the sensation type, the problem takes on an entirely different aspect, for immediate reality spells to him security. Especially is this so to the extravert, for he rests secure on facts. They are to him solid rocks on which to stand. But even to the man of introverted sensation, the image called up by the object (though it may differ from the concrete objective reality) is a thing in itself; not a collection of evolving potentials. If, therefore, his security is not to become static, rigid, no longer capable of change or growth, he must admit the clarifying perception of the evolving potential of life; of that which is developing from the womb of time.

In this perception, the present loses its absolute sovereignty. Through being freed from its domination, one perceives the present as part of a greater life force. In accepting intuition one touches upon the relativity of time. This, therefore, is an initiation to one who has heretofore lived in the moment, in immediacy, a realization that the present moment can have deep meaning only when it is seen in connection with the potentials of past and future.

In an active phantasy a woman heard a child calling. Following the voice, she realized that the child was shut in a small, windowless room. She knew the child to be there but could find no way in. Then suddenly she heard the rushing of wind. As it passed she saw a bird beating itself against the wall. A little opening appeared and the bird flew in. This opening seemed too small to admit even the bird, but quite irrationally she found herself pushing through, following the bird. Then the walls crumbled and she was holding by the hand a small neglected-looking child.

The bird was the intuitive perception which came upon the wind of the spirit, and in following it she found the Puer Eternus, the new attitude, the redeemer, a child who had been shut into the shrinking walls of factual reality.

The inferior function frequently appears as a child. In one dream, feeling appeared as a dirty, ill-clad boy, who drew closer and closer to the hearth fire until, when the fire had warmed him, he burst into a strangely beautiful song which the dreamer felt was one that he had heard long ago in childhood. To another he came as an uncouth child, who suddenly appeared in a university classroom—the uncared-for thinking function in search of instruction.

It is this child within the self which must be accepted, cared for, loved with the kind of love that understands and develops. One must take the child of pain and sorrow and neglect, living in one's own unconscious, and find through caring for it the living value of which it is the image. Or it may be that the image is of a primitive or inferior man, or of an animal—an instinctual force submerged in the shadows. It may take on an aspect threatening to the conscious. For when a submerged function is raised to consciousness, the energy which it holds is released. This energy may have an elemental strength, for it carries with it the dynamic force of the unconscious. Then one may be swept away by the affect, as though the whole collective experience of this idea or emotion became activated and one's entire being fell under the dominance of an archetype. Such irrational possessions by the affect may depose the conscious ruling function, just as the submerged masses rising in a revolution overthrow the monarch. Feeling may first appear as uncontrollable emotion, intuition as incontrovertible truth. For to find salvation in the inferior function does not mean just to perceive it and to use it where you can. It means to go over to it, to recognize it as the most important thing in your life—the actual savior—to know that without its intervention you will never be whole. The following dream illustrates the process of a new integration made possible through the mediation of the inferior function:

"Two slave women stand motionless by the wall. They look beseechingly at an open door. I feel that another woman should be there. For some time it is still, then into the room comes a figure of power and cruelty. On his jet-black face is a look of malignant triumph. He looks fixedly at the two women. He would force them to bring to him the woman who has escaped, or he will destroy them. Fear grows in them and they call in a weird, high, chanting voice, 'We four now! We four now!' Then they are silent. I hear quickly falling footsteps, the missing woman enters.

She sees the man and stands rigid, looking straight into his eyes. There is both terror and amazing courage in her figure. She makes no attempt either to advance or to escape. I feel that he is about to perpetrate some indescribable cruelty and try to close my eyes. Slowly his face changes. A light grows upon it. The cruelty goes from his eyes. There is a mysterious smile upon his lips. I cannot tell whether he is now a creature of good or of evil, but I know he has great power. But the woman has brought about a deliverance. It is she who now commands. I wake feeling that I am in the presence of a mystery."

It was some time before the dream faded. Then, apparently irrelevantly, there came to her the realization of the actual life situation in which she was at the time caught, a situation which she was struggling to hold on to because she felt it contained a potential of good, a potential which she was determined not to relinquish. As she reviewed this now, she saw it in a new light. Certain facts, certain ugly realities that she had been determined not to see, showed themselves with unmistakable clarity. They forced themselves upon her attention. It might be that those actual facts must be accepted instead of the desired possibilities. Almost grimly, she began to look these in the face, as the women in the dream had faced the tyrant.

Suddenly she realized that this woman who could face the tyrant must represent her own sensation function, the function which would enable her to face present realities—to see things as they actually were. She was an intuitive feeling type. Her feeling, which was warm and alive, was often led away by her intuition, which could not bear the contradiction of hard facts. When these intruded, her thinking became opinionated, because she could not sacrifice her intuition to reality. At the time of this dream, she was caught in one of these typical situations. The dream remained with her, and its full meaning was worked out very slowly. The dark man, in varying but recognizable images, had appeared in her dreams before as a form of the Animus. She had seen how an idea suddenly arising within herself could dominate her and make her ruthless in her determination to make the situation conform to the intuition that possessed her. Her thinking (which at such times became unconscious) had been taken over by the Animus.

Now she could see that the "four" represented the four functions. If the dream could bear this interpretation, then it was the portrayal of an extremely unconscious situation. The Animus (who now governs her thinking) threatens her intuition and feeling (her superior and assisting functions). As for her fourth function, her sensation, it is so deeply buried in the unconscious that at first it does not even appear at all. It has "escaped;" it is at once deep in the unconscious and yet, in some mysterious way, still at liberty—still able to affect her salvation.

The dream also shows the dual nature of images; for here this dark and malignant Animus demands, with threats, the appearance of the one function which will transform him. She had, of course, a theoretical knowledge of the four functions; but hitherto it had had no vital significance for her. Hence, she feels that she is "in the presence of a mystery." For suddenly, she perceives the living reality of what had before been so much theory.

This sensation function had not been present in her conscious adaptation. She had hated facts as stupid, dull, confusing. The pursuit of the potential had seemed to her the only desirable way; and in this pursuit of the potential, she had never stopped to examine her day-by-day realities. Her neglected function of sensation—the reality function—is, therefore, the savior. But when the Animus is confronted with it in the dream, he is not completely transformed. She is merely permitted to perceive his dual nature: "I cannot tell whether he is now a creature of good or of evil."

The dream suggests a solution for her problem. By trying to face the reality in every side of her life, she would begin to realize that before she could really become a well-balanced person she must train her thinking, which up to now she had taken for granted as being good enough, but which in reality often fell under the power of the Animus. She would have to use her sensation as a constant check upon her thinking, a function which had always been partially in the unconscious. So through the reliance upon the despised function she would eventually achieve what was expressed in the cry, "We four now!"—that is, a consciousness of the four functions.

This dream deals very clearly with a stage in the process of individuation, that is, the discovery and acceptance of one's own unique being. Ideally, this stage in the process would be the raising to consciousness of, and the establishing of a complete balance between, the four functions. Practically, it is an awareness of the four functions, both in their conscious and unconscious manifestations. This awareness, as it increases, creates a new center of the psyche—the *self;* a center more valid for life than mere ego-consciousness.

In the book of the Shepherd of Hermas, men come from the four corners of the earth, each bringing a stone. As these are placed together they fuse and become a tower, which is now a single stone formed from the fusion. This is an allegory of the union of the elements of the self into a single being. So when the elements of the psyche are fused, they too become a united whole. This is a *concept,* rather than a condition ever completely achieved.

But the elements which must be fused for the integration of the self cannot be described merely in terms of the four functions. The harmonious relation of the inner and the outer is not to be defined, even by such a phrase as a balance between introversion and extraversion. It is a realization of the connection between the archetypal symbol and the individual experience. A first step in this realization is an acceptance of one's own unique nature and an attempt to discover oneself as one really is.

The concept of the self dawns very slowly; it is at first as though one saw something minute in the middle of chaos. One woman described it in this way:

"When I thought of that other self—that *me*—I could see far away in a nest of gray clouds a little shrivelled pea. Always I had a fear that if I tried to take it up it would vanish into dust and there would be nothing there. But one day, in great fear, I knew I must go toward it, look at it, take it in my hands. As I did so, it turned into a little ivory die with five on the top and three on the face toward me. Then, as I held it, it grew larger and the numbers changed to seven and four. My fear increased and I wanted to throw it away, but I had taken it up and knew that I must carry it. I cannot describe the struggle that took place within me, but at last I accepted it and felt a great peace come upon me."

Her conscious determination to let this phantasy have its way, and her acceptance of its meaning, marked the beginning of a deep inner change. Her life had been a bitter struggle with resentments, angers, tempestuous demands for love, futile attempts to overcome "the devil inside herself" and to force other people to acknowledge their own devils, who, she felt, were always menacing her from without. It had been a passionate search for spiritual values with no knowledge of where they could be found, or of any way to find them except through a continual warfare against everything that "ought not to be."

Now came this strange, though at first only momentary, peace; not from deciding what ought to be, but from accepting what was. In deciding to take up the small shrivelled pea, she felt she was acknowledging her own insufficiency and might discover that she had no self worth the finding. As with most of us, it seemed easier not to know, not to put this to the test. If she really took it up, then she must accept the truth about herself and assume whatever responsibility the knowledge might involve.

She had hoped that in her hour of need a saving symbol would arise—a star which would guide her away from herself to a more "spiritual" plane. Instead the symbol was the ivory die, to her the symbol of a forbidden thing. She began to study the symbol quietly so as to find its connection with herself. I must abridge her associations, which came slowly over a long period of time:

"From early childhood I was taught to regard dice as 'things of the devil.' They were used by low people for gaming. We lived in the West, near an Indian reservation. My father loved the Indians and he and I used often to be with them, but to my mother they were 'a heathen people,' and she refused to see anything but the times when they drank and threw dice with the traders; so dice became the symbol of 'their evil ways.' First, the dice meant to me taking up all that evil I have tried so violently to repress, accepting the unacceptable, acknowledging myself as I am instead of admitting only the value of what I ought to be.

"Five is the number of relationship. I have longed for relationship but have never been able to find it. Something always goes wrong. I think I have found someone I can love and who will love me, and then I am disappointed. They never measure up to my expectations. I find something mean or selfish, and before I know it we are estranged and the relationship is shattered.

I have tried to put this number in the wrong place—does it belong on the die, must I accept not only myself as I am but also people as they are, not as I would try to *force them* to be?

"Three is the symbol of the Trinity. This has never meant much to me, a remote Father, Son, and Holy Ghost, something I should accept but which in reality meant little. But now on the die the three changes to four. This is the Indian's mystic number. It is also the number of individuation—something is added to the Trinity. Can it be the devil? Is there a meeting within the self of a dark principle which unites it all in a foursquare reality? The devil was always a very present image in my childhood. All that seemed to me pleasurable—the simple life of the Indians, the lure of idleness in the sunshine watching the trees, the emotions that swept through me, often destructive but also full of energy, my own carnal nature—these always were in the 'power of darkness' and the dark elements within myself were the work of the devil. It is perhaps the earth, the deep feminine instincts which I have secretly feared that this fourth element represents, the instinctual elements of myself as a woman.

"Seven has always carried to my mind the significance of completeness and mystic unity and fulfillment. It, too, is found upon the die.

"This symbol (the die) is three dimensional. It is the cube, it has the reality of substance. It does not merely express 'the flat plane of consciousness,' but height and depth. From its center radiations may go out in every direction. This cube, therefore, may symbolize the center of the psyche, including both the conscious and the unconscious.

"This, then, is what I must accept. I as I am, with the good and the bad, as attentive to the good as to the bad, to the bad as to the good, identifying with neither side—seeing both the negative and the positive as realities, and knowing them for what they are. This same attitude I must hold toward others and toward life, and only out of such an experience really accepted and lived can come a central peace."

It is difficult for our consciousness to accept as a deep religious experience the saving symbol when it appears in terms of such simple everyday objects—the shriveled pea and the ivory die —yet when she accepted it, the new irrational elements appeared in the numbers which differ from those to be found on any dice and which, when studied, revealed the deeper meaning of this apparently trivial concept. In this combination of elements, which she would never consciously have put together, she saw a new relation between herself and the symbols, which up to now had been meaningless because they seemed to have no real connection with her own life.

The importance of this experience lay in the fact that it was her own and arose from within herself. Through the conscious acceptance of it, she made a connection with religious concepts in a way which gave them a new meaning and a positive inner reality—they became alive in her. Thus the experience acted as a healing agent in her life. She saw things in a new relation, they assumed new values. It is this intervention of consciousness which enables us to make a connection between the archetype which arises within us and our own vital need, and to see life from a new level. Then, as old experiences of life return to us, we can meet them in a new way. Even the die, which seemed to her a trivial image, had a form which appears in many dreams, for it is the foursquare stone and is spoken of in the search for the philosophers' stone.

The following dream makes use of this image of the crystal in form like the cube, the die:

"I dreamed that I was awakened from deep sleep by a sense of a portentous happening. I saw a strange red light reflected on the snow, it was fire. Then the dream changed. I was wandering in the burned ruins of my own house, searching for something I knew I must find. I turned over the charred masses and came upon a foursquare stone, small and like a crystal. As I took it in my hand, I woke."

Here, the dreamer awakes from the deep sleep of unconsciousness and sees the fire, apparently outside but really within his own house. That is, an inner flame is destroying his old adaptation. Fire may arise from spontaneous combustion. To the ancient Hindus, it was the god Agni, the living spirit who was contained in the inert substance and leaped forth from it. In the dream, an energy has burst forth from the old adaptation and will destroy it. This is what had been happening to the dreamer. A new energy had been growing in his unconscious and had destroyed the old security. But when the apparent destruction has occurred, something of great worth remains, the foursquare crystal, the essential value. And for this he must search diligently, even as in the parable one searched for the pearl of great price.

This foursquare stone, or the crystal, appears frequently in dreams. In the Eastern philosophy, it is spoken of as the diamond body, the indestructible essence. In alchemy, it is the philosophers' stone, the lapis, symbolizing the treasure at the center of the psyche. In other forms this central value appears as the living germ, the seed kernel, the golden flower; that is, as the potential of growth latent within the psyche.

Frequently these symbols make their appearance not merely in the dreams of modern occidental man but in his unconscious paintings, which quite spontaneously take on the form of a circle in the center of which such a symbol appears.

Through the acceptance of the symbol as it comes to us, we reach a place of *original experience*, that is, a place where we set aside traditional and systematized concepts to examine that which arises within us. This brings us back to a direct contact with the psychic processes of our own nature and, since nature is creative life, to the creative power in our own psyche. For the self is ever created and creating. As we ourselves become newly created, the energy flowing through us seeks an outlet in creation. It may be in new life experience, or it may seek a concrete form. True creation seeks to find a fitting body for that which has come to life within the self. It differs from ambition, for that is an experience of the ego which struggles for personal success. The self creates in order to give visibility to the inner essence that has become manifest.

When the symbols have been formulated in definite creed or dogma, there is danger that they will no longer be living images moving with the dynamic creative force of individual experience, but, like images of marble, will be viewed as forms of beauty outside the self. If this happens, life is again projected, not lived.

So, at each step, we find the necessity for accepting the living reality of our own individual life. We must become active agents in our own experience, and in this way find our relation to our own destiny, the part which is ours to play.

If the great images were in our control, we could predetermine the way in which this creative process should move; we could decide upon the pattern of the self to be created. But these forces are far greater than any personal element. They enter our lives unbidden. They may force upon us the very thing of which we desire to remain unconscious, and if we are not strong enough to meet them, may turn into destructive forces instead of creative ones. Nor is it possible to say when these great images will appear. We cannot say they will remain dormant in the deep unconscious until we have met all our personal experiences. We cannot say, "First I will meet this, then I will meet that;" for we have no power over the archetype. We are determinants of our destiny only in so far as we are willing and able to become conscious, to find our relation to the archetypal forces in connection with our own individual value. If we try to use them for ourselves, we find it is only their shadows we have grasped, and the only magic we obtain is the dark energy of the Shadow, which in the end leads us back into unconsciousness.

A man had dreamed of a great crimson rose lying upon a white velvet cushion. To him it expressed fullness of life, *rosa mundi*, the rose of the world. One day the dream picture reappeared as a visual image, the rose was full blown, almost ready to fade. Then from the center a strange fountain of energy began to flow out to every part. The petals changed. They became living gold. The cushion on which the rose had lain became a cube of clear crystal, and eternally the fountain of energy flowed out from the living center. Then the image faded. He tried to concentrate and call it up again, but the image took its own form. He saw the crystal, but this time it was of ice, and upon it was a spider through whose veins flowed the ice of living death. A third time the vision came. This time he saw a sphere of light, in which were the rose upon the crystal and the spider on the crystal ice. Between them was a small flame shaped like a living bud, standing forever in the center. This was to him the flame of the spirit—the essence of the self, maintaining its middle way between the eternal images of the light and the shadow.

In describing an experience of this sort, it is necessary again to emphasize that such a vision portrays in ancient images a concept which lies deep in the collective unconscious—the concept of the integration of an imperishable self. Into this vision also enters the old idea of the middle way—that is, the way that is found between the forces of good and evil, forces eternally active.

This is a very abstract picture. The forces appear to be eternally separated, and the self holds its central position unaffected by either. In reality, one attains this middle way, first through a consciousness of the dual nature of the instinctual forces within the psyche, and then through the integration of a central self which, while continually experiencing these forces, is not identified with either their good or their evil aspects—that is, does not become identical with the emotional affect.

The working out of this process of integration is quite clearly shown in the following dream:

"I saw an Indian woman standing on a great plain, looking off at the far horizon. She was very, very old, and yet she stood as strong and erect as though she were still young. I went up to her. She turned and began to walk toward a faint line of distant flame; I knew I was to follow. We came to a circle of fire. This the woman entered; I knew I must also go through. Though I felt the flames, they did not burn me. Inside was another circle of fire. The woman passed through this, and again I followed. Inside the inner flame there was a center of cool stillness. I knew that there were other women about me, but I could not see them. Then the woman spoke. Her words were clear and cadenced: 'You have come to the inmost place, the place of remembering and of reassembling, for woman must remember all the experiences of life until they are understood in their deepest meaning. She must accept the pain of remembering and understanding, for the small things become small and the great become great, not through forgetting but through remembering.' Then the woman was gone and I was alone."

In this dream, the circle of protection again appears. Here it is the "fire within the fire," the inmost place, a place where through remembrance the elements of the self are to be held in consciousness and a new understanding reached. Such an understanding of "experience" essentially means the understanding of the forces within the psyche which have been active agents, or even the factors—the makers—of experience. This brings one to a realization of the self as something far beyond ego-consciousness.

It is the whole man, both the conscious and the illimitable unconscious, and it is also the center of the whole—here portrayed as a center of cool stillness within the fire. And in this center appears as a symbol of wisdom the Indian woman, old and yet young, whose voice prepares her for the symbol which is still to appear when the process of "remembering and reassembling" has taken place.

This dream brought a feeling of peace and of quiet. This might seem quite irrational, since the realization that it is the forces within which have determined so much of our life might overpower one with a sense of failure and of impotence. But in this "reassembling" there comes also an acceptance of the Self, the saving element is also within the psyche. Something new is integrated which is apart from the affect. There is a unique entity which experiences the emotion yet is separate from the emotion, which experiences the images of the unconscious yet is not overwhelmed by them.

In this way, the supra-personal force—the power of God within the psyche—gives the symbol a new, individual value, whereby one can accept life as something to be lived in its fullness, as one's own attempt and one's own experience.

X. A BRIEF EXPERIENCE IN ANALYSIS

BECAUSE OF the infinite variations in the activities of the inner life one can give little idea in a theoretical discussion of the interplay of the images or of how an understanding of them may change and recreate our lives.

It is necessary to emphasize the fact that this activity of the unconscious is ceaseless whether we regard it or not. We cannot say that it is "purposeful," having as a goal the creation of the self, any more than we can say a waterfall has a purpose toward producing electricity: it is full of energy, of creative power, which can be used and directed by an understanding mind. But just as there are energies in the material world, so there are energies in the inner world. They are greater than the self, yet contained within the self. These energies may be directed toward a creative end, or they may be ignored and continue in the unconscious, showing themselves in such occasional outbursts as we have described in some of the material in previous chapters.

Contemplation of the inner image has not come into being with analytical psychology. Throughout the ages men have concentrated upon an image, or upon a spiritual concept embodied in a redeeming symbol, and have thereby activated forces within the self. Nor is the honest attempt to know and face one's own motives and inner realities anything new. All we can claim for analytical psychology is that it provides a new technique for understanding and directing the inner activity through the individual experience.

It is difficult to explain just why, when the problems of life are considered in an analysis, one becomes conscious of dreams and the various activities of the unconscious, but this is the common occurrence. People who say "I never dream," suddenly find dreams intruding. They begin to be aware, first, that dreams hover on the brink of consciousness. Then they remember an image from a dream and by concentrating on it the dream is remembered; and then the activity becomes more apparent and they recall their dreams more and more clearly.

This process can be understood only if it can be seen in its actual working. I am therefore giving a number of case histories exactly as they occurred so that the reader may see the process and also its relation to the life problem. I have tried to select instances illustrative of various types of experience. In each case all the material has been in the hands of the analysant, in most instances for a period of years. It has been checked as to its complete accuracy and is of much greater evidential value because of this. It is the analysants, therefore, who make possible the publication of the remaining chapters.

The true value of analysis is that it establishes a contact with the unconscious, whereby one may obtain nourishment for the conscious life. In this sense, therefore, an analysis is never complete any more than the life processes of growth and development are complete. It does not assume that the "analyzed" person is a fixed and finished product, but only that he has acquired a new way of meeting life problems. An analysis may be short or long depending on the individual need. It may deal with a single difficulty or stage of life or it may demand an exhaustive examination of the personal unconscious and a long synthetic period of reconstruction and reintegration. Its purpose is to serve life by removing obstacles and freeing the energy. The age-old necessity for such an experience is depicted in the myth of the hero who slays the dragon and makes available the treasure. That is, the energy which has been buried is released from the regressive power in the unconscious and free to go out into life.

Such an experience of setting free the libido (life energy) is given in the following case history; that of a young person. It illustrates the necessity for breaking the dominance of the parental image before the ego can make its own choice of a way of life. This analysis covered a period of about three weeks; it showed a way out of an existing impasse, and indicated a new way of adaptation not only acceptable to the conscious but also in keeping with the promptings of the unconscious.

The analysis took so short a time because the problem involved was specifically the removal of an obstacle. Though one can have no theoretical attitude as to the length of an analysis, youth is concerned with living and with learning from actual experience, and so, very frequently, when the immediate difficulty is removed, a young person quite rightly chooses life rather than a complete analysis.

This analysant was a young man of excellent mentality and real ability. Yet he failed repeatedly in his college entrance examinations. He was apparently eager for college. There was no undue pressure. There was no criticism of these repeated failures on the part of the parents. In fact, every effort was made to see that no "inferiority complex" should be set up because of any criticism. The parents were quite properly convinced of his ability to do his job, and gave him every encouragement possible. After the first failure, he went to a tutoring school and did such excellent work that the master said it was really not possible for him to fail. Yet fail he did, in spite of the fact that he went into the examinations with enthusiasm and optimism. At certain points, his mind "went blank," and he had no idea why this should happen. A few hours after the examination, he remembered several things completely forgotten during the hours when he needed them, and suddenly realized several most stupid blunders that he had made.

This failure could not be laid to any form of amnesia, for his mind did not go blank at other times, nor could it be laid to an inability to meet emergencies, because he had been confronted by several emergencies which he had met very well indeed. His own bewildered comment was that some part of him or other was "just a damn' fool," and he did not know why.

He was genuinely disappointed at giving up college, feeling that he had no right to waste the family money any longer. He took a job. At first, this seemed a solution. He was full of energy and resourcefulness and was promoted rapidly, but suddenly, with no apparent cause, his ability deserted him again and he was confronted by dismissal. This time he was quite fortunately on his own. His parents were at a distance. He was without funds, and he turned to a friendly analyst, not really for analysis but for counsel and help, as one would go to any trusted friend in a real emergency.

Here was a baffling situation. The analyst did not know the answer any more than the boy did, but felt intuitively that this was no time to embark upon a lengthy analysis. Nor was this young man a neurotic. He was a very normal young person, temporarily blocked by some force that he could not recognize or control. Acting upon this intuition, the analyst made the suggestion that up to the present time the boy had probably never done what he really wanted. This suggestion was met with indignant denial, both as offering him an excuse which he had no right to take, and as a possible reflection on his parents, who, he felt, had always helped him but had never tried to force him.

The suggestion was then made that since the old way had so completely failed, he should give this new idea twenty-four hours trial. The suggestion interested him, and he agreed to try it without reservations. A temporary loan was made on condition that he should go out and do whatever he pleased for the next twenty-four hours, trying not to block any possibility which rose in him as a thing to be desired. The analyst even went so far as to say, "If you have always secretly desired to get drunk, that is all right so far as I am concerned, but don't go and get drunk just because you think it will be a desperate and manly gesture. Act upon the impulse, no matter what anyone else would think about it."

The immorality of such a suggestion almost started a resistance. It was hard for him consciously to accept such a reward for failure, but he was too good a sport and too genuinely interested to let these resistances have their way. His first desire was to go somewhere where he could hear music, and he went to a restaurant quite too expensive for a young man who had just lost his job. He sat for a long time at the table, more interested in the new idea than in his food, when suddenly he had an impulse to draw. He left abruptly, and going to his own room in a state of excited curiosity to discover what was stirring within him, he drew the picture, given in the picture section (plate 40).

The next day he brought this picture to the analyst. His first explanation was, "I know that it is all inside of me. The beast is crushing the woman between his teeth. She is a part of me that wants to live and, somehow, the other side of me is killing her. But the beast is crying, he is sorry himself. In the tree is the thing in me that laughs at my failures. It has something to do with them. The tree is dead, but it ought to be alive."

This was a vivid inner drama suddenly portrayed by the unconscious. The beast he could see as his conscious willing, his determination to achieve success. But when he was asked, "Why is the beast killing the woman if he does not want to?" he answered spontaneously, "Because he has to." And through this spontaneous answer came the realization that his conscious willing was directed by a greater force of which he was unconscious.

But who was the woman? What did she want? What could she give to him if she were liberated? He felt that in some way she alone could make the dead tree live and blossom; that she could keep his energy alive and not let it fail him at his greatest hours of need. Clearly, then, she was an Anima figure, representing not a living woman but his own creative values existing in the unconscious, which now were held by this beast so that he was deprived of their energy. And the face in the tree which mocked him he recognized as something deep down within himself which knew that he could never succeed if the beast were allowed to have its way.

Though he was bewildered at the paradoxical situation which made him admit that his chosen way was not in accordance with any inner choice, he saw that the picture presented a reality within himself and not anything suggested from without. But something more was still necessary. These forces that had pushed him on to failure must also reveal to him their purpose and in that revelation show both the cause of his failure and the way out. For the way out must be the way of the inner desire which had been too strong for his conscious choice.

Then came a second picture, produced the next day. This showed the beast transformed and rising above the city (plate 41). Though the beast's face was now that of a woman, his intuition made him feel that it was now, in some strange way, a combination of the beast and of the woman the beast had held captive. It was an oriental face, and its headdress was of a kind that one often sees in illustrations of articles on the East. But the unconscious had made use of this fairly familiar picture to illustrate its own purpose. He did not draw this picture because he had seen a similar one, but because the idea which it embodied had a particular bearing on his present situation. He thought of the Orient as a place closely connected with unconscious values, as the source of a type of artistic creation. This face, he felt, was rising above a city which represented to him our Western materialism and success, the kind of success that one side of him wanted but which destroyed the other side. Now the face, the transformed beast, drawing power from his released energy, represented by the Anima figure, rises above the extraverted success which he had believed to be his own choice. He was greatly surprised to find that he had drawn the ears as serpents. He had not even known that he had done so until his attention was called to it. The serpents he felt to be instinctual wisdom, which would make him able to hear the inner voice and to know what his unconscious was trying to say to him. What was his own instinctual unique way of life, which he had not yet been able to find?

Hovering near these serpent ears were black and white birds. The black and white suggested the opposites of the unconscious. The birds are intuitive thought. His first association was "a little bird told me," which he said meant to him, "I had a hunch about it." These birds representing intuitive thought must give him the answer arising from his own unconscious. Now all of his attention which had been directed upon outer events was turned upon these inner perceptions, and as a result of the change of direction of his attention, inner pictures continued to rise clearly.

In phantasy, he perceived a great star which was to him the new light that he must follow. He started to draw it and to draw an image of himself looking up at it; but, as he drew, there rose between himself and the star's brightness a figure shaped like a black tombstone. To his amazement, this figure associated itself with his father. The face upon the tombstone had even an actual suggestion of the father's features and, for the first time, he recognized that the beast also in some way suggested his father. This confused him, for he and his father had always had a fine relationship, and his father had always left him "perfectly free." But now he began to untangle the twisted threads of conscious and unconscious desires. He had greatly admired his father, and had talked things over with him quite unreservedly. In these talks, he had taken over his father's ideas about the value of the professional life and of a college training as part of the equipment of a gentleman. He had absorbed these ideas as though through spiritual pores. They had seemed to become his own. He saw with his father's eyes, thought with his thoughts. Yet all this was quite without his conscious realization. It was another case of father identification.

Then certain associations brought up early interests in drawing and in color, which he had repressed in favor of the more manly sides of life in a preparatory school. As he worked out these associations, he drew another picture in which a curved wall appeared between himself and the tombstone; the tombstone turned white, and he felt himself that this wall shut him away from the tombstone but not from the star. It did not surprise him then to find that the face on the tombstone had become friendly.

Then came a picture in which a white figure rose out of a black background, and the hand which the figure extended had six fingers. This he called the "hand of authority," and recalled a time when he and his father had discussed a statue which represented patriarchal authority. It seemed to him that this figure had also had a hand with six fingers, but he could not remember whether this was actually true or not.

Now he saw that he had been ruled not only by the identification with his own father, but by an archetypal image of masculine authority. This figure he had heard speaking when he had repressed his creative desire in favor of what he believed to be the more masculine way. It was, therefore, not just the image of *his* father, but the image of *the* father, the authority which demands masculine success. In the corner of the picture was a symbol, which he had felt impelled to draw, although he had no idea of its meaning and had never seen anything resembling it. It actually was an ancient Chinese symbol which represented the masculine creative potential. This potential until now had remained undeveloped.

The climax of the series was a picture of a figure rising out of a swamp, impelled by hands that he thought were those of the analyst. He spoke of this figure as himself, but it was that of an old man with a long beard. Obviously, this was one of those impersonal representations that come from the deeper layers of the unconscious, the archetypal Wise Old Man who represents inner wisdom, the figure which each man must find within himself and which speaks to him from his own unconscious. Nor were the hands in this picture those of the analyst, but the representations of that energy of the unconscious which could lift the wisdom above the quagmire which had held it down. They stood, therefore, in contrast to the hand of authority, which had repressed the intuitive wisdom.

This drawing showed him that, had it not been for his past failures, his whole life would have been a subtly concealed but more tragic failure. For, in the acceptance of his father's ideals, he would have lost the opportunity of finding his own real values.

During the period when he had been drawing these pictures he had continued to let his impulses arise and had tried to see where they would lead him. He began to realize that his interest in drawing had not been confined to these products of the unconscious, but was much more far reaching. He wanted to go to art exhibits and to paint pictures himself. He begrudged time spent on other things. There was an intensity in this interest that surprised him. The energy which the beast had held was evidently released and taking its own way. In fact, he reconnected with a very vital part of himself from which he had become disconnected when, in preparatory school, he had sacrificed his artistic creative desires to the accepted demands of "manly" education. So a masculine strength and determination (the beast) had reluctantly laid hold on the woman and attempted to crush out her life. The release of the old man from the swamp he now saw as the liberation of masculine wisdom (an image of the Logos principle). Here it was the principle which would help him to find the *form* for his life, so that he would use his masculine energies in accordance with the dictates of his own being instead of in a way destructive to his innate capacity. This released the energy of the unconscious, which lifted the masculine image from the quagmire.

The energy thus released found its outlet in a creative activity which satisfied him. Therefore, a continued analysis of the unconscious at this time might only have tied up in phantasy the energy which was ready to go out into life. I do not mean that all the young man's problems, or even the one of his identification, were forever solved by this dramatic experience. He has needed help at other times and from other sources, but the immediate difficulty had been removed.

He started in an art school, but was, of course, confronted by the necessity of earning his own living. To his own surprise, the release of his energy was so great that he was able to take a job much more uninteresting than the one he had lost, and also to go to a night school where he could continue his drawing. He was now carrying a double load of work, whereas before he had found the single job too difficult.

The journey is much easier when one is rowing with the currents rather than against them. In this young man's case there was no longer a deep undercurrent in the unconscious pulling him away from the goal he had consciously chosen. He found, therefore, that he was able to carry responsibilities instead of needing the device of failure to free him from them; because they had now become the means of obtaining an end which he really desired.

Such a sudden dramatic denouement was not magically guaranteed because of the youth of the analysant. Young people who are full of neurotic inhibitions and are afraid of life may need to do a great deal of analytical work, but always the effort is the same—to get them back into life as soon as possible, even though they may need to return for frequent help. Analysis is not a substitute for actual experience. This youth was just starting out to find his own way in life and to make his own mistakes. This experience did not turn him out "analyzed" and finished. What it did do was to make it possible for him to set out on his own path, seek out his own experiences, learn from his own mistakes, gain incentive from his own successes. It also gave him a realization of some force within himself from which he could obtain energy in future times of difficulty. He came asking for advice, but in such a case the kindliest advice could not help, for it would again be giving ideals and patterns from without. Instead, he was helped to perceive the images moving in his own unconscious, which alone could give him his own solution. For the answer always comes from within. The creative energy of the unconscious is always on our side if we can become understandingly aware of it.

This boy already had a sympathetic parental bond; he was not a misunderstood child seeking a loving parent, but a youth baffled by his own inner confusion. The help which he needed could come only from someone who had an understanding of the unconscious, which would not be possible for the most loving parent untrained in this technique of interpretation. On the other hand, an overtheoretical attitude would have forced the boy into the acceptance of a long analysis on the assumption that everyone is benefited by a "complete analysis," a completely unwarranted assumption. In this case, the process was analytical, but the analyst was not following a fixed plan of analytical procedure. The analyst's own understanding of the unconscious was at the youth's disposal for the interpretation of material which the unconscious gave. There was no demand that a lengthy analysis should take the place of a life process, or that anything should be done except to find the way out of the immediate impasse.

The young man had reached this impasse because of an identification with the father, and since identification is an unconscious process, he had to investigate the unconscious in order to find out what really had happened. Only by seeing the images that rose when his conscious no longer dictated the way could he possibly have imagined his father as a figure of death standing between himself and his own star of destiny. But since this was the existing situation in the unconscious, it became apparent when he let these images appear. With the appearance and development of these images, the bond which had held him was broken and his ego was set free.

XI. DREAMS OF MOTHER AND ANIMA

These dreams deal with the image of the Anima as she appeared in the first phase of the analysis of a young man. They have been selected from a series of about two hundred dreams. The order of their appearance has not been changed, but many other dreams dealing with different phases of his problem have been omitted. It has been necessary also to abbreviate the associations and to eliminate all material of a purely personal character. The images are here considered in their deeper symbolic aspect. These archetypal images, while having a distinct bearing on the personal difficulties of the dreamer, are illustrative of a typical problem which may be met by any man. Hence, although personal to this dreamer, they are also profoundly impersonal.

His earlier dreams, vague in form, dealt with the fixation upon the mother. In them the mother appeared as the love object with definite sexual attraction. Such dreams are common in adolescence (either chronological or psychological adolescence), when life has not yet been freed from the parental pattern. These dreams were, of course, unacceptable to the conscious and were dismissed as disagreeable intrusions. Since the dreamer could not understand the psychological aspect—their bearing upon his own infantile dependence—they impressed him with a feeling of guilt and distrust of himself and he "forgot them." Yet the vague images so excluded from consciousness continued to have a powerful influence upon all his so-called conscious decisions. They exaggerated the ambivalent attitude to the actual mother, so that both positive and negative decisions were influenced by fear of her or admiration for her. Could he at that time have seen these dreams in their symbolic aspect as the problem of overcoming the mother, which is part of the development of every youth, he might have come to grips with his problem earlier.

In his case, the problem was heightened both by the outer situation and by temperament. Through necessity of circumstance, the mother had carried for him not only the image of love and protection but also the image of authority normally carried by the father. Temperamentally the young man was emotional, artistic, irrational (an intuitive in type) and in too close contact with the unconscious.

The fears aggravated by his introverted intuitive perceptions clustered about the actual mother and reinforced the power of his personal projections upon her. These fears had made him, in his earlier youth, assume a premature independence. This he could not maintain without constant inner conflict, because his choice of a way was dictated by negative emotions rather than understanding of his essential values. The fear of his mother was in part justified because he was bound to her by a deep tie of love and gratitude, and also hated her because of her concentration upon him and her insistence upon his developing his very real talents, for unconsciously she looked to him to live out his dead father's life. She was unable to free her own energy from the relation and to use it for her individual development, or in another marriage. Her overanxious love put upon him a silent but continuous pressure to live up to "his best abilities." The pressure of her demand on him increased his fear of the world and kept him tied to the childish image. Consciously, she left him free; unconsciously, she never left him to himself. The things she desired for him were actually more his own than those he chose, but her pressure made them her way rather than his.

The dreams dated back a number of years but rose to memory from time to time. The first few dreams which were remembered in detail came before analysis. They were so vivid that he wrote them down. The first of these is given in its entirety, so that the mood and temperamental attitude may be understood through the way in which the detail is written. The others are abbreviated, only the material dealing with the Mother-Anima problem being presented. The development of the image rather than the literary form of the dream is considered of importance.

"I was on the lawn of my grandmother's place, where I was born and where my mother lived before she was married. There were some big crows in the oak tree beside the house, and a group of men were preparing to shoot them down. This seemed wicked to me; in fact it gave me a very strange pang, but I could do nothing about it. One by one the crows, who made no efforts to escape or protest, were shot out of the tree.

"Then mother came home from somewhere. She was going to be married, she said. She was young, in her teens or early twenties, and she didn't care a hang about me and my dependence on her. She went on packing up her things to leave her parents' household, strangely determined and silent and removed, apparently without emotion, just calm and assured—and intensely, quietly determined. I was shut out, along with the rest. It was strange that she should be going away to her own life, to be married to some man I did not know; it made me wonder and it hurt me a little too, for I felt very small and defenseless, thrown back into the past.

"Then the wedding. It was to take place at the Willards' house down the road, that old dark mausoleum of suburban bourgeoisie, its aura so deeply connected with mother's childhood. The wedding party, or ceremony, was in the basement, a short flight of stairs down from the basement vestibule I was in; a sort of sub-basement. It was all lit down there and there were a good many people. When I got there, I found she had become a little girl again, of perhaps fourteen years.

"This young girl was someone with whom I had a deep spiritual connection, as if she had been a sister or a playmate from whom I had never been separated since birth, and with whom I had always been in love, with that piercing, helpless, almost painful love which sensitive children sometimes experience, which is really deep and lasting, yet tragic because it cannot be consummated. It was strange that she was being married to an unknown man, and she so young. I hovered on the sidelines in a kind of suspense, neither suffering nor rejoicing, but just waiting to see it through; with a growing sense, however, that this wedding was something I was being wrongfully detained by, and that I must soon depart. Finally, I did make up my mind to go without seeing the wedding through, and I started up the steps to the outside. But just then the child left her bridegroom and the whole affair and came running after me, her lovely face anxious and pale, her small body trembling with excitement and emotion; she caught up to me on the lower part of the stairway and implored me, with her hand on my arm, not to leave. I said I had to. She besought me desperately, with tears in her eyes. I loved her like death, I had always loved her; but I had to go, I was determined to go, I longed for the open air and the out of doors and the path to my own life which lay out there. I told her I could not stay, she must not try to make me. She said it was *I* she loved, it was *I* she really wanted to marry. But I turned to go on up the stairs, warning her not to come with me.

"She did come with me, still tearfully imploring me not to go. I knew I should have to hurt her, to shake her off, to convince her I must break with her. Quickly I turned and slapped her wrist cruelly. This surprised her so that she let go of me, giving me a second's time to make my escape into the open. My eyes were filled with tears at leaving her, at hurting her; she was so small and brave and pitiful, the lovely flower-child in the short white dress, with her intense gray-blue eyes. I had always loved her, she had always been part of me, but it was right to leave. I was glad to be out in the real world."

Writing out the dream, he added, "Crows, during a period of my childhood, I considered my own private property; I had an especial fondness for them, and liked to imagine that I knew all crows and all crows knew me."

He sees reluctantly that these birds, childish identifications, must be shot. Once this is done, the dream changes. At first the mother is to leave him for her own life. This is what he consciously believes he wants, yet in the dream it is a source of anguish to him. Then he pictures her as a young child, appealing to him. He would see her dependent upon him, needing his protection. She is dressed in white, the color of innocence. He wishes to stay with her, but feels that it is she who is making the demand. This was in accordance with the reality of the situation. Objectively, he believed that he could not leave home because she needed him; unconsciously, he was both unwilling and unable to break his infantile dependence upon her and yet, in a more subtle way, *she* was holding him back, for her unconscious had put upon him the demand that he should fulfill the unrealized ambitions of her own marriage, that he should live out his father's life. Therefore, she was demanding of him what she should find for herself, either in individual life or in a marriage relationship.

Here he is assailed by the emotion which was most confusing to him in real life; his desire to remain with her disguised as protectiveness and pity. In the dream, just as this emotion reaches its height, he slaps the child. His unconscious, that is, has tried to reduce the mother entirely to the level of a child; but it has also warned him that the relationship, on any terms, cannot be maintained without peril, and that he must escape from the surroundings of his childhood.

Then, having attempted to escape from his problem by throwing himself into artistic activities, there came a dream of great beauty, which remained with him as a vivid experience of reality.

"It was in a verdant valley in spring. There was a small pastoral village, not of this age. There were two beautiful young girls, naked each, one with dark hair, one with light. They were strange, wild, lonely creatures, immature. I had never seen either before, but I had a sense of having been deeply related to them from childhood or earlier. I was in love with them, deeply.

"As I approached them, they began to move away, so I followed. Whereas at first they had not been ten feet away from me, they began to get farther and farther away. They went to the foot of the pasture-mountain and began to climb, turning and waving their hands sadly at me. As they climbed, they sang. No words can describe the wildness, the magic beauty of that singing, which seemed like an echo from an immortal muse's song of long ago.

"I stopped when I came to the foot of the mountain. I could not follow them, madly as I desired them. I should never have any contact with them; they were lost to me. Still they turned their faces back to me as they climbed, still they waved their hands. Still the sustained notes of that marvelous singing echoed down from the mountain."

He reluctantly sees them go, conscious of the beauty of their song but knowing that the heights that they inhabit cannot now be his. This youth is too near to the collective images. He has been in great danger of living wholly in phantasy and of regarding the demands of reality as a bad dream. Here he sees the two sides of the Anima, the light and the dark undifferentiated, as they are when a person is in the grip of the unconscious. As he wakes, he feels both sorrow that he must remain in the valley, and a sense of exhilaration at the experience. It also seems to him that, though they are seen in the dream as two, yet they are as one; and that this image which they represent holds for him some future promise.

In actual life, the temptation to follow the Anima was not overcome, because he was constantly drifting away into phantasy and evading the problems of his outer life. This situation was made clear in the following dream:

He is attempting to make a relationship, as a man, with Eileen, a girl who in actual life represented to him a love image; but they are going to bed by daylight, like two children, and when he gets into bed he finds that the girl is his mother. She disappears, and he is in her car, with his grandmother. He is waiting for the return of the girl, who has gone to get her wedding dress. He sees her coming. She is in white. This is his mother whom he is to marry, for Eileen would be wearing red. White was to him the color of childish innocence, and red the color of passion, of fire, and of life. He woke with a feeling of despair and a realization that he was caught in an ancestral pattern, in a childish relation to his mother and grandmother, and was unable to make any real relation with the girl he loved. And again he hated his mother, feeling that it was she who had done this to him.

This picture of his ignominious failure threw him back on his old inferiority. He felt that he had no value of his own. Then came a dream which showed what was stealing away these values: He is in "his own house" but an enemy is stealing away all his possessions. He feels this to be a man against whom he is powerless, for he cannot see him. All his possessions are being carried out, yet he cannot see who is doing this. He pretends he knows and, calling the enemy by a name which suggests a bogey in a child's story, shouts in a high, childish voice, "I know you, High Pieham." He searches frantically from room to room; he shouts, "I see you, High Pieham," but the maurauder is invisible. Now his house is empty; he rushes out and sees the enemy in the woodshed, but it is a little old woman "in a long, coarse brown dress like a gunny sack. She hurried to escape. As she ran, she turned her face around toward me . . . her face was plain and ugly and expressionless. I caught her easily. As I threw her down with my hand on her throat, she seemed to shrivel to something like a pasteboard woman. When I cut off her head with the axe, there was nothing to it, there was no sense of triumph, she was not a flesh and blood woman."

At this time, in his conscious life, he was alternately possessed by, was wandering to and fro between, two contradictory ideas. First, that he himself was an inferior being, possessing no values by which he could establish himself as a man. Second, that he was potentially a great character and that the entire social order was against him. Now his unconscious showed him that the enemy was in his own house; it was his shadow, the negative aspect of himself, still invisible to him, which was stealing away his values. When he tried to come to grips with it, the only aspect of it which he could perceive was that sterile and lifeless form of the Anima, the unsustaining phantasy, which took him away from life instead of giving him energy, which he had substituted for reality and which, when met, had no more substance than a cardboard witch.

In the next dream he is back in a town where he had once been in college, but the house in which he is living is furnished like his grandmother's house and he is living with his mother. He is puttering about, putting away small articles, straightening out bureau drawers. His mother is scornful of his occupation. She is interested in a strange, shadowy man. Then his mother goes out and after a little while he follows to join her at a restaurant where she will buy his dinner. The restaurant is full of young people of his age or younger. They are laughing and talking, appearing confident and happy. Suddenly he feels strangely embarrassed, he is conscious that his arms are bare to the shoulder and that his sweater hangs loosely about him like a woman's garment. They will see it and ridicule him. Then he catches sight of his mother at a table near by. She is laughing and talking with a male companion. She is young, beautiful, and she is wearing his blue suit. He sees that this suit is no longer gray-blue, but a bright, luminous color which almost seems to give off light. She looks at him, he feels, mockingly. He will show his scorn of her and of her companion; he will bow ironically and pass on; but instead he finds that his muscles do not obey him, and he genuflects to her.

Although in the dream he is in a town of his own choosing (a town where in actuality his mother has never been) it is still the home of his grandmother and he is living with his mother. In the retreat of his own room, he can satisfy himself with trivial little jobs (like a woman puttering with household details), but when he gets in the world outside he sees himself surrounded by people who know their own way. Then he becomes conscious that his garment has changed its form and is like the garb of a woman. Here he sees that his ineffectiveness lies not only in being dependent upon the mother for support (looking to her to give him his dinner) but also, he perceives, in her having stolen away his essential masculinity, his blue suit. This suit is now of a peculiar living blue, suggesting to him "spiritual and intellectual clarity, the Gnostic Logos color." It is, therefore, the very essence of his own masculinity which he believes she has taken from him. At this time he feels that she has herself found her own way (that is, that she has made friends with her own Animus and begun to find the values of her own masculine side). But he feels, too, that through the combination of his economic dependence and her silent but continuous pressure to make him accept her values as his own, she has stolen from him his masculine garment. He would like to show his scorn of her, but against his conscious desire he makes obeisance to her.

Even though this mother image, now a combination of mother, Anima, and archetypal or Divine Mother, is still to him the biological mother and his return to her is infantile dependence, he perceives in this dream that the idea of mother contains for him a value to which his unconscious bows. What this value really is he cannot tell until he has gone farther with the solution of his personal problem. Meanwhile, in the next dream, the Anima comes to him in a new guise:

He is on a lonely road by the sea; behind him is a familiar city which he has left. There is an atmosphere of gloom—almost darkness—and he is quite alone. He sees coming toward him a young woman walking with free, long steps. Even in the dim light he notices her red hair, like flame. As she passes, he feels her presence as though a magnetic current was set in motion. After she has passed, he turns and makes a gesture of salute, which she answers. Instantly, there is a great explosion in the sky over the city. He is terrified, but the woman continues quietly on her way to the town. He has an impulse to follow her, but is restrained by fear of the explosion and of the perils which he may find in the city.

This is his first encounter with this woman of the flamelike hair. She will appear again in his dream experiences. The affect of this dream shows its deep importance. For days this figure retained its vivid impression of reality and power. He could neither forget her nor understand her. Here the Anima, the mysterious woman, personifies that intuition which could guide him in his life of adventure if he would follow her. He has by this time come to grips with his solitary unrelated phantasy, and discovered its unreality (the cardboard witch). Now he can see the other side of the Anima, the reality side of his inner life, an intuition of the next step. This figure would lead him back to the city, that is, back to his actual life in the world of men, where he would use his energy in his normal masculine development. The excitement of this encounter is symbolized by the great explosion (the fear, the release of tension, the desire, all those intense irrational emotions). He thinks this is a destruction in the city, but it is only in the heavens. The city is unharmed and the woman continues on her road there. He longs to follow but is afraid and so is once more alone.

In the next dream, the Anima appears again as Eileen. They meet, but discover that she is six inches taller than he—her stature is greater than his, they cannot achieve relationship, they must part. They are in a room full of people, including his mother, who is aware of his pitiful tragedy but sternly unsympathetic. All the assembly are well dressed, but he is in his pyjamas (he has no Persona, he is in the garment suited to his unconscious—his moods and womanish inadequacies). The young woman tells him that though they must part, he will find the answer to his situation in the words of a poem that he himself has written, a poem about the recreation of a self which can take on new patterns and fit into new forms of life—that is, in an answer arising within himself as part of his own masculine creative power.

Here for the first time the Anima appears in her true introverted aspect connecting him with the creative part of the unconscious. It is to this power that he must look to find his energy as a man and the strength with which to make his own way. The dream says that his stature is not yet great enough for marriage (a real relation with the Anima). Since this is so, the woman leaves him, having indicated what he should do.

In the next dream, he is again with his mother, but this time in the village where Eileen lives. He goes out to find her. She will have nothing to do with him, for she is accompanied by X, a simple, successful, conventional young man. He associated this young man with the normal ego which was not yet his, an ego which could achieve a right relation to the Anima. Hence Eileen prefers X.

In the dream, he now becomes aware of another figure, a young girl, manifestly inferior, who makes advances to him. He decides that if he cannot have a real relation he will accept the sexual substitute. He follows her to her home. It is squalid, its occupants sordid. She comes out to him, but he feels a repulsion for her. The merely sexual offered no solution for his problem.

In the next dream he is working in a store, earning his own living at a job which seems dull but worth while as bringing him to a new experience. It is to break something into small bits which can be contained and reassembled in a bowl. The dream depicts the analytical process, in which the elements of the personality are first separated by analysis and then synthesized, fused into a new substance. It also points out the fact that, for this young man, the inner synthesis can take place only through his acceptance of a routine job which, though dull, gives him a chance to support himself. The young man would have been delighted to concentrate upon the collective aspects of a symbol so ancient and widespread as that of the bowl, but he needed to see its direct application to his personal life.

The next part of the dream brought him back to the problem of the Anima. He is now in a pasture. There he finds the girl asleep, dressed in white (the garment of youth before worn by the mother), but her sleep is so sound that he can only half rouse her (she is still too much in the unconscious). He knows he must leave her, but this time feels that he will find her again. He kisses her, but she does not really waken.

Then again the dream shifts. He is embarking on a river boat. He feels this to be a journey he must take. He carries under his arm a few possessions which are the only personal objects that he can take with him. Suddenly his mother appears at his side telling him that he must change boats at the next landing. Though he still resents her, he feels that she is right and that at this time he must accept her guidance. He is on the upper deck. The change to the other boat must be made quickly. Where are his possessions? They were on the deck below. His mother will bring them—no—she is again on the deck beside him and is completely unmindful of his pain at losing them. The new boat is going south, the other had been going north; yet he knows that this boat is the right one. The north to him is associated with independent adventure, with breaking from social collective demands and following the irrational desires; the south associated with work and with analysis. Here the personal associations were more important than symbolic aspects of north and south, although north as intuition and south as feeling and sensation had a meaning. This dream showed him a new aspect of the mother. She partook of the nature of the introverted Anima, acting (as he put it) as conscience and guide, a voice that must be followed.

As a result of the discussion of this dream, he saw qualities that she possessed, qualities which were also his, but which he had never accepted and used. It was as though the breaking up process with which the dream began were now actually taking place and he could see the elements of his mother-inheritance as separated and to be used in a new fusion. He still deeply resents her utter disregard of the small objects which are so precious to him. This was true in real life. She often acted ruthlessly, brushing away as valueless things dear to him, yet now he feels that this very ruthlessness may for a time be a quality he must accept in himself; in an emergency he must be able to sacrifice even some of the things dear to him if they would delay him and so prevent his going the new way. But he feels too that he could have preserved these if he had been conscious of what was happening and had not left them "in the lower part of the boat." It is really his own heedlessness that is to blame.

In this dream, there is a distinct progression, a new sense of values, a willingness to see in the elements which he has rejected a saving element. The mother now takes on a new aspect. He can begin to see her impersonally as a psychological figure representing factors of his own unconscious which he must listen to and follow. In this way the process of depersonalization (becoming free of the mother) has begun.

And now in the next dream he meets the Anima in a "gracious, restraining aspect." She appears once again as a woman with red, flamelike hair, although in the dream he feels that it is his first meeting with her. They enter into conversation. What she tells him he knows to be true. He asks her to eat with him, and they go to a place where there is music. She tells him that they must not dance to this "hot" music, for they are as yet strange to each other and in their excitement they could go too fast and "burn themselves out." He feels her restraint to be born of wisdom and that he must learn to understand her words first. This dream made him accept a fact which he had previously ignored. He had always been so excited by the images of his unconscious that they had had a power to plunge him into moods of elation or despair. And in his feeling relations he had grasped intuitive potentials and been swept on by emotional excitement, with disregard of all except the desired element, often to disillusionment. It is these emotional excitements, these moods, which are the "hot" music which in the dance with the Anima might make them burn themselves out.

Now in the next dream he makes further progress in his discovery and understanding of the Anima. He is in a house with a young woman who in real life always seemed to him a courageous person foredoomed because of inheritance and environment. He must get her out of the house to where she can get a sight of the open ocean and the buoys. But fate has married her to a man he does not know but who holds her in his power. It would be dangerous if this husband discovered that he was talking to her, helping her and showing her the open sea. He does not know this husband but fears his power. "I never saw him, but I felt him *around* all the time, even when I was alone with her, and I feared him." When he now sees her, she has been fighting with her mother in a futile battle against her inescapable doom. The husband is not visible. They go down to the water's edge. He sees in the distance a sailing ship, beautiful in the sunlight. It comes nearer. It changes and becomes only an ugly flat scow. He says to her: "It looked at first like a beautiful four-master." Then he points out to her the buoys which mark the channel to the open ocean by which they might escape. But they must go back. Otherwise her husband, to whom she is bound, will discover them. He tells her wistfully that she has not even heard a whistling buoy—it is far out—perhaps, some day!

Here appears the Anima in another form, that of the unconscious mood, in this instance the despair which often sweeps over him. She is the daughter of doom, wedded to the shadow, which keeps her from life and freedom. As yet they can only *look* at the way of escape; he cannot yet free her from the Shadow. The Shadow is still invisible. The change in the appearance of the ship corresponds to the dreamer's own sense that what is remote is beautiful, while that which is at hand is dull and ugly.

In the next dream he is working in an office. One of the girls approaches him with a suggestion of seduction. Then other girls in the office attack her and undress her. She has a man's genitals. Here other images from the unconscious reveal the fact that the Anima has taken over the masculinity which is properly the attribute of his ego. This makes her revolting and any relation with her impossible.

In the next dream Eileen comes to him. He discovers that she has grown chin whiskers. This showed that the danger unmasked in the former dream was real. His unconscious was carrying masculine values that belonged to his conscious. Also he was expecting real women to carry certain masculine responsibilities.

In the next of the Anima dreams, Eileen appears driving an automobile in which several people are riding. A trolley car is "proceeding in orderly fashion" but, as it stops, the woman drives ahead at full speed and there is a violent collision. The trolley car he associates with middle-class traveling. It runs on tracks laid down, it is humdrum, uninteresting (his attitude toward ordinary conventions). The Anima, running violently against this, brings the occupants of the car to disaster. That is, if he yields to his irrational unconscious impulses, they will wreck his necessary daily routine.

There was then a long series of dreams dealing with the problem of finding his place as a man in the workaday world and thereby recovering the masculine attributes which had been lost in the unconscious. Then came a dream in which he finds himself again on a river boat, this time going north, to take up his own life in the world. From the boat he sees that the house where he has lived with his mother has been gutted by flames in the night. Though brick, it has burned like wood, as though the flame had sprung from within. Suddenly he realizes that he has left his mother asleep there. This realization is in turn blotted out by a greater fear. Has he left there the record of his dreams and also his other possessions; that is, has he again started out too soon without taking with him the things which should have become part of his conscious life? He must go back. Then he sees his mother as removed far away in her own life, burned in the fire, yet alive. No, she is dead. He wishes to be glad of this but cannot. He feels that if his mother is really dead, then the dream book has been destroyed also. At this time he had a great desire to wrench himself out of the old life as an assertion of independence and to go "my own way" without discovering what his own way really was. This would be like a death of the mother, in which all potentials of new value would be destroyed. She would be *really* dead; she would not be "alive in another place," a place in which her positive values for him might appear. In this event, his dream book, which represented his understanding and integration of the values of the unconscious, would also be destroyed. Actually, to leave home at this time would be destructive, for it would again be only an escape.

In the next Anima dream he is in the north, "far, far up in a place of intolerable loneliness and beauty." He feels that he must start south to find "reality and my own true conscience again." But he dallies on the way, attracted into a store by expensive sport outfits "for the playboy life I envisaged." Then he is in his mother's car (though he thinks of the journey as his return, to find his own truth, still the energy which carries him is the mother's). The road is lonely. A headlight lens falls in the road and shatters into fragments (he has lost his intuitive perception). He gathers the fragments from the road and puts them in the grass. Lest someone step on them there, he picks them all up

DREAMS OF MOTHER AND ANIMA   159

again and puts them in a ditch. Then, going back to the car, fearing that he will be hurt by someone else, he flattens himself against the running board as other cars pass. He even thrusts his head in the window of the car to hide from the passers-by. Then he sees there is plenty of room, that he is hiding from a nonexistent danger. Yet he is overcome by panic. (This is a picture of his own oversensitivity, his excessive fear of what he may do to people and of what they may do to him.)

Although vague thoughts of the ignominy of seeking security flash through his mind, he finds that he has taken refuge in a strange house in which he is "in the power of an old crank whose ideas of diagnosis and procedure were prearranged and predictable. She was omniscient, and of course knew just what was right and wrong for me. I must submit. I was in her power." She takes him into a room "lighted by false sunlight," strips him and gives him a strait jacket which looks like black winter underwear. There is a young woman there who is acting under the direction of the old woman. She seems to tell him that he is powerless. (The youthful Anima image now also under the control of the Terrible Mother.) He suddenly remembers the analyst, who appears to him as a "true Gnostic." (Here an image of the Anima in a positive aspect, who would connect him with real wisdom.) But though the effort to connect with her seems "almost to wake him up" the dream continues with his struggle to put on the strait jacket, which is too small. All the time, the inner struggle to defy the "omniscient bitch" is going on. Suddenly, he pulls off the garment and dashes from the room.

This part of the dream represents the fact that he saw the world itself as the Terrible Mother. One of his difficulties had been his fear that in accepting any conformity to social order, or any position which offered him financial independence, he would lose his own unique values. His idea of the social order was that men became slaves, automatons, that they were made to live according to rules and regulations—in short, they were pressed into stereotyped molds represented in the dream by the strait jacket which was too small for him. The Terrible Mother now has the Anima as her servant, and in this capacity the Anima speaks only through his negative fears. It is she who says, "The world is terrible, cruel, omniscient—you will lose your freedom—

your self. See what this other mother will do to you." But in the dream he is conscious that this is only a "spell." He vaguely hears the other voice, the voice of wisdom within himself, which he here embodies in the analyst—"a true Gnostic"—really the wisdom he can find when he has faced the problem of the Anima.

In another dream, he finds himself a wage slave in a factory, another form of the strait jacket.

In the next dream, the same subjugation continues. He is a guard in the subway, to him the dreariest of occupations. He makes mistakes, he runs to and fro. Then the train stops and a colored woman with a small boy stands in the doorway and tells him a "joke," a story of a "temperamental" elephant who kicked a stone which hurt a small dog and then a black cat dropped on the dog's back and clawed him cruelly. The negress laughs and laughs. "*She* is the black cat—she is laughing at me. I am the dog." Here the negress, the black Anima, is mocking him—would hurt him cruelly. The elephant is to him a quiet, strong, earth animal, a type of dependable instinctive force; but here it too is an agent of cruelty—the stone so carelessly kicked starts the pattern of malicious chance. At this time, he saw the whole world as cruel and himself as subject to evil chance. He was the victim of the black Anima.

Then came a period in which these black moods were subjected to conscious scrutiny. Other dream images arose for consideration. Then again he sees the red-haired girl, now "an adventurous out-of-door girl of warm feeling, liked by everyone and full of friendliness." She is working in a restaurant and too busy to talk then, but asks him to participate in a "party" next day. He lingers, though he feels he has work to do. He sneaks into the kitchen and makes himself cocoa. He hopes no one will see him, but finds the girl looking at him, though she says nothing. He is ashamed, but stammers explanations—"It is so little, it is not worth paying for. I will make it do for supper too." Still she says nothing. (His is the attitude of the man who feels life owes him a living. Asking so little, he should not pay for what he gets. But the Anima stands in silent criticism.)

In the next stage of the dream, he is at the party. It is a cross-country race in which the one who can beat the girl will receive her as a reward. Here he realizes that though she is apparently near and visible, she is surrounded by "a dark aura" and he has never really seen her face, nor does he during the entire dream. This aura is not evil, but more an energy which she possesses. At first he keeps abreast of her and carries on a sort of subtle courtship. Then they reach a lake. He notes with surprise that the surface of the lake is not level but conforms to the contours of the rolling land, so that its depth never varies. The girl plunges in and he after her, but she easily outswims him, and on reaching the land he finds that all the contestants, including the girl, have vanished. It is in that strange lake (the waters of the unconscious conforming in defiance of natural law to the contours of the land, the conscious) that he loses her. He finds himself penniless on a long, hilly road, unable to take a bus home.

In this dream, the Anima is again the elusive, the mysterious one whose face cannot be seen although he appears to look upon it. Really to see her, he would have to prove himself a worthy antagonist and this he is as yet unable to do, and so in the old discouraging way he finds himself helpless to meet external difficulties.

In the next dream, he finds himself once more living with the mother in the old Chicago apartment. As a result of the discussions of this dream, he realized that his various attempts at independence had been merely infantile rebellions, that they left him still childishly dependent, that he could really become a man only by finding his own way.

Both before and after this, he had many dreams of a very beautiful and intelligent horse, who was especially the dreamer's own. It meant to him his own unique energy. It was always one special horse that he had lost and for which he was searching. At one point, he follows a trail leading to a ranch where he knows the horse to be. It is night when he arrives and stormy—a vivid flash of lightning cleaves the sky. He sees the horses by the fence but, even in the vivid light, he cannot tell which one is his. He feels panic. (He no longer knows the essential element of his own nature—which of these images is his own instinctual energy.) In other dreams, he was still searching for this horse.

After a period of confusion and regression, he dreams that he is on his way to Detroit, which in his conscious life represents a step forward in his chosen work. But he finds himself instead in Marcy, a lonely hill village which once meant to him being on his own. The place now seems to him inexpressibly dreary. Then he sees again the red-haired girl and starts to make love to her. But the love-making is unreal and turns into a sort of play. It is night. There is no inn, only an empty house where once he lived. Where shall he sleep? This attempt has brought him to no place of his own. Where is Detroit, the place of real independence? Why is he here in the place which meant merely childish rebellion? Why is the relation to the Anima unreal?

This question he had to answer, and to do so he had to work out a long series of dreams and to review many phases of his so-called conscious life which really had been directed by unconscious images which had been given strength by his emotions—his Anima. The destruction of ideas of independence based merely on negativity brought him to a reconsideration of Marcy, where he had made his first attempt to carry the responsibility of his own life. This attempt had been based on a wrong assumption, but in abandoning it he had also given up his fight for psychological adulthood—his real masculinity.

Soon after this, he found a way of living which involved some apparent dependence but which was based upon real individual choice. Then came a dream which answered the question asked in the dream about Detroit.

He is back in Marcy and there to his joy he finds his own horse which he had lost long before. It was only a colt when he left it, but now it is a strong and vigorous horse. (His energy has really been developing in the unconscious without his knowledge.) He is to leave this place, he knows, forever; not, this time, in his mother's car, but on his own horse. Although the house is bare, it is he himself who has dismantled it, leaving it clean and ready for a new occupant, and packing up what he wishes to save of old possessions. His mother, who is there, is now a shadowy figure. He is concerned only with helping her to get away safely, in order to be free to go his own way with his horse. Then, while he is considering what he is to do with his mother, a strange thing happens. She seems to faint. Her face grows gray, and she twists and shrivels and gradually disappears.

"I think she died then, because she just 'went out like a light' and did not reappear." (With the discovery of his own real energy the biological mother—the Terrible Mother—"goes out like a light." That is, she vanishes from his psychic life without apparent struggle on his part, because *he* no longer energizes her image.)

Now he is free—so he thinks—but to his surprise he finds himself in the company of a young poet, whom in real life he has alternately admired for his brilliance and despised for his weakness, false assumptions, negativity, and self-pitying irresponsibility. Although in real life he had broken from the acquaintance, he sees this figure as his new companion, but he sees him clearly. This is his Shadow, the side of himself with which he must now reckon. The Shadow has appeared before, but as a mysterious invisible energy operating in the dark (see High Pieham dream) or as the invisible husband who holds the Anima in his power.

Until now the mother image has stood between himself and a clear perception of these shadowy sides of himself. While he remained a child, he could not deal with his own Shadow. Now he perceives it in a figure which combines his own unrealized possibilities with the weaknesses of his own nature, which have until now kept him from making these possibilities into something real. It is now this Shadow with which he must deal. With the disappearance of the problem of the mother, a new problem arises.

After he had dealt with this problem, both consciously and unconsciously, for some time, the image of the Anima again appeared, no longer in bondage either to the mother or the Shadow.

XII. DREAM ANALYSIS IN LATER LIFE

A WOMAN in late middle age came to analysis because she felt that her life was barren of opportunities, that people were critical of her, and that she had been unjustly treated. She also had a growing fear of a tension within herself which at times made her feel that something might give way, and that she might even become insane. She came to analysis with no real idea of changing herself, but to find some kind of magic by which she could change other people and outer circumstances; assuming that the inner tension would vanish with a change in her outer life.

Her first hour was devoted to a description of her present situation, though it was not so much a description of actual circumstances as a voicing of dogmatic ideas about what ought to be and of opinions about people whose attitude she felt to be entirely wrong. In fact, from the very first the conversation was usurped by the Animus, who talked through her lips. Her resentment at the moment was caused by the loss of an important position; a loss which she said was due to some "weak, sentimental women" who were jealous of her ability and would not allow her to carry out ideas which were very much better than theirs.

In the second hour of analysis, she was asked whether any special experience, beyond the loss of her position, had made her feel the need of help. She then admitted that, the summer before, she had had a dream which had obsessed her and which she was not able to dismiss. The dream was as follows:

"I saw my sister in the water, and in great danger. I called out, 'Keep your head out of the water, don't go under.' But she paid no attention and sank down into the depths, and disappeared from the dream. I then found myself in a boat which I had supposed was secure, but which now was breaking, and my own peril was imminent."

She spoke of her sister as of unstable emotional temperament, delicate in health, full of fear of life and taking refuge in "an old-fashioned religious attitude." In early middle life this sister became insane. "Later I learned that she had had an abnormal fear of sexual relations in her marriage, and it was darkly hinted that her husband had driven her to insanity." She could see why her sister had been drowned. What the dream meant to her at this point was that she herself might be going insane.

In answer to further questions she told of her situation at the time of the dream. She had been traveling with a professional woman, but their relationship had degenerated into a contest for power; and she had deeply resented the fact that this woman had then gone off with other people and left her to shift for herself. She had also been a good deal in the company of a clergyman and his wife. He was an intellectual man and had been interested in her capacity for discussion, but she had so snubbed his wife that this relation had also ended in disaster.

The other situation of the summer, and one which was now affecting her deeply, was that she had been paid some slight attentions by an elderly man, a scholar, a friend of her family's, and ever since she had been living in a phantasy of a possible marriage with him. In this phantasy she had entirely remade marriage to suit herself. She described it as a community of mind, and recalled a remark she had made earlier in life that though she might be married, she would never have intercourse. This she still felt to be possible in an "ideal marriage." This, then, was the actual situation from which the dream arose.

Though she admitted that the summer had been a complete failure, she could not see the elements in herself which had made it so. Nor could she see that the boat was her old adaptation, which could not fail to break, and that she must find a new form of security.

Any attempt to show her the real meaning was met by a flood of argument and an attempt to draw the analyst into a discussion. No other dreams came for some time because she was consciously so busy trying to pick the analyst's brains, trying to find out whether she really knew her job, and trying to discover what all the intellectual theories behind an analysis were.

She took copious notes and would return to her next appointment with a classroom copybook in which these notes reappeared in the form of short essays. These she would insist upon reading out. Some of the topics which she discussed in this manner were: "Static or dynamic attitudes toward religion;" "Disposition of libido;" "Bergson's *élan vital*;" "Phantasy and sexuality;" "Place of Joan of Arc in the life of the ideal;" "Emotional trauma and psychic injury;" "India and America;" "Stages of growth in the psychic life;" "Selfishness or self evaluation?"

She said that these were ideas which she had gleaned from analysis, though the analyst could not help feeling that these ideas had gone out in petticoats and returned in pants and that so far the analysant had done little more than successfully block any intuitive thought that might arise from within herself. But her neurotic fears were now so insistent that she did not dare leave the analysis and attempt a return to her old adaptation.

The first new dream which she brought was the following: "I found myself going through an underground passage, and was afraid of the man following me; I thought he was a priest!"

She found this dream very confusing, because the priest represented to her a renunciation of the "lower side of life." Now in this dream, the figure was fraught with terror and was following her as a menace. At first the only feelings of fear that she could connect with it were those of too great austerity and too great conformity to a religious code.

In analyzing this figure as an enemy pursuing her down the dark passage of her own unconscious, she saw it as dogmatic idealism which denies normal life. But immediately this became an interesting concept, and she could not understand why it had filled her with terror. She had caught a fleeting glimpse of the Animus whom she would recognize later. Then she recalled a dream which she had had years ago, and which she had tried to repress.

"I had a feeling that a terrible presence had come into the room, though I saw nothing; I felt that this horror was creeping upon me. I woke screaming, and as I woke I suddenly felt a black man was trying to get into bed with me."

The man was her image of primitive sexuality which she feared might overpower her. She was, in fact, beset with sexual desires and phantasies, which filled her with a sense of shame, as though they were temptations of the devil. Because she denied the value of normal instincts, she now saw them overpowering her as a bestial and terrifying black man. But she could not see that the priest's figure of sterile idealism was something to be feared as greatly as the black's figure of primitive sexuality.

The analyst asked, "Why are you so afraid of your own sexuality?" and was answered by a flood of remonstrances and an astonishment that any woman could ask such a question, and not herself realize how revolting it all was.

This question activated her memories of a woman-Mrs. Z— who had long dominated her life. She had met this woman at a time when she was a motherless girl, full of adolescent dreams of ideal love, and had projected upon her the image of Spiritual Mother. She turned to this woman when she was in great confusion about her first love affair, with a man who was unhappily married; the the older woman, instead of giving her sympathetic understanding, had upbraided her and filled her with shame that she could have thought of having any relationship (even platonic friendship) with a married man. That he had once kissed her became a guilty secret which she must try to expiate.

Now, quite unconsciously, she was trying through the experience with the elderly scholar to relive her first love affair, giving it the ideal solution which the Spiritual Mother had demanded of her in her youth.

At this time she recalled another long-repressed dream which had come to her after this first love affair was over:

"I saw a corpse with a face old and wan and despairing. Then I perceived that it was my own dead body. The face was like a death mask, but the hair was a bright, vivid gold. I gathered this hair as one would gather a harvest from a field."

She had felt at the time as though she herself "had died of shame." And now, even after all these years, she wept over the recollection of her dead youth. She remembered telling the dream to the older woman, who brushed it aside as unimportant, and gave a long lecture on the superiority of the spirit to the flesh.

So, instead of harvesting the gold, she had buried her instinctual feeling, and weighed it down with her sense of shame. Thus she had made her first separation from her life as a woman, and in obedience to the Mother had accepted the Animus (sterile intellectual ideas) in the place of a living relationship, instead of trying to discover what was the reality of the situation and whether or not she could gain understanding from its experience.

After dealing with the associations of this remembered dream, the first new one was:

"I faced a closed door with a combination lock. If I only knew—if I could possibly find the combination—then I could open the door and be happy." Again came the old sentimental excuses; it was too late; her life was wasted; she wept over the closed door instead of trying to find the combination.

Frequently the early dreams show the problem to be met during the course of the analysis. Three important dreams had now come to her. The first, of the boat which was no longer safe, showed the peril of her present adaptation. The second, of the priest, showed in one of his many roles the Animus, that figure around whom so much of her analysis was to revolve. The third, of the combination lock, showed that there was no one rule of conduct of right and wrong by which she could proceed, but that the door could be opened only by a combination which was at present completely unknown to her.

The deeper meaning of these dreams was lost upon her, because she could get no emotional connection with them. There followed a period in which she again attempted to make analysis an intellectual discussion. Then the dreams began again:

"I had been riding on top of a Fifth Avenue bus with an older cousin. I was going down the staircase to get off, and tried to help her down, but could not seem to get hold of her hand. I went into a house alone. Looking out of the window, I saw no one, but I felt her ghostly presence in the garden."

Her associations: "The Fifth Avenue bus is a time-waster and very boring; one should travel in the fastest way possible. My elderly cousin lived a completely conventional life according to the ideas of the Victorian period. She was a dominating, powerful type of person, and I did not like her at all."

These meagre associations were all that she was able to supply. The analyst suggested that the persons moving in a dream were subjective elements and together they worked out the following explanation, which interested her intellectually but did not "take" emotionally. The top of the bus meant that she was in a position above the ordinary crowd on the street (that is, above ordinary relationships). Her elderly cousin represented a side of herself. Then she was, as she supposed, alone in the house, but became aware that the cousin, although now invisible, was really moving about the garden as a ghostly presence. That is, in her garden of life this element, this ghost or image, was still a living and moving factor. Here the unseen Shadow makes its presence felt. She consciously saw herself as a vital intellectual person and had an overyouthful image of this self, but others could easily recognize in her what the cousin represented.

At this time she again met the elderly scholar with whom she was carrying on the intellectualized love phantasy. He made some slight advances and suggested that there was more in marriage than the sharing of noble thoughts. In fact he made a slightly humorous allusion to the large double bed that was in his room. She felt he had been crude, and retired into priggishness. She did not realize what a monumental heroism it was for any man to attempt a sexual advance with a woman whose armor of virtues was like that of the iron maiden. After her indignant repulse he withdrew, and met her with only cold reserve.

He was just recovering from an illness, and having failed to meet him with any human warmth, she substituted pity for his lonely life and talked of how sad it was for a man to have only servants about when he was ill. She became very emotional over this, pouring into her pictures of his isolation all her own problems. She became deeply concerned over his lack of power to make a feeling contact; she projected her own problems over onto him; she pitied him for the very things which were her own limitations. But instead of doing anything about it she took refuge in writing what she thought to be a poem. In it, material rising out of the unconscious is so sentimentally elaborated that a brief extract from it will suffice:

> Why do you come so often unbidden to my door,
> And force your way in uninvited? What are you seeking?
> I only see your face and the hungry eyes
> That search and search for I know not what.
> To me you are an unknown guest

> For nothing articulate passes between us.
> Yet you come and come. Could you but speak
> And tell me why you come and what is that nameless sorrow
> That is in your heart, dear other soul,
> The weary head could rest here on my breast,
> For the mother soul of the universe is within me,
> And gives me to dispense to others her soothing power.
> I would lay my hand on your eyelids
> And softly touch your forehead, and again
> You would feel your own mother come to nurture you,
> As when you were a child. Rest and peace are here
> For you, comfort and joy in full measure.
> Then come and receive the gift of the great earth mother to
>   the children of men.

She used the idealistic sentimentality of this phantasy as an escape from the actual problem. The man did not need an unreal mother; he needed a real woman. As yet, she did not know what a real woman was. But to reduce the man to the position of a lost and pitiful child, and to exalt herself to the seat of the all-compassionate, all-loving mother, gave her an inflation which she mistook for security.

By identification with this great archetypal image she could blind herself to her own pitiful failures as a woman. So, this phantasy only added to her sense of futility and resentment. Why could not others recognize the beauty and nobility of the spiritual choice? Why did none of the recognition nor any of the inner peace of a great soul come to her? She had accepted so little of human experience that she could not see that in reality she was living out the shadow side of this image through a cruelly arrogant attitude toward the man. He did not wish to be met as a pitiful child, but as a sensitive person whose human needs were recognized and met by the intuitive understanding and warm feeling of a woman who was herself learning how to accept and give in a human experience.

After a brief period in which there were outbursts of futile emotionalism, more childhood associations, intellectual arguments, resentments and bitternesses, there came the following dream:

"The head of a wooden horse is looking at me mournfully. A veil is drawn over it, a sound of weeping heard."

The horse with its long, mournful, intellectual face looked, she said, like the man with whom she was involved at this time. She also associated the animal with the wooden horse of Troy. She said the man was as dead as the wooden horse, but that hidden inside the horse of Troy were soldiers who could destroy the enemy and take the city. As she told this dream she herself assumed the same long, mournful expression.

Again it was suggested that the dream might be subjective, that she was perhaps projecting upon the man qualities which were within herself, that it was *she* who was holding living values within a wooden intellectual attitude. Quite involuntarily she said, "Why that is what rebirth must mean." She now connected the veil with the veiled mysteries, the weeping with an echo of human sorrow, the living values enclosed in the wooden horse with energy that might still be released from the prison of a dead attitude. She sentimentalized the dream as she had the "poem"; it was not possible then to connect it with her own reality situation—to see that it would be through the release of the despised function, her feeling, that rebirth could come. She wished to regard herself as a potential "priestess of the veiled mysteries."

But the rebirth came to her in a most unacceptable way, for the energy which was released was her own feeling in a most infantile and undeveloped form. She had expected an army of men (like the Animus figures on whom she had depended) to come out of the horse, but instead there was released a demanding child.

She now began to make intensely childish demands upon the analyst, seeking from her the type of love which she had needed as a little child. She was only two years old when her mother died, and she had been taken care of by so many people—passed about the family so often—that she had felt no safety in anything. She had not been able to attain a sense of security in any woman, because a whole succession of them had passed through her childhood.

The only person who had had any continuity in her childhood had been her father. Although he had been often away from home, she remembered the times when he had put his hands through the bars of her crib and held hers. This was almost her first memory. This early association had been the foundation of a deep attachment which had lasted through all the years. Unfortunately, as she grew older, her desire to please him and to make him proud of her had made her struggle for types of professional achievement which she felt he admired and which helped to build up her Animus attitude.

Yet even with him there had been no secure relationship, for every time he went away on business she was afraid that he would never come back. When she was only about five years old, two little friends of hers had died very suddenly, and this had made her feel as though another danger had always to be reckoned with, the lurking danger of sudden death. She should have been a gay, eager, extraverted little girl. Instead she was a combination of fear and misplaced energy.

In view of all this, her present situation was pathetically understandable, and she needed a very tender appreciation of a certain rightness in her demands. But, unhappily, so much of the poison of power had now entered into her that she would violate the very relationship which she rightly craved. She emphasized hysterical self-pity and neurotic fears of insanity as reasons why she must and should be loved, so that her own present attitude made it impossible for her to receive the very thing which would have been the first proper nourishment of her emotional life. She would have used the analysis, as some children use sickness and night terrors, to make the mother give them the attention that they demand, and to keep her subject to their needs. She had to accept the necessity for allowing these emotions to come up, and to recognize that she herself must assume to them the attitude of a mother to a sick child. Then, with the sympathetic help of someone else who also understood them, she could slowly educate and train them, till they had developed a form that could be rightly used in adult life. Like all really living processes, this meant slow growth.

While she was still trying to put the entire burden upon the analyst, there came this dream:

"I am in Y's room. There is a table on which is food in disorder. I say to myself, 'So this is the way she keeps her room.' No one is visible. I listen to hear if anyone is coming, and hear a muffled sound of weeping which comes from the closet where she has shut herself up."

Y was a woman who had lived only in a bloodless and ideal

religion and in a profession where she had expressed herself as being dedicated to beauty. The food in the mind of the dreamer symbolized comradeship and communion. Here the food on the table was disordered and abandoned. Now Y has shut herself away with her own grief. This woman had said to the dreamer at one time, "I have never really lived." The appearance of this figure showed how little the dreamer herself had done about her own self-pity. She was astonished and somewhat indignant at the suggestion that after all, in the dream, the closet door was not locked, no stern figure stood guarding it. She could, if she wished, stop crying and come out and put her table in order.

Deep down behind her conscious attitude she had a feeling that if she were denied the joys of life she might be permitted the luxury of woe. Discussion of this dream revealed many unrecognized negative feelings toward the analyst. She resisted the discussion of them on the ground that they were not loyal and had great difficulty in seeing that whatever really exists, no matter how deeply buried, affects the situation between two people, and the thing that matters is finding out the truth.

At last she was able to see that these resentments must be brought into the open, that they were part of an analysis, and could be considered impersonally, even though they dealt with personal feelings. Some of these were that the analyst had had human relationships which the patient had never known; she had been married and probably understood only the problems of married women; she undoubtedly had a scorn for spinsters; she had "crude" ideas of sexuality; she had had a mother relation in childhood, and could not understand loneliness, and so on and on.

It was useless at this point to try to show her that each person has his own problem, and that the meaning of life is to find out how to meet one's *own* difficulty. She wanted to find out the problems of the analyst—which, of course, was not the subject in hand—and if any simple questions were answered, she was immediately bent on proving that her own affairs were *much* more difficult.

This attempt at forcing an Animus battle was broken by periods of self-pity and outbursts of unrelated emotion in which she demanded that the analyst become the all-pitying mother. Instead of being the Earth Mother of her phantasy, she took the part of the child, a more genuine situation. But the Animus was so strong that it was he who fed upon any love and understanding that was given, and not the neglected child of feeling who needed it. So that for a long time the Animus acted like a tapeworm; he ate all the child should have.

Then, in a vivid dream, the Animus appeared in a different form, a form which she was not yet able to accept:

"M is lying in bed; she throws off the clothes; her father is standing at the head of the bed. When she is naked, I say, 'It is time for me to go.' I leave the room."

M represented to her a completely intellectual, conventional woman who lived according to an ancestral code, deciding all questions of personal values by the rules, as it were, of a moral and ethical book of etiquette. She had the same worship of opinions and the same sexual repressions as the dreamer. Now M strips off her clothes and is naked before the father. But the dreamer cannot see this side of herself exposed, so she leaves the room, as has been her habit whenever naked truths were exposed to view.

The father in this dream was a man very different from her own father, a shadowy archetypal figure, representing a figure of understanding within herself before which she *should* be naked.

She then discussed her own father, reluctantly telling of her distrust of his sexuality and yet her secret desire for small physical attentions from him. These aroused emotions which filled her with a sense of confusion because she could not understand their meaning. In some obscure way she connected her sexual phantasies —of which she was deeply ashamed—with these confused memories. This shame had been intensified by the teachings of the woman mentioned before, who had become her mother image. With great grief she told one of her carefully guarded secrets, which was that this woman had in her last illness repudiated the dreamer as being unfit. It had been one of her most disastrous experiences, and had left her with a feeling that she could never be accepted by a truly good and pure woman, and a hope that though relationship was barred to her, she could at least make a success of her professional life.

In the next dream another woman friend says to her, "Look at your face. It is getting wrinkled."

Her interpretation of this is interesting because it showed a change in attitude. She did not launch into a tirade against life because she was growing old, but felt that the dream was trying to tell her that she was neglecting her feminine values and because of this they were growing wrinkled or faded. She had a dawning perception of her inner problem, for which she might become responsible, and which she could change from within.

Then in a nightmare she was in the power of a witch-woman. Many fears were released by this dream, fears which she was not yet ready to discuss. She was sufficiently familiar with psychological interpretations of images to recognize this witch-woman as one of the aspects of the Terrible Mother, but she was unwilling to allow her spontaneous associations to arise so that she could discover its relation to her immediate problem. She was beginning to wish for a personal relation with the analyst but projected this desire, and feared that the analyst wished a relation so that she might gain power over her through the emotions aroused in the analysis. This new mother might "put into her" new and dangerous ideas, might rouse improper emotions, work a dark magic on her. She hinted at the "dark side" of woman friendships but considered that a discussion of them would be "irrelevant." So she relegated the witch-woman to the past as only the old mother image (the image of Z) returning.

It was quite true that she had never succeeded in breaking the power of this old mother image and so this aspect, which was also true, was the one considered. This led once more to the discussion of her fears of sexuality (so accentuated by the teachings of Z). She reiterated her belief that her sister's sexual difficulties had caused her insanity. Her need to break the identification with her sister was apparently paramount. The associations which arose in this connection occupied many hours. Her vague intuitions concerning the "terrors" of her sister's marriage, the remarks that had been let fall about her brother-in-law's responsibility for her sister's illness, all of these had to be brought to consciousness and their influence upon her present attitude discussed. The old fears which had been instilled by the former mother were still active and this aspect of the witch-woman was very real. That this material was of utmost importance at this time was shown by the following dream:

An old friend appeared, looking healthy and happy, and told

her that her sick and dependent sister was dead. A sense of quiet came to her, as though the fears which had centered around her identification with her sister had broken and fallen away.

At this time of quiet, she dreamed that the door of her bedroom was sliding back and forth, opening and shutting of itself. She had, for the first time, an intuition that something greater than her own small ego was taking charge of her life; that something from the unconscious was opening and closing the door and that she could only wait to see what would come in.

Then, in a dream, she saw the figure of a woman connected with one of her unfortunate professional experiences. This woman now appeared in gentle and loving guise, and as she reviewed this old situation, which was the one she had so resentfully related in her first hour of analysis, she saw it in a new light. She saw that in her attempts to dominate she had thrust aside as "old-fashioned and sentimental" a woman who had loved and admired her. She had lost her position as a result of a battle which she had herself forced.

Up to this point she had mourned only the loss of a position, but now she saw that she had lost something more valuable, which was the love of her friend. In the light of this new discovery she reviewed the other "unjust" situations, and found that in every one of them the same destructive force had been at work in her. As this realization dawned upon her, she saw that even more tragic than the loss of her friends had been the loss of her own ability to love, and with that realization something new stirred within her.

A flood of emotion poured out toward the analyst, and she wished to relive with her the friendship which she might have had with her professional colleague. These emotions which she projected upon the analyst were turbulent and undeveloped. They were soon followed by phantasies of close physical relationship with her. The phantasies in turn brought back memories of her girlhood, when homosexuality was never mentioned, but only hinted at as a monstrous form of perversion. She now became terribly afraid that through analysis she would be given over to the power of these phantasies and so become "a monster."

At first she resisted the analyst's attempts to show her that any emotion which is violently repressed will find its outlet in infantile sexual phantasy. When she could accept this explanation, it was possible to discuss the whole problem of homosexuality. That this could mean a deep friendship between persons of the same sex, one not accompanied by sexual acts, was an entirely new concept to her. The discussion of this carried her far into the problem of modern woman, for she still depersonalized her material and preferred its historical aspect. She had seen the feminist movement only as an assertion of woman's rights, not as an effort of woman to become conscious and to complete herself as an individual. She saw the resultant banding together of women only as a part of a political warfare between man and woman. She could see from her own analysis that any effort to become conscious necessarily liberates repressed elements and that these frequently appear in turbulent form. While her predisposition in favor of the Animus made her feel that any militancy, and its attendant violences, were necessary phases, the wave of homosexuality which was a part of this close affiliation was to her monstrous and incomprehensible. She could not see that underneath this, when the emotional wave had passed, there lay something permanent and valuable, something which remained in more conscious relations between women and which gave to their friendships a new understanding of their life as women and their growing individuality. She still felt that if an experience roused evil phantasies then one must give up the entire experience as evil.

It was suggested that the old adage, "Don't throw out the baby with the bath," might apply here, that perhaps one should save the values of feeling and try to understand the phantasies. She could only see that the water was soiled and the whole thing should be thrown out.

At this point came the first dream of companionship with any man:

"I am riding horseback with X along a wood path; there is a pleasant sense of companionship, but the horse I am riding has a little swaying motion like that of a hobby horse. I said, 'I have dropped my glasses and I must go back to find them.'"

X was a man whom she had known for many years, having for him a kind of tolerant affection, considering him her intellectual inferior. But in the dream it was she who was riding the childish hobbyhorse. That is, it was *her* instinctual libido which was still in the nursery. To see the situation as it really was, she needed to go back and get her spectacles; she must look at him again from a more adult point of view. She desired love, but saw no possibility of it in her life. She had lost the man of her intellectual phantasy; she despised as unintellectual the man with whom she was riding in her dream.

Then the corpse with the golden hair reappeared as a visual image, and when she acted on the suggestion that she should live with the phantasy as she would with an actual outer experience, and write down all she felt impelled to, she produced a long sentimental phantasy which gave to this strange dream of her youth a new meaning. If she could understand the old failures, see what forces in herself had produced them, and trust the new attitude, she would still be able to harvest values from the dead past, for the energy—the growing hair—was still alive.

She was beginning to think that she could, but she still had to reckon with the infantilism of her new-born feeling. The old Animus had a bit to say right here. He had been in power for so long that he would not so easily step down and let the woman take possession. She immediately wanted to use her new-found energy in the old ways, thinking that her "new attitude" would protect her from old disasters. She determined that, in spite of her age, she would "make good." She sought out her intellectual friends with a scheme for new work. She turned from the unconscious. The first attempts met with success. She felt she had a new attitude toward her professional ideals—a "more spiritual attitude." A dream interposed:

"I saw a man walking up a path which seemed near the Matterhorn. It was a clear-cut atmosphere. It was all ice, snow, and cold blue sky. He was walking straight into the cold snow singing a hymn of praise very exultantly. When I awoke my feeling was that he was turning away from the earth and walking into the snowfields with no conception of his danger."

The Animus, turning away from human things, was seeking the snow-clad heights. His hymn of praise recalled to her the spiritual exaltation she had felt long ago when she had read Swedenborg's *Visions* and had imagined herself "wedded to an ideal." Now, looking at the figure in the dream, she saw that this intellectual exaltation had carried her into regions of ice.

The next dream showed the contrasting reality:

"I saw five neglected, forlorn children, the oldest a boy of about twelve. They were waiting for their parents. Somebody told me that their first parents had been carried off by bandits and that I must take the children in and take care of them myself."

"Somebody" was the voice within herself, which told her that she must save the children from the Animus, the bandit who carried off her feeling. The boy represented to her the Puer Eternus, the new attempt; the other four children her own four functions, her feeling, thinking, sensation and intuition, that is, all the sides of herself, which had been deprived of love and care by the Animus and were therefore neglected. Her job was not to climb the icy height, but to care for these children.

After this, in a dream, she found herself married to a boy of seventeen, living with him very pleasantly but without having sexual intercourse. This brought up the fact that she still unconsciously desired to have a childish relation with a man in which she would not have to accept the responsibilities of her own sexuality.

Next she was sitting on the lap of a man with black hair and beard. She felt very happy but became anxious and said, "Do not let my father see you kiss me." Again the thought of any adult relationship with a man was barred by her desire to remain a child.

After this she found herself with a group of peasant women. One of them held up an open book for her to read, but it was in an unknown language. This showed her how far away she was from the attitude of the simple peasant women and how much of the earth wisdom which they knew was to her written in an unknown language. That is, there is something which women know, and with which she has not yet made any connection. This brought her again to the consideration of the essential values of woman. This unknown book was a knowledge of the part a real woman plays in life.

Again she first considered the "historic aspects." She was deeply interested in the primitive wisdom which ordains that before a man is initiated into his tribal manhood he shall live apart, seeing only the men of the tribe who instruct him in the mysteries of manhood, and that the girl shall, in the woman house, learn what is a woman's life. This wisdom she began to desire for herself. In the discussion of this she saw the difference between knowledge and wisdom; and that an understanding of the Eros principle meant not merely a personal relation which satisfied the ego but involved a willingness to serve life, to study the human value contained in each individual experience. This knowledge of woman's nature she perceived could be constellated and developed through right relations with women. She must learn to read this book offered her by these peasant women whose wisdom about life was a far different thing from her intellectual concepts.

Then she dreamed that she saw her father lying on his face and ran up to him and found him dead. After this she had a great sense of freedom. She assumed that now the old ties that had bound her to the father were completely gone.

But "death" in the unconscious often means death of an aspect or attitude. From her father she had received a concept of woman values far different from that which had been revealed through the previous dream. By his concentration upon her intellectual achievements he had dominated her ambitions. The death at this time represented the death of the old Animus attitudes developed through her relation to him. As future dreams showed, the father image in all its aspects was not dead, but by accepting the concept of woman values revealed by the dream of the peasant women, the father as negative, intellectual Animus could die.

Her next dream was:

"I went to see B. As soon as I looked at her I noticed something peculiar about her face. I saw that she had three eyes; one was in the center of the forehead. Somehow I knew that the third eye had been made out of the left eye. She told me casually that her mother was dead. As I left, someone helped me on with a coat, a blue one. I said it was not mine and took it off and put on my own, which was brown."

This cousin was a feeling intuitive, who seemed to have an almost magic power of understanding the unconscious reactions of men. Hence the third eye in the dream, for the third eye is a symbol of intuition. The fact that the third eye was formed from the left eye indicates that this was introverted intuition, which perceives the images of the unconscious. The cousin tells her that her mother is dead. The cousin represents intuition; the mother, the ideas derived from her early relation with the older woman, Z. Therefore the death of the mother represents the death of the old ideas that had long ruled her, releasing her intuition so that it could be used in connection with feeling. So, also, if she could free herself from the opinions taken over from her father, she would be free of his dominance through the Animus. This was the situation symbolized by the death of the father in the previous dream—a situation indicated but not yet achieved. Now, having heard the cousin's announcement, she is offered a blue coat, which she interprets as the garment of spiritual freedom. But she is not yet ready for it and so once more puts on her old brown coat. She was very sure in her associations that she should have taken this new blue garment, but, after all, the brown one was the color of earth, and she had many simple earth values to accept before she could be ready for a new garment, so perhaps the choice in the dream was not so unwise a one as the dreamer decided it to be.

All this emotion was so new to her that she could not understand it. She could only become conscious of a flood of desire for the cousin. She longed to be accepted by her in an emotional type of friendship.

Then a dream came to her which at first frightened her by its homosexual implications:

"I was lying in bed with another woman. Suddenly the corridor was thronged with a rushing mob. A procession of nobles who ignored me passed in the distance. A large, white-haired woman entered, closed the door, and said there was nothing to fear."

The mob she thought of as all the revolutionary, turbulent elements of her unconscious. They were of a very different order from her old ruling ideas, which were now of no use to her. She felt the mob had been let loose by the fact that she was in bed with another woman. Yet the older, wiser woman said to her, "There is nothing to fear."

These words seemed to be true, for as she discussed them

with the analyst her fears disappeared; she saw that what she actually desired was not a physical experience but a feeling relation with another woman and a deeper connection with the real woman side of herself. The word "homosexuality," with its suggestion of physical acts, had so terrified her that she had feared any real friendship with a woman. In the former discussion of homosexuality she had intellectually accepted the values of woman friendship: now, through her dream she saw that a change had also taken place in her unconscious attitude. For here the affirmation came from within herself.

A real feeling transference now took the place of the old intellectual attitude toward analysis. This new feeling for woman made it possible for her to go back to her earlier experiences with the dominant mother, Z, who had made her so desperately ashamed of her first love, and had filled her with a sense of fear about her own feelings. She could now discuss in detail all the emotions that had overpowered her when this woman had, before her death, repudiated her as being unworthy. This humiliation had acted as a barrier between herself and all other women, causing a fear that she might again be rejected. Though she now saw how false the other woman's attitude had been, and how unfair the repudiation of herself, she still desired in her unconscious a relation with the perfect mother. It was as this perfect mother that she now saw the analyst. Then came the following dream:

"I was in the great cathedral at Chartres. I stood in front of the blue window, the window of the Mother of God; and as I looked at it, I saw that the celestial mother was you."

"Yes," said the analyst, "and was there any more to the dream?"

The expression of rapt devotion changed to one of perplexity. "Nothing," she said, "except for one small thing that I cannot understand at all. Someone standing near me said, 'Yes, but you must remember that her name is Sophia.'"

Sophia, in the Gnostic writings, was an image of wisdom, but also one of the four Divine Harlots, the heavenly mother who came to earth to minister to the wants of man. Although the dreamer had never heard of the Gnostics, this name had come to her in her dream as a substitute for the name of Mary, and the discussion of it released a flood of repressed ideas about the analyst.

The projection upon the analyst of a too-celestial image awakened in the unconscious an image of the analyst which went to the opposite extreme. And the next step was to bring both of these images out of the stained-glass window and connect them with her feeling for a woman who could no more carry the burden of an ideal image than she could.

She went back again into all her own personal material and once more reviewed the relationship with that former mother image. She could see now how this woman had destroyed for her every human experience by insisting always that she should follow the bodiless ideal; how she had turned her from reality for fear she would find that in some way it appealed to her "lower nature." Then she realized why this woman had died in bitterness and anger. It was because she had remained unconscious of the desire for power which underlay her wish to be a spiritual teacher; because having herself married without love and for ambitious reasons, she resented others having life experiences for which she secretly longed but which she had rigidly denied herself. No one is more bitter against life than the person who has not lived, and there is no one more cruel in judging the young than the older person who secretly regrets his own unlived youth.

With this understanding came a liberation from the dreamer's feeling of inferiority and guilt and self-depreciation, for she saw that her early Spiritual Mother had repudiated her, not for any uncleanliness or depravity in herself, but because she still had a potential of life that the older woman had thrown away.

In the discussion of this woman's cruelty she recalled having been told that her own sexuality was "a taint in the blood" inherited from her father. This had made her feel cut off from relationships, and in her loneliness she had taken refuge in masturbation, which stimulated phantasy and daydreams. It was unbelievably difficult for her to tell this; she had concealed it up till now; and was convinced that no decent person could ever have done such a thing.

The analyst spoke of Aladdin's Lamp, an old myth of masturbation. In the story, when the lamp is rubbed, wishes are fulfilled, the palace of the king is carried up into the air, one travels on a magic carpet, and lives in an enchanted world, substituting dreams for reality. This is what she had done, and in understanding it as a very common experience, and one which another woman could discuss so simply, she was relieved of the burden of secret and particular guilt which she had carried for years.

She then began to consider her connections with other women. Her nearest friend, L, was a woman of very gentle feelings, somewhat younger than herself. The dreamer had played upon the childlike side of her friend; she had wished always to be the counsellor, always to do the giving. Often she had forced gifts that were reluctantly received, and then had been angered because the recipient had not felt bound to her by ties of gratitude. She had sought a dependent and then resented her as a clinging vine. She also felt that L was not self-assertive enough in her life with others, though she was herself always trying to make L turn to her for guidance. She had needed the gentle affection which her friend could give but was unwilling to admit this need.

Slowly there came to her the perception that L had quite as much to give as she had, and that the most difficult thing is to achieve relationship in which one can receive as simply as one gives. Until now she had always to be the child or the mother in a relation; now she saw she must stand upon a footing of equality as an adult.

Such perceptions come long before an actual attainment in experience. She made the first beginning of this new kind of friendship and was much pleased with herself, but she was still like a child who, having been good, expects a sugarplum from life. But instead of a sugarplum she received what to her was a rebuff.

Her friend L had many other demands on her time and many other human responsibilities; also she had a mother whose necessities appealed to her sympathy, so that she could not clearly see a right to her own independence. Now, when the dreamer made demands for a too-intimate and absorbing friendship, it seemed to her that L pushed these away. She tried to force her new psychological understanding, and to make the friend "free of the mother"; but L had her own ideas and held to them. She therefore felt cut off just at the start of this newly-accepted experience; the old self-pity came back, and she returned to her own infantile demands for love, which again took the form of her right to an understanding mother. She then produced the following phantasy:

Earth Mother Speaks

"I hear a child crying out through the years
'I want my mother, my mother, my mother.'
Oh child, will you never stop weeping?
Must I always hear the sound of that ceaseless sobbing?
Must I always feel the loneliness of the child heart?
They gave you toys to play with,
They sent you story books to read,
But they couldn't answer your questions.
Neither could they bring her back again.
So you nurse your childish sorrow,
And the wound grows deeper within.
What is it you want of me, child heart?
Why are you always calling me?
How can I heal the wound?"

The Child Answers

"Hold me close in your great strong arms,
Arms that surround the whole round earth.
Calm me and soothe me, oh mother of men.
Make me as one with you, ample of girth.
Wait until I draw one deep full breath
Full of the scent of your warm soft breast.
The scent of the milk that flows ever forth.
The mother's milk that spells for us rest.
Sing me the song that you used to sing,
Oh mother of mine, in the sweet long-ago.
The song of a rose bush that grew in the light."

"Oh, indoor rose bush, wait patiently there;
Someday you will bloom and gain your sight,
The eternal rose with petals fair."

She tried to relate this to a deep impersonal experience, and dwelt at length upon the mystical meaning of the rose, and the impersonal force of motherhood. But in reality she turned that force back upon herself in waves of self-pity, and demanded that the analyst should be the all-understanding mother.

In this return to the same oft-repeated emotion we see how in an analysis one goes back and back to deeper levels until the earliest memories have been unearthed from the personal unconscious and the new attitude strengthened. So the same problems connected with the mother image returned again and again, and had to be met with patience and understanding. For one must be willing to go back over the same ground until finally both the conscious and the unconscious have accepted the new way that has been indicated.

The phantasy of the earth mother and child was used, as the others had been, as an escape into the impersonal, an attempt to identify with an idea. It surprised her that other people did not realize the very beautiful feeling which she considered herself to have attained. She was resentful of any obstacles that came in her way, as though life itself were an unappreciative mother. Again the attitude that the fault was not hers but life's returned. So, since she had again taken from a phantasy little but an inflated idea of herself, she once more regressed to the old Animus attitude.

She was now trying to work out a friendship with a younger woman who had recently come into her life through proximity of environment. In this relationship she was determined to assume the role of guide and philosopher as well as friend. She wished to control the younger woman according to her ideas of what a young woman should do, and tried to become censor of her morals. She was quite certain that she was doing all this for the good of the younger woman and for some time repudiated admission of the power impulses within herself.

During her many discussions of this relationship, she showed a naive desire to have everything formulated in advance. She wished to decide just what to say in her next conversation and was quite indignant if the young woman's replies were unexpected and upset her cues. She could not wait for the situation to develop —she must prearrange it all. In fact *she* again must open and close the doors and decide what should come in. She also wished from the young woman respect due to age and demanded an equal respect for the Animus and all its opinions. Quite naturally, therefore, the friendship could not materialize, and the young woman vanished from her life, leaving her resentful of what she considered ingratitude.

At this time she had to have a slight operation and the terror which she felt at the anesthetic showed her how deep was her resistance to losing conscious control. The woman who had so influenced her youth had warned her against ever taking an anesthetic in any form. She saw now that this woman, too, had feared to lose conscious control, because through that, the things which she hated and despised in her own self might come to the surface and be shown to other people. Had she this same fear?

At the time of the operation, when she was losing consciousness, she was haunted by the face of a dark-skinned, primitive man and had a sense that it was he whom she must meet when she returned to the conscious world. Although to her surprise she went through this operation very easily, it had activated her old fears. Taking an anesthetic was giving oneself over to the power of the unconscious. To put oneself in the hands of an analyst was to do the same thing.

This fear of a power which would render her helpless was projected upon the analyst even after she had apparently forgotten her fears of the actual operation. Her old distrust of woman was again aroused. Once more she confused the analyst with the former mother image. Again she feared the dark primitive side which she had perceived as she went under the influence of the anesthetic, and which she knew she must face when she returned to consciousness.

She plunged deeply into extraverted activities, saying that she must use her energy, which had become much greater with her renewal of physical health. Immediately the Animus reactions returned and she dreamed that she had overhastily boarded a train which she found carried no passengers, only piles and piles of baggage. She felt no emotional connection with this dream because she was so sure that she needed to be busy, and could not see all these numerous activities as so much impedimenta. Therefore her next dream was to her especially startling and arresting.

"I saw an old man with the skin of a corpse. He had a mortar and pestle and was grinding something that seemed to be an old scarf. Then I saw that the scarf looked as though it were made of chaff and husks. I thought to myself, 'This is strange food that he is preparing.'"

She was very confused when she woke. The old man was so

real that he had seemed actually to be in the room. Then she saw him as the image of the Animus, and the food he was preparing as the husks and chaff of old laws and old opinions. She hated the remembrance of this food; she could no longer accept it; she felt an inner change take place; and knew that she had made a choice of great importance. Both the conscious and the unconscious had told her that her old power attitudes, though she might fall into them again, would never again give her even the illusion of nourishment.

Immediately she had another dream of the death of her father. It was from the father that she had taken on her old opinions. It was not strange that he should die when she had to turn from outworn things.

She had dreamed twice before of the death of her father, and apparently little had happened; but this third dream followed on the heels of a genuine choice where she had consciously decided that she could no longer permit the old power principle to guide her. Therefore the dream of the father's death was something that had happened within her in relation to her Animus problem; and was no longer merely a suggestion of the unconscious accepted as an intellectual possibility, but a deep emotional experience. This meant that she had consciously refused the autonomous power of the Animus. The old form was dead; what would the new form be? For the Animus is a personification of psychic energy, and cannot be killed but only transformed.

Shortly afterwards she said, "A strange thing happened to me last night. I woke, and there in my open window stood an Irish harper. He said, 'Follow me.' I saw him as clearly as I have ever seen any living being, and I heard his voice as distinctly, but I had a feeling that though he was there in my room, he was also far away. As I looked at him, I seemed to go way back in time and to a far-distant country."

She was asked, "What did you do about it?"

"Why I thought about it a little, and then I turned over and went to sleep."

Here the Animus reappeared, not as something determining her life in the world, but as the spiritual Animus, telling her to follow him into an inner world where she might experience the images of the unconscious.

She was asked, "Why didn't you follow him?"

But she was so accustomed to thinking of experience in terms of the outer world that at first the only way of following him that suggested itself to her was literally to go out of the window after him. Then she saw how one may hold in mind a dream image until, activated by the inner concentration, it begins to move and act autonomously, as though it had a separate life of its own. That night she called back the harper, that is, she lay quiet in the darkness thinking about him, concentrating upon his image until it reappeared.

Then, in a phantasy in which the inner world became as vivid as the outer, she did follow him. He led over winding paths until she came to a hillside, where she was met by an Irish piper and by a little black pig who ran to her and looked up at her with human eyes. She heard the harper's voice say, "The piper of God and the black pig of Ireland."

This phantasy perplexed her. Why should the piper of God be in the company of the black pig? Even though in the dream he had looked at her humorously, she felt the black pig was not a celestial companion for the piper. She therefore made one of her flights into the ideal and produced a sentimental and evasive phantasy of the harper who had come without the black pig.

> Oh, Harper green, where are you straying?
> My heart is sad, my spirits graying.
> So long ago I heard you playing,
> The song so far away,
> Its faint, sweet ringing and echo on the wind.
> Play, Harper green, the breeze is blowing,
> The sea shines bright, the morn's a-glowing.
> Today is fair beyond our knowing,
> For beauty weaves about our going,
> An ever-fresh enchantment.

But the incongruous companions of the dream were not so easily dismissed. They returned again. Her associations with the black pig were first of the Valley of the Black Pig as described in *The Wind Bloweth*, the place where the witches met their masters, a dark valley filled with images of crude bestiality. It was her first experience of these images which lie deeper than the personal unconscious. It took her into this dark valley of fear, which she was reluctant to enter because she might find that all these images were alive within herself. Then it occurred to her that the little pig was not a loathsome and fearsome sight but rather an attractive little black pig who looked at her with a twinkle in his eye as though he would say, "The piper of God likes me. You might too, you know."

She accepted this suggestion only theoretically. She could see that it might be a good idea, but as an actuality she had a good deal of scorn for those simple things which the little pig would enjoy. She therefore fled with the piper of God and left the little pig at home. She tried to find the message of the harper through studying the myths of Ireland and wrote a series of phantasies which occupied her for a period of several months.

During this time the dreams practically ceased; a strange split took place between her outer and inner life. She had times of great serenity, yet the feeling which came to her at introverted times she was unable to carry over into her outer life.

One of the phantasies concerned Boana, and her acceptance of the pain involved in the birth of her three sons, who in this phantasy were called Joy, Sorrow, and Love. She gave them these names although she did not know that, according to the legend, Boana was the mother of Angus Og, the Irish cupid. She had the idea that through the acceptance of this experience in phantasy would come the birth of the new individual. She expected in this to accomplish something which could only be accomplished by relating the phantasy to her actual situation.

Next she attempted the following verse, again using unconscious material as the basis for a literary effort:

The Three Noble Strains

Three harpers came to Queen Maeve's hall
(My heart cries out " 'Tis a lonely way")
And they took their stand by the carven wall,
And sorrow-strain they played first of all,
(The wind moans in my heart night and day).

The next strain they played was a song of joy
(Oh, flower of my heart, your petals are white)
It rang through the hall like the laugh of a boy,
Glad, exultant; clear through pain's alloy,
(So piercing sweet is the wind tonight).

The last strain came like a soothing hand,
(Rest, dear heart, by the water's way)
For they played of the sun on the golden strand,
The low lap of water, the sleeping sand.
(Oh wind, sing soft to the drowsy day).

Here the three sons become three harpers in the hall of the queen and the phantasy ends with the paradisiacal solution, where she was soothed and comforted as a child but makes no contact with these forces as a woman.

Then from an unexpected quarter came an opportunity to go back into work of the kind that she had done years ago. She started with enthusiasm, but had difficulties with two other women who were both unfortunately Animus-ridden, so that the hours of analysis were mostly occupied by struggling with the old problem of projection, although she now tried to distinguish what actually existed in other people from what had its origin in herself. She also used much more love in her actual work, which was with little children.

One day, however, her opinions came directly into conflict with the opinions of the two other women. Animus thumbed nose at Animus; all of her old power demands rose from the unconscious and overwhelmed her. The only thing she considered was having her way in this emergency, and she got it. She felt triumphant and exultant for a brief moment, but was aghast when, as a result of her triumph, she was dismissed, and dismissed so suddenly that she had no chance to correct the mistake which she had made.

She felt as though she had been in the grip of a monster, and saw the negative Animus for what he really was.

One night she woke with a feeling that something was trying to write itself, and the following phantasy was written without any conscious sense of direction:

I had always said—"These are mine—no one shall have them
And no one shall take them from me."
But robbers crept in through my door while I slept
And stole away my all—my most precious treasures were gone—
All I had hoarded for a lifetime.
I searched frantically for them.

There were so many of them I could not count them all at first.
But one by one as the days went by, I missed them,
And each day when I discovered an added theft
I wept bitterly. How I hated the robbers!
How I berated the cruel fate that sent them to my door.
"No one shall come in again to take what is mine.
What I have now, I shall keep against all marauders."
And my heart grew hard and bitter to have struggled
So long to amass a little gold—a few keepsakes—
And in one night to lose them all!
But spring came and a high wind rose at midnight.
I heard it coming and was afraid and carefully bolted the door.
"Not even the wind shall enter here without my permission," I said.
Then as I slept, a strange thing happened;
The wind burst through the bolts and blew the door open.
I woke suddenly and saw it ajar, and rose to close it again,
When lo, the door shut of itself.
I gazed in wonder, for there I saw
Spread out across the doorway
A delicate tracery of living green
In pattern exquisite and rare of nature's handiwork,
Soft and tender as young ferns that open at the touch of spring.

Nothing could show more clearly the impotence of an old Animus attitude clutching at the small values left in conscious (extraverted or outer) life, when against it a new force is preparing itself in the unconscious. Here she was consciously clutching at the petty remnants of the values which she had always desired, but greater forces had been working in the unconscious and these took no account of the barriers and securities which her conscious erected. At midnight—the time when the forces of the unconscious are greatest—came the high wind, the moving energy of the spirit, and broke her locks and bars and swept through her room, leaving—not the objects which her conscious still preserved—but a living green plant, a symbol of spring, of new life. The plant grows according to its own living germ. What is in the seed is manifest in the flower.

The wind is an archetype of the living spirit; it is the breath of a god, or rather of a god force which may be for good or for evil. A wind heralded the coming of the Pentecostal fire; "and suddenly there came from heaven a sound as of the rushing of a mighty wind, and it filled all the house where they were sitting."

A "cold gust of wind that makes you shudder" precedes a nocturnal god of a primitive African tribe, who is called "the maker of fear."

Her reaction to this phantasy was one of terror of the great impersonal force which it depicted. She could accept the beauty of the living plant, but she could not accept the way in which it came; for only theoretically could she conceive of a life not directed by conscious desire. In the analytical process, something had been happening which could not have happened if the door had been closed to the unconscious. When she followed the harper, the spiritual Animus, she voluntarily went into the realm of the collective unconscious. So her life was lived upon two levels; her conscious life growing more barren and meager, her unconscious life more vivid and compelling. It was not only fear of the great wind which overwhelmed her, it was fear of the living green plant. However beautiful she might see it to be, it had grown without her knowledge; its life was beyond her control. It brought with it a realization that she could no longer retain her old opinions as to what was of value.

At this point she was like a person living in two worlds, able to pass from one to the other, but unable to make any connection between their contents. This may sound like a schizophrenic condition; but in reality there was nothing abnormal about it, since she was completely aware of which world she was in and knew that the experiences of the one eventually must become related to those of the other. Important changes were taking place in the unconscious, but they had not yet reached such a point of intensity that they could be translated into conscious life without a tremendous struggle.

Into her relationship with X, the man who had appeared in her hobbyhorse dream, an instinctual quality was beginning to enter. This she refused to accept. She projected her awakening sexuality upon him; it was he who was aroused, not she. Then she tried to impress him with the superior value of her experiences in the unconscious. X, however, was unimpressed; he was vulgarly perceptive of the reality of the situation. So she let her Animus deal with him, treating him with the loftiest contempt, and fled back to phantasy. This was the result:

> The golden hair is flying out on the wind,
> The sun draws shining glints from it,
> It burns and crackles like flames of fire;
> Leaping, darting, pulsating on the head of the woman,
> A strange energy possesses it, a seeking, devouring passion,
> A subtle, searching, burning flame.
> It unwinds itself from her head,
> Like a gorgeous snake it uncoils,
> Stealing out through the air to envelop, to suck in.
> Ah, it is the touch of the man's flesh the woman longs for.
> See, the hair coils around him
> Drawing him closer and closer.
> The fire leaps through him, the flame of hair encircles his neck,
> Arm meets arm, and breast meets breast.
> Still the fire burns, still blows the wind,
> Whirling and dancing still faster and faster,
> The two figures clasped together
> Eddy through space, like a mote in the sun.

But there was no escape. She had turned from her sexuality in the personal world, only to meet it here in its collective and unconscious aspect. The Animus appears as a demon. The hair is instinctual energy, which is used by the Animus to possess and destroy man; so that the ecstasy becomes a dance of death.

The wind, the living plant; again the wind, the demon. She had now seen this great force in both its aspects. But what had been left behind after its first visitation was still alive. She emerged from this phantasy, saw the destruction which the Animus had brought about in her personal life, and was able to say, "This is what I have done," instead of "X has done this to me."

For the first time she made a connection between the two worlds and saw that her inner experiences were taking part in her outer life, and that what seemed a large impersonal phantasy represented, in fact, a barren effort of the Animus for personal supremacy.

The cry that rose in her now was the one that at some time must come to every human being who realizes his own insignificance in relation to the great unconscious forces, the cry for a savior. This has to be found in the function which has been neglected; but she was not yet ready to look for him there; she saw him as a hero figure. She had been studying the Irish myths, and her phantasies clustered around the figure of Cuchulain. She saw him with the "seven lights in his eyes and seven colors about his head," changing into many forms and performing many deeds of valor, but, in a final phantasy, as scaling the icy heights.

In phantasy, then, he had started in a most promising way to overcome the dangers of the unconscious; but had ended as a personification of one of these dangers, as the Animus figure of the Matterhorn dream.

It was some weeks before she felt again that she had come to a decisive place. Now in phantasy she saw Cuchulain standing at a ford, and holding in his hand a spear with a sharp head and a long, inflated bag in the place of a shaft.

This fantasy was drawn from an old legend which touched more closely upon her own problem than she realized. It concerned the battle of the herds. Queen Maeve had in her possession the bull which the men of Ulster wished to obtain, but the bull could be won back only by the conqueror in single combat, a combat which would take place at the ford between the two lands. All of the men of Ulster were afflicted with a mysterious weakness. At the moment of combat they were attacked by pains like those of childbirth, and suddenly became weak as a woman in labor. None of the Ulster men could vanquish a warrior sent by Maeve until Cuchulain was born of God and a woman of Ulster. He took his stand at the ford, and one by one, Maeve's warriors came out to him and he vanquished them. At last, to his consternation, he saw approaching him his best friend, who had been ensnared by Maeve. Knowing that all of his usual weapons would have no effect upon this one who had gathered strength from Maeve herself, he drew his magic spear, called Gaebold, which means "bag of wind" or Spirit Breath. This he threw in the water, upstream; it floated down and pierced the body of his friend who died as though afflicted by thirty wounds. So the men of Ulster obtained the bull from Queen Maeve.

Here is a picture of men who have lost their manhood because it has been taken from them by Maeve, the queen of magic. She represents the Anima figure who is both the woman image that tempts man, and the feminine forces in his own unconscious that overpower him. Overpowered by these forces, the men become like women in pain and their strength goes from them until Cuchulain, the hero, resisting the enchantment, sacrifices what is dearest to him, and by the breath of the spirit overcomes the spell and wins back the virility of man as symbolized by the bull.

Here is *the other side* of her own picture, for she, a woman, had been overpowered by the masculine forces in her own unconscious. It was her Animus, her desire for power and domination, that took from her her woman values at the time when she most needed them, just as the Anima magic overcame the men of Ulster when they most needed their strength at the moment of mortal combat.

This was a pivotal point of her analysis. Now with every failure her desire to face herself grew, and more and more she tried to understand and relate the unconscious material to her own personal problem. The effort for a time was almost too much for her. She saw the unconscious as alive with besetting devils, as a great battle ground of shadows:

Shadows there are, yes, shadows manifold,
Grim shapes a-many, of fiend with sneering, wagging tongue,
Of tempting devil red, and satyr shape,
Thrown out upon the screen of time.
Some see fair angels also,
Saints of pious mien, heroes and saviors.
Who contend against the evil crew,
What are these shadowy forms?
Are they but phantoms of a mind diseased?
Or can we find by tracing a solitary way through the cave's labyrinth
The deep central fire that throws the shadow?
Oh, living fire, send here a gleam of light,
For shadows dark are gathering.

When she wrote this, such was her confusion that she thought of giving up the analysis altogether.

She began again to consider the harper, who had first led her into this limbo of contradictory images. She knew that he, her spiritual Animus, could help her to separate herself from them and relate herself to them; but the effort needed for such interpretation was more than she could consciously undertake. But the unconscious produced this phantasy:

Oh Mother Tree, lift me up among your green branches,
Let me hear again the wind among the healing leaves.
My wound will not heal in the shadow of your trunk.
I long for the life-giving juices of spring-flowing sap.
Mother Tree, dear Mother Tree, heal me and strengthen me.
I feel the sap beginning to flow,
I feel it rising from the buried roots of all the ages,
It surges and pushes through the veins.

Here was a new image of the mother, an image bringing her into contact with life itself. She was not an infant demanding the love of a special mother, but an individual who asked for strength from the great earth forces. Again she sensed only dimly the meaning of this, yet she did feel that something within herself was asking for nourishment, something less infantile than the child seeking the personal mother. Such an experience is the beginning of the supra-personal in an analytical process. It is an approach to the collective unconscious, which makes one ready to obtain the mana, that is the dynamic energy of the archetype, as one cannot through an attempt at identification.

The harper, she realized, had by no means deserted her. He was the positive aspect of the Animus, which gave her understanding, and stood in opposition to the negative aspect, which pulled her back into unconsciousness. Now the following dream occurred:

"I was with M, gathering botanical specimens. We found some mushrooms. I was quite indignant when M said they were to be catalogued and taken home to her mother. I said, 'No, they are to be eaten by me.'"

She was very fond of mushrooms; also they represented something which grew in a single night, like an irrational value suddenly appearing from the unconscious. The Animus-ridden woman who has appeared before in her dreams wished to catalogue these and sacrifice them to the mother, that is to say, she would put them into a rationalized and intellectualized form, and give them to the mother as the dreamer had been wont to sacrifice such values to her old mother image. But the dreamer said, "No, I am going to eat them." She is going to accept their nourishment.

At this time she was really seeing a good deal of M. She accepted the dream as not only subjective but also as dealing with the objective aspects of the friendship. She tried to make the relation more real but found that it now had little meaning for her because M brought to the relation little save an intellectual Animus. With her change in values, she felt that L, whom she had once patronized, was growing to mean more and more in her life; but just at this time L had to take over certain responsibilities for a younger member of the family. The two came together to see the dreamer, who was overcome by a most unexpected torrent of jealousy and reacted in a cruel and unfeeling way.

Within a few days she had another bitter quarrel with X because he would not look at life in the way which she felt was broad and open-minded. It would almost seem as if those mushrooms had been toadstools and had produced strange reactions in the unconscious. The only gain was that she saw these onslaughts from the unconscious as affects which she must learn to control, and in both cases she did something about them. She accepted her responsibility and tried to repair the damage that she had done.

Her next dream was of a blind man and a lame man walking in a tunnel. She had her own interpretation of this dream. To her the blind man was one who could not see except with the intellect. He was therefore blind to all the inner and irrational things, and the lame man was one who was afraid to feel. He could only limp out into life; he could not run out to meet what came to him. The tunnel was a deep place in the unconscious which must be gone through if one would come out into the light of a new attitude. She felt that she herself was in this tunnel. She perceived that she might come out into a new connection with life, where her feeling would no longer step haltingly, nor would her eyes be blind to hidden values. Again, came early memories of the things which had blinded and lamed her. But again she could not meet the issue, she could not accept reality.

She was beginning to be really interested in X, but instead of admitting that she might be falling in love with him she tried to see how she could be a "good influence" to him. Then in a dream she saw the little black pig again, sitting and looking at her very humorously. He was an aspect of the situation which she did not care to face, and on waking she concentrated austerely on the image of the piper of God. She began to think that she could care very much for X, and through her feeling help him develop "a nobler side."

For several weeks she lived in this illusion, seeing herself as she wished the man might see her, while X, on his side, made it perfectly clear that a woman of this kind did not appeal to him. Then she woke one night and heard a voice saying, "You are bringing in contraband goods," and it flashed upon her that she was trying to smuggle in sterile ideals which were not real, instead of admitting and bringing in her instinctual feeling. This was very shocking to her, for she saw how these old forces in the unconscious were still at work. Now she fell into a fit of deep depression, because life was not the beautiful thing she had imagined it to be. She bitterly blamed the man for not fitting her pattern. Had he been different, spiritual, and intellectual, then all would have been well. She was once more controlled by the Animus.

But he was not so secure in his power as he had once been, and this was very soon illustrated in a dream. She dreamed that she was sitting at a clergyman's table—the clergyman mentioned on page 165—and was suddenly oppressed by fear of his wife, who was looking straight at her. That is, she was becoming afraid of her own woman's intuition which could see her real relation to the Animus. It was self-knowledge that she feared.

In her next dream she saw her sister ill; the face was old and worn, but she was wearing a brilliant kimono and her hair was dressed in schoolgirl fashion. Her old attitude toward the instinctual was sickly and adolescent. She dismissed this dream as meaning nothing at all, but the next dream came with startling intensity!

"I fell upon my face, and could not rise because of the heavy load upon my back."

All this time she was pursuing intellectual interests, deciding that the feeling that had come to her was not worth bothering about. She was distressed by infantile sexual phantasies. The heavy load of repressions which she was carrying in the unconscious had got her down, and she was not able to rise.

Next she found herself tugging at a square, boxlike, outdoor toilet. She had a distraught feeling that she must find some way to cleanse and disinfect this. She wished to be cleansed of these infantile phantasies but she did not realize that the way to do this was to bring her feeling back to the conscious and use it in a reality situation. In spite of the strong affect that this dream aroused, she again turned away from it as meaningless, and took refuge in some extremely interesting philosophical books. But the unconscious was still at work, and the next dream was so vivid that she could not forget it or consider it meaningless.

"I saw a beautiful songbird in a cage. The cage was on the floor and tipped up slightly on the left side. Then I saw a cat creeping toward it; I was terrified for the bird, but I was powerless to move, and the cat looked at me and said, 'The next time that bird comes down to eat, I will catch and devour it.'"

She was too frightened to try to think out this dream clearly, but for days she seemed to see the cat following her. The cat personified the stealthy quality of the Animus, which would creep up on any happy intuitive feeling she might possess, and so she had good reason for being afraid.

It so happened that her summer vacation was almost due, and now she decided, instead of staying near X, to make a literary pilgrimage. She felt that in so doing she would not only further her professional interests, but would discover "her own myth of individuation." Then suddenly in the night, she woke confronted by a very independent little pig, sitting firmly upon the top of a small square house.

The house she associated with the symbol of individuation, in its three dimensional "foursquare" form, and in this she was perfectly correct. The pig had appeared in her dreams as someone who was always himself; and this real meaning of individuation, which is finding one's own reality, she failed to see. She wished to find her individuation by turning away from what she really was, and by identifying with the chosen image of her unconscious. She therefore went her own way; and shortly after she dreamed again of the priest whom she had seen in the first new dream she had brought to analysis. Now, instead of pursuing her down the passage, he said three times, "I love you, I love you, I love you."

Instead of realizing that she was being wooed by the Animus she thought this quite as it should be—a sort of ideal reunion with the divine. She was therefore a bit disconcerted that in the next dream she should find herself on high stilts and in great danger of falling, the stilts, of course, being the ideas upon which she had mounted instead of standing upon her own feet.

After this, she found herself eating with Russian monarchists. There was a deliciously adventurous sense of intrigue and poison, but she was quite clearly with the monarchists; she had nothing to do with the masses, all those turbulent lower emotions she had excluded.

Then M appeared again in her dream; she was trying to enter into an affectionate relationship with her, but for some reason this seemed no longer possible. Here M appears as her shadow side, the side which makes its alliance with the Animus, this side which she can no longer accept.

In the next dream she was filled with anxiety for a little dog, for an older dog had bitten off his legs and tail. These were the two sides of herself which were at war—the power and the feeling. In the dream she was appalled by the cruelty of the big dog, yet this represented what her power side really did to her feeling.

In her next dream she saw a little naked boy with red hair alone in an empty room. As she looked at him she should have known that he was her neglected child of feeling, whom she must nurse and cherish, but instead she tried to identify with him, seeing him as the image of her own loneliness, and becoming overwhelmed with self-pity. It was not long, therefore, before she had dismissed the dream as merely incidental. She continued with her literary pursuits, and came back from her journey with nothing more to show than seven sonnets of an extraordinary sterility.

She was glad to return to her friendships and to her professional life. As for X, she did not think that he was of much importance. But X, when he appeared, proved to be very disconcerting. Not merely was he demanding a decision with regard to their relationship, but a demand had also risen in her. More disconcerting still, the dream of the little red-headed boy returned to her memory in a most vivid and compelling way; she saw him now, not as her own loneliness, but as a personification of the Eros principle, in the only form in which it could come to her because of her neglect of it.

For two months more the struggle which had been so insistently outlined in her unconscious material was lived out in her conscious life. Then the dreams began to show which way the struggle was going. One night she dreamed that she was reading an old Gaelic manuscript, but she was called away to clean the spots from the bath tub.

The Gaelic manuscript associated with the "ideal phantasies" which she had heretofore written as an escape from facing her own realities—cleaning her own house. She took the dream very literally and for some time concentrated upon the purely personal aspects of her analysis. She struggled with the old power attitude, the old fears and suspicions.

This honest attempt brought her face to face with the fact that she was not yet ready to accept life as it came to her, but that deep down she still wished to predetermine how and when experience should come. So she wished nothing to happen until she was ready to meet it in what she considered a right way. She had now placed her emphasis upon her inner change but she had forgotten that one cannot hold life back until any decided time. While she was struggling with this the following dream arose: She saw an Irish hero at a grave, and over the mound were written the words, "Come by night or come by day, but come."

She felt that the hero standing by the grave and the one within the earth were the same. It was as though this dream showed her the past and the future at the same time; if the words over the mound could be accepted, the Irish hero would emerge from the grave. From the dead past a new spirit would rise, but only at a time of its own choosing. Would she continue to reduce this relationship to a matter of personal convenience, to an experience which she could accept when and how it pleased her to do so? Or would she see that any experience common to humanity, if it is really to mean anything, must be met and lived out on a level deeper than the merely personal? Would she dictate to the Eros principle or would she serve it?

Facing these questions, she came to see that this dream dealt with the mystery of rebirth. The symbols it had used were those of initiation into the mysteries. The initiant is "buried" in a hollow tree or a grave. During this burial his past self—the infantile, personal aspects of life—dies, and when he emerges, he is "reborn." He now partakes of the nature of the God and is able to serve him. Just as the initiant had voluntarily to enter the grave, so she had to give up her way of life, her old Animus attitude. That is, she must no longer serve the Animus, but serve the new principle that was born within her, that of love.

It was a crucial point in her analysis; it meant a realization of the fact that life was larger than herself. It was no longer a question of her particular act, her particular decision; but of her acceptance of the experience of love. While she was trying to understand what this would really mean in her life, she had the following dream: She was bound to a pillar with a chain that was fastened only by a string, and this string she cut. She had been chained by old Animus ideas, old restrictions, but these bonds had lost their power; she was fastened only by a string which she could easily cut.

This dream made use of another rebirth symbol, that of cutting the umbilical cord—the cord which binds one to the old infantile, unconscious adaptation. But to her it directly applied to her immediate situation. What was the string that was holding her to the past? She was no longer chained, she could free herself if she wanted to. Now she realized that the string which she had to cut was her old prejudice against an unconventional sexuality. It was a childish desire for a secure relationship which would give her the outer as well as the inner values. It was the desire for all that her ego craved of safety and personal position that bound her now.

She saw that X was offering her not merely sexuality but a love which necessarily included it. She cut the string, therefore, and fully accepted the relationship.

This acceptance was by no means easy. The choice which she had made determined her ultimate destination but in no way brought her to the desired end. The new way was quite as difficult —in some ways even more difficult—than the old had been; the forces inside herself which she had thought left behind traveled with her and their voices still insinuated. She had acted upon the dream. She had, in cutting the cord, definitely decided to accept life as it came, to commit herself to her own life experience, but she still had to fight every step of the way. She expected green pastures and quiet waters—she found a rocky, difficult way. The newly born attitude had to fight for life.

In the first place, X was held in a marriage which had long-since ceased to exist as a reality but to which he was held by a sense of duty to the unfortunate woman who had left him. In the second place, there was still resistance in her unconscious. In the third place, X had not been transformed into the ideal lover for whom she had secretly hoped; he was still much the same person, still just as amused at her "higher values."

So the old inner struggle began again, *though on a more conscious level*. As of old, she wished to remake life so that it would fit her ideas about it; she wished to change both the outer circumstances of their relationship and the man himself; and this will to power warred with her newly awakened feeling.

In her next dream: "I open my door and find X waiting and close the door in his face."

Was this a statement of what she had wished actually to do? Had she made a great mistake? She had expected a single act to accomplish what only years of development and understanding could do; she was still far from an understanding of the meaning of a real relationship. Consequently part of herself, disappointed, wished to shut the door upon the whole thing.

She dreamed of a dog shut in a cellar and poisoned. Could this be her instinctual side poisoned by living in its lower form? There were dreams of toilets, with unclean details, of negroes, of herself seated at a table with a dirty cloth. These dreams made her realize that she had not completely abandoned her old attitude, that she had overestimated her freedom from it. The unconscious undervalued what she had done because consciously she had expected too much from it. What she had done meant nothing of permanent value unless she could make it part of a far greater experience, an experience of love. For without love she would only have taken a step down into the cellar where this new food would indeed prove poison, and she had not yet learned to love. She had not "completed a relationship," she had only made a meager beginning.

It was not sexuality, but her attitude toward sexuality that mattered. Since so many of her old inhibitions had clustered about this (in fact her early definitions of "good" and "bad" were formulated on this basis), it had been overemphasized in her fear and sense of guilt. Now it must not be overemphasized in value; for it was not the pivotal point. She was in danger of saying, "I have given all for love." If power and self-love were still dominant she would gain nothing. If this step was merely an assertion of a new opinion about life it would be futile. Was it the Animus or the woman who had taken this step? Which one would profit by the new-found freedom?

After earnestly considering the question, she dreamed that a young woman came to her home whom she first criticized bitterly and then accepted with gladness. Then she dreamed that she was seated at a table, which was bare but clean, and had on it a bowl of lovely autumn fruits, which she connected with the harvest that had come to her in her autumn time of life. The dream seemed to show that the woman rather than the Animus had acted.

But now a decided difference of opinion arose between her and X, and she tried to enforce her own ideas. She did not change his mind, but she did change his mood. She had again allowed the Animus to speak, and quite naturally the man's Anima answered. He felt only anger and irritation toward her.

She then dreamed that she and her sister stood beside her sister's dead child and that suddenly, in the midst of her despair, she cried out, "No, she is not really dead, I hear her breathing." In life, her sister had destroyed her marriage relation; now the side of herself which was like her sister might wreck this relationship with X, and she determined to nurse it back to life at whatever cost to herself.

Just after this she had a dream in which she was frightened by seeing her favorite dog run out to the end of a pier and plunge into the ocean. She was sure the waves would overpower him and he would be drowned, but she heard a voice say, "The tide will carry it in." In the present situation, that is, she could only wait for the tide to turn. But she had never learned to wait; and she began to try to compensate for her apparent failure by writing a highly theoretical book. She dreamed:

"I was trying to write; the ink was thick. I tried to get the ink out and dipped down with my pen and pulled out a long, stringy worm. Something within me cried, 'Throw it out.' As soon as it reached the air it changed into a huge, red-brown serpent that encircled the sky and earth. Then as I looked at it, it faded. The same voice within me said, 'You should have killed it.' But deeper down inside I knew that I had had a glimpse of some force greater than anything I had ever imagined."

This dream filled her with a profound terror. Feeling the tremendous power represented by this serpent, she was appalled at the thought that by what she had done in her own life she had tried to reduce it, as far as she was concerned, to a mere worm shut in her inkpot. By beginning the relation with X she had released something far too great to be limited to her writing. Yet even after she had seen the magnitude of this force, something within her—the Animus—had said that she should have killed it.

She was both shocked and frightened by the realization that the Animus might lead her to destroy anything which she could not herself manage and limit. She saw as never before that the Animus could be a deadly power, destroying for her the greatest positive values. She tried to understand the image of the serpent, reading about the oriental concepts of the Kundalini serpent as a psychological force.

(Kundalini, the serpent, is a manifestation of Sakti, the female principle, a form of woman power which is pure wisdom. This woman wisdom is like a stream of wisdom that runs through differentiated knowledge and produces a fusion—a oneness. It differs from masculine knowledge, which has a tendency to shape and to differentiate. When Kundalini is wakened the masculine tension of formulated insight becomes loosened, freer—that is the essence of Kundalini.

In modern psychology she is the force moving of itself in the psyche—the objectification of images. To activate the archetype means to awaken the divine force and to begin the development of the supra-personal—the non-ego. It forms a connection between the past, existing in the psyche in the archetypal images, and the present as it appears to ego-consciousness. It is not an inflation but a differentiation by which one discovers a relation between the ego and the supra-personal. It therefore, through finding a relation to the past, makes possible a basis of intuition in regard to the future. It puts one in the stream of life energy. Kundalini is the same principle as the Sotor, the savior serpent of the Gnostics. Shut into her inkpot the Kundalini serpent was no longer earth wisdom but sterile rationalization—not a female principle but an activity of the Animus.)

Although she could not grasp the whole significance of the image, she was certain that it represented a value more than personal. She never wholly lost her sense of the importance of this dream and of its significance for her; but there were still times when it seemed to have no effect upon her daily life.

In her next dream she was seated at a table where there was no food (that is, she had not yet found real nourishment in the relationship with X), but a voice said, "Wait, you will be fed soon." Again the unconscious was saying to her, "Wait;" yet again she decided to hurry. Once more she tried, with very poor results, to manage the relationship. In her next dream, she sat in an upper room, eating cake. In an inner court below, a forlorn child was taking food out of a garbage can. So long as her ego, high up in an inflation, was eating the cake of self-satisfaction, her new feeling remained a forlorn, improperly fed, child.

The next dream was: "I heard a knock at the door, and when I opened it, I saw X standing there with a small branch of bright green leaves and red berries which he had brought me. As he came in, he stepped on my foot and hurt me." This, indeed, he did in many ways. She did not see what she could do about it, but the next dream gave her the clue: "I was crossing the street with L" (the friend in real life who always represented to her gentle, feminine feeling). "There was no traffic policeman, and as we came to the middle of the road I became terrified and said to her, 'You must take the lead.'" There was no traffic policeman at the dangerous crossing she had come to in life. She had transgressed the conventional code, and therefore could expect no directions from the guardians of society. It was only her own intuitive feeling that could now guide her safely.

This was easier dreamed than done. X was going through a very difficult experience which was both humiliating and demanding of his closest attention. Now, just when she should have given love, she asked that love should be given to her. Instead of being willing to wait quietly and help him, wherever she could in this difficult situation, she insisted that he must give more time to her, that their love was the most important thing in the world.

Then she dreamed that she was seated in the gallery of an old church, listening to a sermon. She heard, outside, the sound of a man in pain. Looking out of a high window, she saw him tied to the head of a massive bed with two children tied on each side. He was goading himself with a whip. Though she was surprised that nothing was done to help him, she did not, herself, come down. Her interpretation of the dream was that X was whipping himself up unnecessarily in this situation; but that he *was* tied to it, and that she was to blame for listening to the sermon, instead of coming down to help. But the dream figure was not that of X. When she realized this, she could accept a more subjective interpretation, that the figure might be that of the Animus in martyr-like attitude, and that the children who were tied might be feeling and intuition, and that she might be listening to theories of love—the sermon—instead of loving.

Then, as often happens in dreams, the unconscious gave her a picture of a contrasting aspect of the Animus. She dreamed that she came into her room and found a man sweeping and cleaning. She said to him, "Who are you?" and he answered, "I have no name." She associated this man at once with the hero of "The Servant in the House." He was the spiritual Animus who, if directed by the Eros principle, could set her house in order.

She saw the meaning of this dream very clearly, and really wished to accept it. But, as far as her everyday life was concerned the dream might just as well have been a play. The spiritual Animus had been an ideal hero; but, when the curtain went down and the lights went up, there was the negative Animus sitting beside her. For when she next met X she was even more demanding and opinionated; her conception of her value to him was even loftier than before. His patience became exhausted and he disappeared from her life.

She went through a period of bitterness; she felt that the whole attempt had been in vain. Again she tried to project the difficulty upon another; this time the man had been to blame. Then she dreamed that she saw her sister-in-law in a pool of shallow water. There was a naked boy beside the pool. Her brother came up and said, "He is dead." But when the brother turned away, she came back and found the boy smiling.

She had always considered her sister-in-law a shallow woman. Now she saw her as a side of herself. Though her brother had not come into the dreams before, he had figured in many of the associations in her analysis. She had a low opinion of his judgment. In fact, whenever her Animus got hungry, he had gone and taken a bite out of the brother. Not that the brother had given him no excuse, for he was a man with a very negative attitude toward life. So, in the dream, the brother represented the negative attitude which said, "There's no use trying." However, when she went back alone to the child, she discovered that he was not dead.

This dream made her feel that her own inner values were still alive even though outer things were in such confusion.

About two months before, M had died suddenly, after a tragic experience in her own family in which an unbending attitude, similar to that of the dreamer, had deeply injured one of the younger generation. Just after this dream of her brother, she went over to see M's sister, with a desire to be of help and comfort. The sister spoke with deep admiration of M, and hoped that she might be able to carry on the principles for which her sister had stood.

The old Animus now arose with a new mask. She must show this poor, misguided, gentler sister how false were all these standards. Completely unaware of how cruelly intolerant one may be toward intolerance, she tried to show the devastating effect that M's rigid morality had had upon the young child in the family. The younger woman was completely shattered. She drew herself together and, with such strength as she could muster, asked her please to leave. Even then she did not understand her own cruelty, but felt that the younger woman was too weak, too bound by old ideas, to see the new way.

That night she dreamed that she looked down a dark passage which led to a bedroom door. There she saw three horrible old men, creeping stealthily from the hall to her room. They slunk close against the wall; there was no sound of their footsteps; their faces were terrible, depraved and cruel.

She woke in such panic that she felt they had actually come upon her. For hours she lay shuddering, not knowing what those apparitions meant. When the day came and she was able to try to face them, she recognized them as images of the Animus forces that had ruled her in her visit to M's sister. The names of the first two came to her immediately—"Cruelty" and "Power." Over the third she puzzled for a long time without being able to put a name to him. Then she remembered her dream of the cat creeping up on the bird. This was the silent, stealthy way that her Animus moved up from the unconscious and she felt that the third old man was "Stealth," a personification of this movement.

No other experience during her analysis had been so revealing to her as this. She had tried with sincerity to see her own inner problem. She had fought her battles with courage. She saw clearly new values that she desired and yet, at the very moment when she had most wished to act from her new-found feeling, the Animus had acted as though she, as a woman, did not exist. An "autonomous complex" had once seemed to her an interesting psychological phrase. Now she saw its grim reality personified in the Animus; for it was indeed an autonomous being who had taken possession of her at the very time when she had intended to act herself.

If this being were indeed stronger than she, what was left her but insanity? Her old fears returned; panic swept her; she fled to the analyst as a terrified child would run to a mother. She must, she would be, cared for.

It was a dreadful last stand, and indeed a moment of grave danger, but the history of the dream life made it clear that the old will to power was at work, seeking to compel the analyst to take over all responsibility. Consequently, the analyst, after discussing the situation with her, left her alone.

Her first reaction was anger and resentment; then again the waves of terror. Two apparently irrelevant flashes of insight came to her. One, like a dash of cold water, that she had been left alone to find her own way out; the other, that she would not have been so abandoned had her danger been completely real. She saw not only that the enemy was within herself, but also that she must find within herself the power with which to meet it. She faced the fear of insanity, trying to see from what it arose and from what it derived its strength.

Then came a deep calm. As she described it, "It had been like being on the vortex of a great whirlpool, whirling around and around, and suddenly stopping and finding oneself at a quiet place in the center." This center was within herself and yet it also contained her. Deeper than events or struggles, stronger than her enemy, was this force within herself, a force of quietness and peace.

She went on her way with a deep feeling of assurance that she could never again be overpowered by her old fear of insanity. She dreamed that she was in a dimly lighted cave, deep down in the earth. In the center was a pool crowded with fish. At her side was the analyst. The cave was the womb, the place of rebirth. In its center is the pool, where swim the fish, the contents of the deep unconscious. She thought of these fish as shad which, with the roe containing innumerable eggs, could be a symbol of feminine fertility. The analyst now seemed to her a woman who was both friend and interpreter. She could no longer demand that such a woman should be the mother carrying all responsibility.

X now came back into her life, expecting to take up the relationship just where it had ended. She had changed so much during his absence that unconsciously she assumed that he had changed too. But he was just the same, and by expecting more understanding than he could give her, she aroused all his old moods and irritations. Here was the beginning of a fine Animus-Anima battle—one that might have destroyed the relationship beyond all hope of repair.

Then she dreamed this dream: "I am trying to disentangle two electric wires. I am afraid that if I cannot do this the lamp will go out."

The electricity represented to her dynamic energy; the lamp, the love in their relationship. The wires were the media through which this energy flowed, and to which she could give two interpretations. They were, subjectively, the Animus and Eros principles; objectively, in connection with her love relation, they were the unconscious entanglement of her Animus and his Anima. The dream said definitely that it was she who must untangle the wires. As a result of asking why it was she who must do this, she saw that the man was fulfilling his masculine obligations in the world and that she could not expect him to perform what was essentially a feminine task, to take the lead in the development of the relation between them. When the Animus directs the woman, the man's Anima is at once aroused, and an Animus-Anima battle usually ensues. It was her job to prevent her Animus from making trouble between them, and, by successfully undertaking it, she brought something quite new into their relationship.

During this time she had begun, in her professional work, to lay more stress upon its effects upon human beings, and less upon its technical perfection. She was now asked to do some work for destitute men, and, coming back from a meeting, spoke of these men's faces as "an interesting picture to hang on the walls of memory."

The unconscious, however, no longer permitted her to see human suffering as a mere decorative picture. That night she dreamed that she was trying to hang a picture on a wall. As she drove in the nail, she heard a sound like the throbbing of a mighty dynamo. She woke with a feeling of awe. There seemed to rise in front of her a sea of men's faces. She realized that in her experience of the afternoon she had treated human suffering as though it were a mere picture—something to look at but not to share in. The dream showed her that, in shutting herself away in the security of her small personal life—her own room—she only put a wall between herself and the energy of the human stream.

The next night there were two dreams. In one she was expostulating with X because he was hiding himself, and in the other she heard him calling her. The sort of demands she was making caused X to withdraw from her, yet he still called to her. He was hiding from the Animus and seeking the woman. Then she dreamed:

"I was going through a corridor, following a woman of my acquaintance who wore a uniform. She took me to a desk where the head worker was sitting. She gave me a badge and said, 'For a position of peril.'"

This woman in real life was a person who had both serenity and poise. The nature of the peril had been stated in the two previous dreams. Now the dreamer was given a badge to show that the serenity she was beginning to acquire would, if she trusted it, carry her through the times when a combination of immature feeling and turbulent emotion might put her again in the power of the Animus.

Then she dreamed that she saw a woman whose hair was arranged in an ordered pattern which suggested a mandala. Although there was this definite arrangement, the hair seemed alive and moving. She recalled the dream of harvesting hair as gold and the phantasy of the hair encircling the man as they danced a dance of death. The energy which, in the early phantasy, had been under the control of the Animus, was now ordered by feeling.

This seemed like a prophecy of the ordered beauty which might ultimately appear as a result of the change and development which had begun. This dream caused some confusion because, like any extraverted intuitive, she tried to see it as applying to the condition of her outer life, and her outer life at this time was far from well ordered.

Although the values of the relationship had grown both for X and for herself, a conflict had arisen as to the outer form which this relationship should take. She found the limitations of an unconventional life increasingly difficult, and was tempted again either to demand immediate marriage or to give up the relationship. She saw X's attitude as merely conventional, forgetting for the time the fact that he was also bound to his legal marriage by a deep sense of duty to the unfortunate woman who had deserted him.

One day, sitting in her room thinking about the situation, she saw, as though it were suspended in the air, a glass of red wine. As she looked, a drop fell into it which she knew was a tear. It retained its shape and remained at the bottom of the glass like a sphere of crystal. This vision gave her a new understanding of what the relation to X involved. The red wine, she knew, was the wine of life, and the tear the human suffering which lay at the very bottom, and which must be accepted.

In the next dream which came she saw a square pool in a setting of green grass, with people bathing in it. She was seated on the bank and was pulling off dead skin, drawing it from right to left, and as she pulled it off it carried away an old sore spot. In the square pool of the unconscious, people were bathing and receiving new life, and at that pool of healing she could pull off the old dead skin that had enclosed her. The pulling off of the dead skin was to her, as to many people, a symbol of rebirth.

Then, again, in a dream X appeared at her door, bearing in his hand a branch with green leaves and red berries. It no longer seemed a dream to her, but a vital experience, and she wrote about it:

Life at the Door

He gave to me a leafy branch
As at the threshold of my door
I stood to greet him and questioned—
Should I let him in?
A lovely, glistening green the leaves were,
With here and there a berry, round and red,
Globes of ripe fruit that tempted me
To taste and share with him their magic substance.
But I refrained, nor would disturb
The lovely symmetry of that green branch with mystic fruit.
Then, as in my hand I held it close
And gazed upon its loveliness,
A mortal pain throbbed through the branch,
And stabbed my hand and foot,
And my side leaped with sudden wound,
For thorns were hid beneath the leaves.
The fruit dripped red with human blood.
My joy was three parts pain
As, with pierced hands and feet and side,
I saw the tragic face of him I crucified,
As at heart's door I kept him waiting.

Although once more she had used a phantasy as a starting point for an attempted literary flight, and although at first she saw herself as one who had achieved the miracle of the stigmata, she was finally able to separate herself from an identification with the suffering savior. Like many other people she had had a phantasy recalling the experience of the saints, but she was able to see that this represented no miraculous experience. In her own life were thorns which had their ugliness and power to wound. The mystic fruit was not merely a lovely symmetry but quite possibly a very simple food which should be eaten, the fruit of a real experience which needed to be digested. She felt a new humility. The fruit could not be of her own choosing, but only what life brought to her. She might have wished for something very different, but what had actually come to her were red berries on a thorny branch in the hands of a man whom she had once scorned as ordinary and unappreciative of higher values.

So once more she tried to accept the unacceptable and worked through long days and nights of alternate happiness and disappointment. She met again her own inner enemies. She began to perceive that her life force moved like a spiral in which, although she had again and again to meet the old temptations, the progress was upward, so that she came back to the same thing on a higher plane. It was not strange that this took her a long time.

Then she dreamed that she dropped the ring which had been given her by X. The setting rolled away but after a patient search she found the stone. The search reminded her of the parable of the finding of the pearl. The stone was to her the essential value for which she was searching. This essential value was the value of love, which heretofore she had placed in an ego setting. It had been the center of her personal desire, not of her whole life as a woman. She must now find a new setting; she must make it the center of her psyche. In this way it became the symbol of the treasure, the precious stone—the individual center.

She then dreamed that she stood waiting patiently for a long time outside her own door. At last she saw a tall, noble-looking woman coming into live with her. It was now the woman, not the Animus, who came in to be her companion. Nevertheless, although she had a new understanding of love, she could still be caught off guard.

Her relationship with X had by this time become much more satisfying to both of them. For this very reason he began to fear that it might endanger his conventional life and said that he must see her less often. Then in a dream she saw him holding a newspaper before his face, and realized that he was putting public opinion between them. This roused all her old power instincts. She was determined that he should put their relationship before everything else. Because to her as a woman this relationship was the most important thing in life, it was difficult for her to see that this was not necessarily true for a man, that he would be accepting a woman's way of life if he allowed this relationship to do something destructive to the position in the world which he felt he must, as a man, maintain.

This was one of the hardest lessons that she had to learn, that it was not for her to decide what should be done, that it was for him to decide whether or not he would keep that newspaper between them.

As a result of this episode she saw much less of X for a time, and tried to direct her energy into more impersonal channels. She tried to apply what she had learned to the other sides of her life. She managed in the professional work which she was doing to consider the feelings of the other people involved, to guard against the intrusions of the Animus, and to be willing at times to take a minor place even when she felt her own work was suffering. She became quite absorbed in her work. Perhaps in no other way could she have restored balance to her life, and become able to see both for herself and for him the need of using in other relations and other activities what had come out of the relation between them.

After a time she had a dream in which she saw a small bantam cock strutting and preening. Suddenly down from the sky swooped a great golden bird which picked up the cock and carried it off. She saw the Animus which had directed her ambitions as a ridiculously self-satisfied little bird carried away by something that had real power and beauty.

Now a change took place in her relation with X. In her desire to remove every vestige of the old dominance of the Animus she swung too far the other way, tried to conform to X's Anima image of a woman. That is, in withdrawing her pressure and demands, in ceasing to try to manipulate him, she tried to change herself into an image quite at variance with her own nature. She acquiesced in all his plans even when they made him neglectful of her perfectly legitimate desires. In doing this she produced a situation as false as the old one.

Fortunately, she became conscious of what she was doing and was able to be frank in showing him what was happening in her own feeling, and how impossible it would be to continue the relation if he could not understand something more of her real need as a woman. She did not demand that he should change, because he "ought" to love her; she simply gave him a lucid picture of the situation. Since her own motives were clear and conscious, she did not rouse his old resentment. Instead he tried to give her more understanding.

Then she dreamed that she was in a tunnel, one end of which had been closed, and that there were only a few more logs to be removed before one could see light ahead. So did the unconscious reassure her of the rightness of her way.

In the next dream she was seated on a jagged rock in the water. To steady herself she touched a smooth black surface which she thought was part of the rock. Then she realized that this was a great snake. She was quite unafraid of it, and threw it down into the water, where it glided quietly away. Then she found that behind her was a naked man. She asked what to do, and as though in answer to a wordless command, she put up her hand and touched his genitals, and felt that in doing this she had accepted herself as a woman and a man as a man. This man was not X but an unknown figure.

In interpreting this dream it was important not to bring in preconceived ideas. It was necessary to take into account her own sense of the dream as impersonal and as not having to do with personal, physical sexuality. What she did in the dream was to her a symbolic act. She remembered old religious rites such as those in which the lingam has the significance of creative power. Without conscious effort on her part this dream related her personal experience to a deep impersonal one. The black snake inspired no fear; it was a great power swimming quietly in the waters of the unconscious.

Then she dreamed that there came a ring at the door; she was apprehensive and asked who was there and heard a harsh, strange voice. As she listened in fear, a light was turned on from outside, and a ribbon of light streamed through the door. This meant to her that the outside world was difficult and harsh, but in conquering her fear of it, accepting it, she had become conscious, and this consciousness was like a light.

Then she dreamed that she was climbing a ladder mounting to the sky. Looking down, she saw the little black pig rolling on his back contentedly, and she said to herself, "I will never be willing to climb to heaven without taking the little black pig along."

The next night she found herself looking down into the heart of a great, delicately-colored oriental poppy. As she looked, the petals slowly floated away, and in its heart she saw a design shaped like a living cross. On it she saw one small spot, a sore. As she awoke, she thought of L. This made her associate the flower with the love which they had for each other. But what was the sore spot? Could it be that her friend's feeling for her was not as clear as her own? That was only a momentary thought—a suggestion of the Animus—which she put aside, for the dream was hers. She thought of the other dreams in which L had appeared, especially the one in which she had been caught in the traffic with no traffic officer to help her. Then L had guided her.

Here L had stood for feminine feeling and intuitive perception which would show her the way of safety. She realized that though the actual relation with L might have a blemish which she must examine, yet the dream had deep, subjective meaning; for it was on *her* cross—her living symbol of individuation—that the spot appeared. But perhaps she could understand it better through a clarification of the existing friendship with L.

When they next met L told her that on that same night she too had a dream. She saw on the bed a tapestry, on which was a beautiful flower, and exclaimed, "There is no blemish on it." She too had, on awakening, thought of the friendship between them.

This was her first experience of a simultaneous dream occurring when between two people the bond in the unconscious is very deep. At first she wanted to return to her original idea that it was merely their friendship which the dream portrayed. But L also had pondered the dream and to her it had the meaning of a concept of feminine values which had developed, at least in part, through their friendship.

As they talked together she realized how much her relation to X had at first been unacceptable to L. L told her how many times she had been tempted to "advise" her and to try to show her the dangers and evils of the choice she was making, but had always known these temptations to arise from power attitudes, and that they must be fought out within herself. L saw love as something that accepted life as it was and people as they were—not as one thought they *ought* to be, and which helped, not dictated. L told her that she had learned from watching this experience how true it was that no one knew what was right for another, or what he *ought to do,* for out of the very thing which would have been to her, L, a disastrous mistake, her friend had come to a new development and an enlargement of life.

She began to see the sore spot that needed healing as the personal wound to her ego when life did not go as she thought it should. Out of this had grown her attempts to change L's ideas, to make L see life in the terms in which it had come to her. In neither case was it the feeling which they had actually attained, but the concept of life, which the dreams had portrayed. Her symbol was the living cross, and the blemish upon it was hers to heal. She could not have life conform to her ego demands. Love was a principle to be served—it was an inner attitude toward life itself. It could not be separated from personal relations, for through those it found its channel for expression—but neither could it be confined to any single relation, or to those few chosen ones that the ego decreed, for it must serve each in its own time and place—it must continue in its own integrity even though the personal aspects changed. Their concepts would always be fundamentally different, the pattern of their lives would never take on the same form but each must develop according to her own individual pattern, and through this understanding their relationship also would take on new value.

After this she dreamed that she saw the Pope; on his face was an expression of great calm and serenity. She asked him why that look had come to him, and he said, "Through the acceptance of bitter reality." What had been her own bitter reality which she had been brought to accept? It was the reality of herself as she really was. It was the fact that her own failures and shortcomings had stood between herself and life—that fundamentally she had been the author of her own greatest misfortunes. But the acceptance of this reality, bitter as it had been, had led to a place of understanding, and therefore to peace and serenity. Not until that reality had been accepted could she also estimate the experiences that came to her.

Once she had thought that the avoidance of suffering, "being happy," was the goal of life; now she saw that it was not by trying to find happiness or by seeking out suffering that one lived but through the understanding of the reality of one's own experience, a reality often "bitter" and difficult but lived because it was one's own. Only after such understanding could the spiritual Animus have any meaning to her. Only then could she see herself not merely in relation to the momentary event but in relation to the life principle behind it.

The Pope meant to her one who interpreted God to the people, one who made clear the mysteries of life. The Animus, in his capacity of interpreter, could help her to understand the images of the unconscious. In this form, as the spiritual Animus, he was very different from the old negative figures of the priest and the father. His authority came through the acceptance of life. She had tried to avoid suffering, yet it was through its acceptance that serenity had come.

She remembered the dream of the serpent Kundalini. The two dreams seemed to meet. Both principles (the male and the female) she saw as forces far greater than herself, yet both energizing and completing the life of every individual. But she could attain this understanding of life only through active living. No contemplation of the images apart from their relation to everyday events could produce any change in her center of being.

In this way she perceived a connection between impersonal forces and her personal life. She had come to analysis to find a way of changing the outer circumstances of her life. Instead, she herself had changed. No new elements had been introduced. Both X and L had been in her life for many years; her work was essentially the same. In fact, her life contained nothing that could not have been hers before, could she only have perceived it.

From now on her unconscious material changed and dealt more with supra-personal images. This did not mean that there were no longer manifestations of the Animus as a destroying factor in her life, but that she had learned to recognize these manifestations as something with which she could deal. She had completed one chapter in her development as an individual. And she saw life not so much as a series of events but as a continuity, a relation to a deep principle.

XIII. PHANTASY

It is not only at night, when consciousness has withdrawn, that images may appear to us in dreams, nor need we wait for the coming of a great vision. We can, through a direction of conscious attention, learn to see the life of the image. We have all had the experience of seeing a face appear or a picture flash upon the screen of consciousness. It intrudes—is gone—and we give it a bare instant of attention.

If, however, we hold one of these fleeting images in our inner vision, it does not vanish, but becomes clearer and more vivid, and, with an increase of our concentration, becomes endowed with life. It may begin to move, perhaps to speak. It is true that, in the dream, figures move and speak; but they appear and disappear entirely at the dictates of the unconscious. In the process known as phantasy—the waking observance of the life of the phantom, or image—their appearance may be prolonged indefinitely. Into phantasy a conscious element enters—that is, a concentration upon the image so that it does not disappear again into the unconscious.

The original image may arise spontaneously, or it may be recalled from the outside world, or from a dream, but, in any case, we do not consciously create such phantasy any more than we consciously create our dreams. We simply turn our attention to the inner world, and thereby energize the original image. Our conscious *direction* is held in abeyance but our conscious *attention* is intensified. There is a voluntary sacrifice of *rational* direction, for these phantasies have nothing to do with our preconceived idea of how things *ought* to develop. Therefore, they frequently show us old, instinctual patterns of behavior which are still alive in the depths of the unconscious and which have to do with the symbolic aspects of life. That is to say, they partake of the nature of "great" dreams and deal almost entirely with archetypal material.

The figures appearing in phantasy have a life of their own, disconnected from our daily life and experience, and they behave in ways quite at variance with ours; for they are not determined by the temporary values of the social collective of our time.

Phantasy differs from daydream because the daydream is a form of escape from reality into a world where fulfillment comes without effort—a personal fairy tale—something woven by the undeveloped ego. The daydream is the childish form of undirected thought. It contains the magic solution—the instant recognition of the wished-for image of the self. The fairy godmother in Cinderella is a typical wish-fulfilling figure; though in the daydream the same happy events are frequently brought about by no fairy figure. But the daydream follows the pattern of the fairy tale. The imagined qualities of the ego are suddenly recognized by the world, not as the result of one's own effort but suddenly, as if by magic. In the daydream the ego is always the central hero.

Daydreams fade as consciousness increases and reality is accepted. Phantasy, on the other hand, is a form of experience which is attained only by people who have paid a good deal of attention to the material of the unconscious. Except in cases of advanced neurosis, where there is sometimes no ability to distinguish between the inner and the outer image, phantasies do not develop involuntarily.

All real works of creation have sprung from creative phantasy. An artist looking upon the canvas sees growing there an image. A sculptor sees the image within the stone and the creation of the image seems but a liberation of a form already contained within the rough and formless substance. Something new comes alive within the artist even before it is given form. So it can be seen that phantasy, even when it is not subsequently given an objective form, does none the less connect man with an irrational creative process. Phantasy is not a personal creation, but it acts creatively upon the life of the individual.

When we have reached an impasse, when we are "in a hole," or have run ourselves into a stone wall, phantasy may show us the way out. It states the problem in symbolic form and suggests the solution, a solution often quite at odds with the old way of life. Through connection with the greater, impersonal images our own personal difficulties frequently change their proportions; and perhaps dwindle, so that they become relatively unimportant in contrast to the new values which are perceived. The special problem, which has been so disturbing, does not cease to exist, but it no longer stands between us and life. The daydream is an escape from reality—the phantasy a connection with realities deeper than the ego or the moment, which liberate us from the fixed and too-often sterile life of consciousness—of the preconceived idea.

The following phantasy came to a person who felt herself to be in a cul-de-sac and did not know how she got there, nor how to find the way out. The phantasy was preceded by this dream:

"I am looking for something. It seems to be a spring, very hard to find. I seem to be groping in semi-darkness under trees and through underbrush; I have to get over a ditch; it is all very vague, but difficult and frightening. I seem to have been there before. I come to an old plaid rug spread out, with crumbs and bits of food on it. I feel that they have been left there for the birds, or for little animals."

For the whole of the next day she thought about this dream and seemed really to be groping in darkness. Then, in active phantasy, she returned to the place where she had been looking for the spring. She concentrated upon the opening scene of the dream, as though she were memorizing the details of some place which she had actually visited. The visual image became clear, and then, with continued concentration, this phantasy began:

"I put myself back to where I was searching for the spring in the woods. There is no opening in the woods, no path, and no way out except the path by which I came. First I think I will plunge off into the woods; I must get to water or to an outlook. Then I remember the food for the animals; they must know where there is water and I will watch and see if they will not show me a way. So I go back to their eating place, lie down on the bank, hear the wind in the trees, see some moss, realize that the earth is living. I suppose I notice it because I am alive; I feel quite peaceful, hear little animals scurrying about, and go to sleep.

"Then I awake and start digging. I dig in the form of a cross—three squares one way, three squares the other. I grow very weary and fall asleep again, and in my sleep I hear the words 'cemetery' and 'core'—the center. I wake up and start digging once more. In the center of the cross I find a fragment of white marble, which I know has come from a child's grave. Then I realize that this hole is the place of my own child's burial, and that I must go deep down underneath this to find the ever-living spring which I am seeking."

This child had died many years before, and though the woman had suffered deeply at his death, she had not realized how great an effect it had had upon her life, nor how much of her feeling had been buried with him. Consciously she loved her other children, but not as she had loved this child, who spontaneously gave feeling to her. With his death she had returned to a certain isolation. What should have been love for the other children found its expression in duty and in anxiety about them. She seemed to have lost all connection with spontaneous feeling; a sense of duty and anxiety are not enough to sustain any active interest in life.

Now the phantasy showed her that this child had represented to her a quality of spontaneous love which she had allowed him to carry for her; and that now she must find a way of releasing it in herself and letting it go out to other people.

In the dream the plaid rug stood for the pleasure that she had always felt during days in the woods when this child was still alive. The appearance of this symbol activated her memories of happier days with the children and this had given her the incentive to phantasy.

These phantasies, of course, may come to a person who is simply interested in the movement of the image, and who observes this as one would a moving picture. In this case, nothing of any value occurs; and there is even danger that one may be caught by its fascination and begin to make it a substitute for directed thought. One is then indulging not in active but in passive phantasy. For the phantasy is of no value unless one tries to understand it and relate it to one's own life situation.

The following case illustrates at greater length how phantasy was used creatively in the life of an individual.

After a profoundly tragic experience a woman found that although consciously she was making every effort to continue her life, she unconsciously wished for death. She would, for example, suddenly hear the squeak of brakes from a taxi in front of which she had absent-mindedly stepped. Although there seemed nothing in her personal life to give it value, she felt that life was something greater than the joy or sorrow of the moment, and that her connection with life was not really broken. Yet something had to be done about the side of herself which wished for death. When she was trying in vain to find some solution of her problem, there came to her a phantasy which had an extraordinary vividness:

"I walked upon the floor of the ocean and came to a great cave. Then I saw this cave to be a huge fish in which was seated a woman. Her head was bowed upon her knees, and her hair fell down in a curtain. She seemed to be in great grief. Then, as I looked at her, she stood up and plaited her hair and took the end of the braid and rubbed it over her heart. The rubbing kindled a spark within her which grew into a fire. With this fire she lighted a torch and held it high above her head. As the light from the torch grew brighter the fish began to dissolve into inky masses that floated away and freed the woman. She rose up through the water, still holding the torch, the light of which was unquenched. Slowly in the waters below the great fish reintegrated.

"As the woman reached the shore she found many piles of sticks laid ready for lighting. She ran from pile to pile touching them into flame. As they kindled, circles of children began to dance about her. Behind the smoke of the fires there appeared a huge, primitive god. The woman went to him and with difficulty climbed upon him and set the torch in his hand. Then the god set her upon the palm of his other hand and rose, holding the torch on high. The light streamed out into the darkness. From between the clawlike toes of the god sprang little streams, and in the mud between them were great newts and other crawling things. Then from the penis of the god flowed a stream that was as clear as crystal, and in it all the crawling things were carried down to the sea. The feet of the god became roots. From the cave of the roots came little men. From the waist down, the god became a tree. Above, his appearance changed to that of the Christ. Then the torch wound itself about his head in a knotted crown, and, as the light streamed from it, the little dwarfs became straight and strong, half man, half god, and the children who encircled the fires became youths and maids, and each one stooped down and gathered a bit of flame and set it within his heart."

Her interpretation of this phantasy was: "Being in the great fish symbolizes entering into the darkness of the unconscious. It associates with Jonah's whale, the great fish which swallowed the hero, in his night journey under the sea. The woman in the great fish of the unconscious is there abandoned to grief. Her fallen hair is the symbol of the giving over to despair. She plaits this, that is, she controls the undirected force of her suffering. She takes it into herself, rubbing the hair upon her heart. Then from love and pain are lighted a fire which frees her from the dark cave. The great fish reintegrates; the dark forces of the unconscious are reassembled, not destroyed.

"When she reaches the shore she lights the fires of human relationship. The god who rises with the torch is at first a primitive god, then a mystical combination of tree-god, the god who is rooted in the earth, and the Christus of love and sacrifice. The light now illumines the world and brings men to their full stature of being. The primeval beasts have been carried down to the sea of the unconscious. The stream which carries them is also a life-giving stream.*

"The next form of life, the Cabiri, the dwarfs, start from the feet that have now become the roots of the growing tree-god, and in the light of the torch which is now become the crown they turn first to men and then to godlike men. The children about the fires grow to youths and maidens who take the fires of love that have been lighted and set the spark in their own breasts."

She felt that through this phantasy she had found an answer to her questions. Then she saw this same woman standing upon a crescent moon. She was clothed in blue and carried a delicate child in her arms. Other children clustered about her feet. Her face was full of tenderness. Other visions of the archetypal mother

---

* Rigveda, 1, 114, 3: "May we obtain your favor, thou man ruling, O Urinating Rudra." Quoted by C. C. Jung in *Psychology of the Unconscious*. page 237.

came, and in the contemplation of these the living woman felt lifted out of herself and filled with a new strength. The mother image seemed to go with her, to move through her. She often saw the image of the woman standing on the hand of the god. She felt able to turn from death back to life, to refuse to bury her feeling in the grave of her past and to use it wherever the needs of others should demand it. This was to her the meaning of the woman who, after she had lighted the many fires upon the shore, stood upon the hand of the god.

There was in the phantasy an element to which she might well have given thought—the god, deeply rooted in earth like the tree of life. This she neglected. She became identified with the woman who was lifted above earth and was looking down upon those who were about the fires but who herself had no real connection with them. What she got at the time from the phantasy was the strength to turn away from death. She identified it with an impersonal image, the Eternal Mother, so that what was once individual love became a *participation mystique* with any and every sorrow.

But just as the love that she gave was impersonal, so was the love and gratitude that she received. The role of eternal mother is not eternally satisfying. It does not take into account the needs of the personal life. She was, after all, a human being with human needs. To this fact, in her preoccupation with the archetype, she had given no real attention. Hence new psychological difficulties arose. Disconcerting dreams appeared; her life, both in its inner and its outer aspect, lost its calm.

Such an identification slowly swallows up the conscious personal life; but in the unconscious all the neglected side is living. The Shadow makes the personal demands that the conscious refuses to consider. Such was the case with this woman. Month by month her confusion increased, until at last she was forced to pay attention to it. She turned again to the unconscious for a solution. Then came the following phantasy:

"I saw a woman standing quietly in a green meadow. She was a peasant woman, dressed in blue with a scarlet cloak thrown over her shoulders. A little animal scuttled out of the bushes and came toward her to be fed. It had the head of a leech, the body of a skunk, and the tail of a beaver. Then I saw that on the ground about the woman were scattered shining silver discs. She stooped and selected two of them and put them over her breasts. The animal scuttled off, moving like a hedgehog, and disappeared in a ditch. She stood quietly looking across the meadow. After a long time, a lamb came up and put its head trustingly in her hand.

"After a little, the woman moved away through the meadow and the little lamb came trotting after. The meadow was full of sunshine, gently gay and sweet with flowers. She walked through the meadow and came to a cottage. There was a white fence about it and a high arched gate with a lantern on one side and a bell on the other. She lifted the latch and went in. The lamb gave a bleat of happiness and trotted into the orchard and lay down under an apple tree. The woman went into the cottage.

"There was a sense of joy, of home-coming, of peace and happiness. She was in a big room with a huge firepalce. She took off her red cloak and threw it on the settee. Then kneeling, she laid a fire of logs and pine cones. She lighted it, and, as the smoke curled up, the aroma of the pine cones filled the room. She hung an iron pot over the fire and threw in many ingredients including bunches of herbs. Then from all about came tumbling little men in brown, wearing pointed caps. They had cups in their hands. The woman filled them from the pot. They dipped their fingers in the liquid and held them up to see which way the wind blew. When they found it was from the north they nodded and drank and then vanished.

"Now about the hearth was a circle of animals, and the woman filled for them little brown bowls. There was a sense of warmth and contentment. Suddenly there was a knowledge of something awful approaching. The animals became rigid as though frozen; only a little fox sitting in front of the woman looked up at her beseechingly. The woman stood motionless. Slowly, as though stepping from the wall itself, a figure entered. It was Death in a great black cloak. The whole room was stabbed with pain.

"Then the woman filled another bowl and offered it to Death to drink. He took it in his hands, but the brown bowl turned into a marble urn, and the warm liquid chilled and congealed. Slowly the urn vanished into vapor; Death withdrew as silently as he had come. The room became dark; the little animals were gone; the woman knelt alone beside the dying embers."

On the next day, without any conscious volition on the woman's part, the phantasy began where it had left off:

"Suddenly I saw the fox, and heard a voice say, 'The fox knows; he only can tell you.' Then the fox spoke and said, 'I, too, have been torn to pieces, but I have been torn to pieces for a sport. Like Osiris and the infant Dionysus, I, too, have been dismembered. I, too, live in an earth house.' Still he looked at me as if trying to say more, but I could hear nothing. He stood looking at me as he had looked at the woman in the earlier part of the phantasy when he was unable to tell her what to do about Death. Then he vanished.

"When I saw the fox again he was lying curled up on a path in the woods. Back of him was the entrance to his hole. He lay curled close, nose on tail, completely motionless as though asleep, but his eyes were alert and watchful. I had a feeling that he would remain thus watchful and alert until the woman of the phantasy was able to understand him better and could hear what he had to say. Then the fox faded out of the picture, and I saw another circle in which was a double five-pointed star of luminous blue. In the center of this great star was a sphere of deep blue. I wondered what this blue star, to me a symbol of relationship, could have to do with the fox.

"Again the pattern of the circle changed. There was still the same sphere of deep blue, but now it was the center of a great wheel of light and energy. The light swept out from the center in a whirling motion, and on the wheel's outer edge were seven figures who seemed to have within themselves small centers of quiet, from which proceeded light to meet the greater light. The figures had the form of seven sages in attitudes of meditation, and in an eighth space on the edge of the circle was a tree of life. Outside all this, as though holding it together, there coiled a great serpent. And outside this again was a circle of clear green light, bounded in its turn by a circle of luminous red. (Plate 79) This vision was as distinct as though it were painted upon the wall of the room."

She painted this picture exactly as it appeared to her. It was the first contact she had with such a tremendous archetypal symbol arising within her own psyche. She felt the mystery and the excitement of it and the feeling that it was her individual experience—something which was really hers but of which she had no real understanding. It was a mystery as yet beyond her interpretation. She concentrated upon the blue center and it seemed as though its quiet began to enter into her. But the next night the phantasy returned.

"The woman appeared, showing great anxiety and perplexity. She carried the red cloak, and, going down the fox hole, spread it over the fox. This seemed to me to be wrong. I tried to enter the phantasy and to direct it consciously. I forced her to take back the cloak. Then she was in great distress. She wrung her hands and looked about for help. She carried the cloak back to the cottage and spread it on the floor, but that was not where it was meant to be. She was frightened and could not rest.

"All day I tried to find what she should do with the red cloak. I was strangely tired. I wished to forbid the phantasy so as to escape whatever it was that it was going to reveal. My own energy was gone but the woman kept reappearing. I wanted her to burn the cloak, but when she carried it to the dying fire and put out her hand, the hand turned into the hand of Death. If she burned the cloak, Death would come to her. I felt that she must die, and I tried to make the phantasy go as I wished it to go, but the woman did not acquiesce.

"At last came a realization that perhaps this woman knew more than I, that I should be willing to watch her and not attempt to command her. She had met Death and he had withdrawn. She had accepted the fox and perhaps knew that the cloak was right for him. He might be a 'Doctor Fox,' that is, a magic animal who possessed instinctual wisdom. Yet for some reason he needed the protection of the cloak. Then a voice said, 'You must not kill your shadow; you must make friends with her.' I went into the cottage and took the woman's hand and told her I was sorry and I would not try to force her, only to understand *with* her. She did not believe me, and looked at me in great fear. I went away over to the end of the settee and sat down. She was like a timid little animal, but by and by she gently crept up to the cloak on the floor, picked it up and stole away. She went down the fox hole, covered up the fox, and, like a tired child, lay down beside the fox and they both went fast asleep.

"At this point the phantasy stopped and I slept. I was awakened by a voice which said, 'There is a black castle where all questions are answered.' I saw the castle rise in front of me. About it was a circle of light. Within the circle was a foursquare pattern of paths and gates. Within this, a moat within a moat. Inside the moat rose the square black castle, a tower at each corner, four towers rising above these. I entered it. In the central hall was a foursquare space of white light in the form of a clear white crystal, which was both emptiness and living light. I felt as though something had integrated within myself, as though there were a center of quiet into which I could retire, and from which I could go out.

"After this, the picture faded, and in its place appeared the fox hole. The woman and the fox were still sleeping. The fox got up and went over and looked at the woman in a protecting way. It seemed quite evident that he was now master of the situation. Then he went back and tugged the red cloak over and dragged it over the woman. Then he straightened himself up, and looked very alert but not at all frightened, and trotted off to the upper world."

After some time, in which she had no phantasy, she again saw the fox curled up in a circle. In a few moments he vanished. She tried to call back the vision of the wheel of light and energy but it would not come. Instead she felt the impulse to paint a picture that was rising within herself. She did not know what was coming till it appeared on the paper. (Plate 77) It came with such a shock that she was dazed. Then the picture took on the clarity of a vision and began to move with an energy of its own.

"The woman walked upon the surface of the water along a silver path. The path led up into the sky to where the moon, a remote silver woman, looked down. The woman walked as though hypnotized, drawn up by a white magic. Behind her from the depths of the dark waters, an octopus rose. The woman was unaware of it. Suddenly the octopus cast out a black vapour. The woman turned and saw it. The moon figure bent lower, and the light path grew brighter, but the woman turned to the octopus and began to battle with it. There was a terrible conflict. One tentacle sought to pierce the woman's body at the place of the womb. She seized this tentacle in both hands and broke it, and with the broken piece, struck at the center of the octopus. Immediately the creature broke in pieces, as a tarantula breaks, and the long tentacles fell apart, and turned into twisted sticks. The sea disappeared.

"The woman was on a plain near the edge of a wood. The twisted black sticks were scattered in front of her, and the center of the octopus had changed to a white bowl containing a flaming liquid. She gathered the sticks and built a fire and placed the bowl upon it. A white vapour came out of the bowl. Then the fire died down and the sticks began to move, at first like half-formed earth creatures. Then they turned to seven priests, in black robes. They lifted the bowl and bore it through the forest to a great cave. They began to chant in a low minor. They placed the bowl upon a rock altar. Then they held in their hands seven tall tapers with pale white beams. They stepped back into the shadows. A space opened back of the altar. The seven priests stood like seven columns. The tapers were no longer in their hands, but the light from them seemed to have gone into the bowl. It changed form until it became the crystal altar of the black castle." (Plate 78)

She now began to review the sequence of her phantasies, and to try to see them as connected experience. She found hitherto neglected significance in the phantasy which began in the great fish, but it was difficult to connect it with the childlike fairy tale of the woman and the fox. This peasant woman was dressed in blue, the color of the spirit; but she was protected by a cloak of red, a color symbolizing the warmth of the Eros principle. Later, this cloak protected the fox, too. At first, she was ready to feed even the leechlike animal. In actual life with the attainment of the impersonal attitude for which she had striven, she had lost discrimination. Her intuitive perceptions were gone, so that she could feed the leech or the skunk with the same compassionate feeling that she would experience toward a lamb. She had been violated by the demands of others who had misused her sympathy because she had become willing to be so violated. The first necessity was self-protection. She saw that when, in the phantasy, the woman stooped and put on the shining breast plates, she shut off the universal flow of motherhood; she protected herself from indiscriminate mother giving. Then the lamb could come up unafraid and she could go with him to the earth house.

First came the little dwarfs, helpers of man, creatures that come in the night to give unseen help to the housewife, the maid or the shoemaker who is in distress. They came as helpers in everyday work. The dwarfs of the first phantasy had grown to god-men; these had no such evolution. They dip their fingers in the bowl cups and hold them up to see which way the wind blows and when they find it is from the north, they nod and drink. The north is the direction of clear intuition. The north star is the star which guides the mariner. Since the wind is north they know things are right so that they can safely drink what is given them in this house.

As they vanish, all the little wood creatures come. These are the instincts with whom she makes friends. But Death enters and every instinct is fear-frozen. Only the little fox remains alert to help her. He is her intuition, an intuition that would serve her if she would let him; an alertness, an awareness. But she has lost the power to hear what he says. It is really he who suggests that she should offer Death the same warm drink that has fed the animals. This act causes Death to withdraw.

Now the voice tells her that it is the fox who understands. She goes down into the earth where he lives to find out his knowledge—earth knowledge. There the little fox lies alert, trying to protect her and doing the best he can, even though he cannot yet make her understand. She sees him lying in the circle, but watchful. But how could the little fox change to the five-pointed star, the archetypal image of relationship? It was only by learning what he knew, by using him—her intuition—to check the judgments of her feeling in her personal life could she find the principle lying back of personal experience, a principle of relationship. He must be accepted first as guide before she could come to the star. Both are protected by the circle; they are both enclosed in mandalas, that is, magic circles protecting the center. It is the fox who protects her personal feeling. It is the five-pointed star which is the eternal symbol of supra-personal love. The two are really manifestations of one truth, and so interchangeable.

Then the picture changes and there appears the third mandala. Here the blue center of spiritual quiet gives forth energy-like flames that revolve as they proceed from it; and heightening of consciousness takes place. In some living way the flames connect the figures of contemplation with the central light; yet these figures maintain their own center of inner calm. Outside these figures the great Kundalini serpent coils, holding the energy enclosed. The circle of green has the color of spring life. The outer red circle is the circle of living desire.

This woman had never heard of mandalas. She had not known a Kundalini mandala existed, and yet one had appeared to her as if painted on her own wall, a picture like those painted in Thibet thousands of years ago. It was a vision too great for immediate comprehension, one that stayed with her as a deep experience to be contemplated and slowly understood.

After this vision the fairy tale phantasy began again. Now the little fox and the woman are together in the earth. As he has first protected her, lying alert on the path near the hole, so now she tries to protect him by covering him with her red cloak. Here a strange element comes into the phantasy, which shows clearly how different it is from something consciously imagined. The real woman tries to command this image woman of the phantasy, but she is of the substance of autonomous complex and will not obey. When the real woman persists and tries to make the phantasy woman burn her cloak, the hand becomes the hand of death. This had no meaning to her until she recalled the words, "You must not kill your shadow; you must make friends with her."

Here she became aware of the fact that this woman in distress was that personal side of her life which she had neglected, the side that could feel terror and confusion, a side that must accept a renewal of life through the simplest instinctual contacts. This showed from what impulse had sprung her desire to direct the phantasy. She wanted this woman to die because she was the personal element in opposition to the archetypal image. To allow this woman to live would mean a loss of security in that identification with the image which lived above human personal needs. It meant returning to all her life of pain as a woman.

These intuitions, only vaguely apprehended, were the cause of her sudden terror and desire to break the phantasy. She saw also that in her concentration upon the center of blue she had again tried to identify with spiritual values when she had not faced her personal realities. The quiet of the center was real, but she could not identify with that experience any more than with the archetypal mother image. If she did this she would again try to kill her "Shadow"—her personal life. She could obtain quiet from the symbol but not use it to evade her problem.

It was difficult to see why this figure was the Shadow, for there was nothing menacing about this woman. But the Shadow is unconsciousness. She had not yet retrieved this woman from life in the unconscious. So she had to go down into the earth—the unconscious—to make friends with her.

When they had become friends, the woman covers over the little fox with the warm red cloak. Then the scene shifts and she hears a voice: "There is a black castle where all questions are answered." She learned afterward that the ancient Chinese symbolism speaks of the yellow castle with the imperishable center. In her vision, the white center, the crystal light, is the center of consciousness. Through consciousness one comes to this imperishable center. This is a concept of an ultimate goal. In reality, complete consciousness can never be attained. The clear light of the crystal symbolizes the light of consciousness and the essence of the integrated self (the imperishable diamond body). The black castle meant to her all the dangers of darkness—the powers of the unconscious. But it is this castle that she must find, that is in the unconscious she must seek for greater consciousness.

It is not through evading the personal life but through searching for consciousness and integration that one can approach the castle where "all questions are answered." Again the concept of the integration of the center is shown as the quest of life. To find this castle would mean to find a new center. It would symbolize a change within herself which was not an identification with an image.

Then, in a return of the phantasy, the little fox covers the woman over and trots into the upper world, where he can function as he should. Her intuition in its personal form is now freed from the unconscious—it can come up into the open. The little fox can help her to interpret her daily life; he can give her intuitions of dangers that she had forgotten. If he is protecting her she will be in touch with her own instincts and will not be carried out of reality. She will have discrimination as to the demands made upon her both from the outside and by her personal desires. Then the experiences of the archetype can give her strength. She can increasingly become able to use the impersonal forces of love without neglecting the needs of her personal life. But she still has to realize how much power lies in the dark forces of the unconscious which has drawn her away from reality.

In the next picture of the phantasy she sees herself standing between the moon mother and the octopus, following, as though in a dream, the light that is luring her away. But the moon symbolizes not only the mother but also the land of dead souls: it is only a reflection of living light, not light itself. She has seen this light as though it were the light of the spirit, and in following the impersonal mother image has felt that she was treading on a pathway of silver light, and moving up to high heaven. But she herself was not an impersonal mother; she was a human being. By identifying with what seemed a beautiful and ideal image she gave enormous power to a hideous one, that of the octopus.

This symbolizes the dark and destructive power of the unconscious, the regressive force which sucks back and destroys individual life. Since she has identified with an impersonal beauty she has to struggle with an impersonal ugliness. That is, the archetype in this unconscious form is itself like a great Shadow, here shown as an octopus. She has to perceive both aspects of the image before she can realize her danger.

When in the phantasy the woman has done this, the picture changes, the body of the octopus becomes a bowl in which a healing drink may be brewed. This mysterious bowl is guarded by seven interpreters of the mysteries who serve at the altar of the castle. Here is the crystal stone, the center; and here are figures which represent the function of the spiritual Animus which can interpret for her deeper mysteries. So the priests are intuition in another realm. The fox gives her understanding of her personal life. The priests interpret the images of the unconscious.

By listening to the fox as well as to the priests she would no longer confuse her personal life with that of impersonal images. She then could gain strength from these images without forgetting that she was a limited human being. She could be herself, related to the forces within but not overcome by them.

But mere perception is not enough. She must really battle with these forces. The phantasy shows her that she is in a place of real peril—that it will take all her courage to grapple with these forces within her psyche, but that it is her only chance of regaining her own individual life. This is a very slow process. Frequently it is months, perhaps years before the full meaning of such an experience becomes integrated *within the self*.

In writing out such a phantasy it sounds as though the conclusion were one actually attained by the individual as soon as the phantasy had reached its end. But psychic growth cannot be hurried any more than the growth of a plant. It must develop. This process of assimilation and integration demands not only a concentration upon the archetypal experience or upon the symbol which has arisen, but a constant attitude of awareness of the action of these forces in our daily life.

It is not enough to meditate upon the Shadow, to admit the danger of the octopus arising from the sea of the unconscious. We must see it when in apparently insignificant form it creeps back into our acts in small unimportant ways. It is not enough to paint a mandala, though the painstaking painting gives a connection which is very real; one must concentrate upon it and realize what it may mean to us in connection with our relation to daily life as well as to deeper realities.

The symbol of the crystal center which appeared in the final picture had a power of new life because it was experienced as *within* her own psyche. It was one manifestation of the god within. What she did in relating it to herself as an individual was now the great question. The study of the phantasy and the painting of the pictures had renewed the energy so needed to break the identification into which she had fallen and to give new and continued understanding if she could continue her inner contact with them. The process is never finished; new symbols arise, new understanding develops, so that the returning experiences have new meaning and are dealt with in new ways.

As we said at the beginning of this chapter, phantasy is not a personal creation. The images arise from levels far deeper than our personal unconscious. They are archetypal in nature. When studied, these images are seen to embody ancient ideas, old symbols, that have contained psychic energy from archaic times. Concentration upon the unconscious may make these symbols arise. Through continued concentration one may obtain an understanding of their meaning, although the symbol always contains the inexpressible element, the as-yet unknown value.

But even this understanding is a mere psychic process having no individual importance unless it is related to life—unless it is externalized through living its meaning to us. The reason for the study of such material is to find out the psychic realities which are within us. Unless we get at these realities again and discover the connection with our own life and the present in which we live, a symbol is only an historical sign. To take over a symbol, or to study it in relation to the past only, has no value—but old truths related to present realities produce in us symbols valid for our time and for the expression of our individual psychic realities. The symbol has the power to concentrate the inner forces, to draw them back into a center so they can be strengthened and re-energized.

The living symbol is therefore a combination of an ancient truth and a developing psychic reality—an expression of a future evolving. New symbols therefore arise slowly, not only in individual life but as an expression of the psychic energy of the collective external world.

XIV. VISIONS

GREAT DREAMS, primarily impressive because of their suprapersonal truth, frequently have a vividness of color and form which make them remain clear to "the inward eye" after the dreamer has returned to the waking world. It is only a step beyond this to the place where the inner material is so intensified that it becomes visible in waking hours. This is the most impressive and arresting way in which the image can appear, because it is a direct invasion by the unconscious of the world of consciousness. Into phantasy an element of consciousness enters; that is, through conscious concentration one continues the life of the phantasy. But the nature of the vision is more autonomous. It is not consciously evoked, though usually it appears only to those who have through long meditation concentrated upon the inner world; nor can its life be lengthened by conscious attention.

As we have seen before, it is difficult to define sharply these various manifestations of the activities of the unconscious because the boundaries are not fixed. The phantasy history given in the previous chapter contains a vision—the mandala which appeared suddenly upon the wall (Plate 79). It is incontrovertibly a vivid experience of the invasion of consciousness by the archetype. The difference between vision and hallucination lies in the attitude of the one to whom this experience comes. If he cannot keep his connection with the conscious world, and confuses the vision with objective reality, it takes on the character of hallucination; and, indeed, unless the person is aware that this material comes from within himself, hallucination it must almost always be. But if he has, through the experience of dreams, come into conscious contact with the images of the unconscious, he recognizes the intensified experiences of the archetypes as vivid pictures of an inner reality. Under such circumstances they are not hallucinations, but visions. They are then material to be deeply studied and understood.

The appearance of the vision in our everyday life is a most unusual occurrence, but the vision is so dynamic an experience of the archetype that some discussion of it must be included in this book. The visions given in this chapter are those of a modern woman and took place when she was living a perfectly everyday life. I have tried to limit my illustrations in every chapter to such material. Yet the vision is so rare a phenomenon that a few familiar historical references may help to give the reader some idea of its influence upon human life.

St. Paul on the road to Damascus beheld a great light and heard the voice proceeding from this ineffable light pronounce words which changed the direction of his life energy. St. Peter, pondering upon the distinctions of race and creed, saw the vision of the cloth descending from the sky and, as he saw within it the unclean beasts, heard the words which brought him to a realization of his own racial prejudice. The visions of St. Francis took him from his father's court to a life of austere simplicity, to his acceptance of and brotherhood with man and beast. Such instances abound in the history of the early Christian church and also in the history and legend of every religion.

The interpretation of the vision depends upon the orientation of the seer. To St. Anthony the vision of woman was an incarnation of the devil; to Dante she was the Anima, the divine guide. Our American Indians still rely upon the great dream or vision which shows them the part they are to play as men of the tribe. But they do not accept as authoritative any vision that comes. It must be pondered upon not only by the initiant but also by the council of tribal wise men. For visions may also come, they say, from misleading and mischievous spirits as well as from the Great Spirit. In every case the vision, like any other experience of the archetype, must speak to the inner condition of the one to whom it comes; it must be interpreted in connection with his own inner reality.

The power of vision seems to belong to the seer and to the creative artist. The visions of Blake, given permanent form upon canvas, are now treasures of art. Dürer's etchings are full of the dark power of the vision. The great visions of Swedenborg, interpreted as authoritative realities instead of archetypal experiences, founded a church. When a vision comes to a prophet or a genius he can make it available to humanity in such a way that its importance is accepted or at least partially recognized, but the vision may also be the heritage of each one of us to whom the inner life is real and vivid. In this case, the effect is shown only in the life of the individual; and that effect will depend upon the willingness of the individual to relate the experience that has come to him to himself.

These visions which follow are described in exactly the form in which they were first written—that is, immediately after the vision was experienced. The words came of themselves, without the woman's conscious direction. Their exaggerated, apocalyptic style has not been altered, since this style has an evidential value.

"I saw myself standing upon a vast plain which was filled with a white light, very clear and penetrating. It stretched away to great distances. It seemed pregnant with life, yet no living thing was upon it. In my hand I held a chalice of white gold, very beautiful but empty. I looked upon it with amazement at its perfection of form. Then I heard a voice say, 'Fling it down, cast it from you.' I was filled with fear so that I began to tremble and the vessel seemed suddenly to become a sinister thing. I cast it upon the ground with great force, when to my astonishment it returned to my hand, this time filled with red wine. The vision faded, leaving me filled with awe and perplexity. What strange peril had lurked in that beautiful cup? Why did it have to be cast away before it contained the wine? Hours after, I heard again the voice, 'The sin of sins lies in nothingness; therefore cast away the vessel of emptiness and accept the wine of life.' I had a fear again at those words, for I knew that this dark wine was a communion with *all* life, not communion of love alone, or of suffering for righteousness' sake, but of all the forces that are alive in the blood stream of humanity."

She is confronted by a mystery, for in the old way which she had before known, it was "they who are without sin" who were secure. Now she is suddenly told by the voice that this very security is the greatest danger, that negation and emptiness offer greater perils than the acceptance of life with its possibilities of both good and evil.

The next vision was obviously related to the preceding one:

"I see a strange rock-bound coast. There is a sense of gathering storm and of anger in the wind. Then, in the vision, there appear great cliffs jutting out almost to the sea. There is a small beach, walled in so closely by the towering cliffs that it is almost like a cave, but open to the sky. I see a crowd of angry men and can hardly tell whether it is their voices or the voice of the wind that sounds like the roar of an angry beast. They have stones in their hands, but one is turning away shielding his eyes with his arm and the stone is dropping from his hand. Then I see on the other side a woman crouching by the rocks. She is terrified; she is also full of horror, yet with her horror is blended some strange fascination. She crouches back, bending over a hollow from which comes a light.

"Then I see that in the hollow is a baby from which the light streams, but the child himself is black. He is crowned by a crown of living light, not of white, but made of flickering flames of every color. They seem to grow from his head into a many-pointed, quivering diadem. As I look, I expect to see the soft brown eyes of a negro baby, but instead his eyes are of a clear, piercing blue. There is a sceptre in his hand but it, too, seems curiously living; on it is a snake's head buried in a mass of jewels, also alive; the most prominent of these is blue, the color of the child's eyes; from this jewel comes a ray of white light.

"At first the child seems naked, but then I see that he is wrapped in straw-like swaddling clothes from which he has thrust his arms. I know that he will break the bands entirely. The woman is in no sense a virgin, more a harlot, but one who has been caught in some great force beyond her understanding. She is full of terror at the being to whom she has given birth, yet she would protect it."

This concept of the black Messiah is not a new one. It comes from a sense of the need of renewal of life from its deepest spring, its lowest forms. This child is the source of light, potentially a source of power, but it is one born of an experience which self-righteous men would reject, just as the men in the vision would stone this woman who had given birth to an unacceptable savior.

Then a very different vision came with the same suddenness:

"I am in a field of dead, dry corn stubbles. There is neither light nor darkness, only a pregnant gray. I hear a voice say, 'Wait.' Then there is, not a wind, but a breath that seems to come up from the earth and to meet a breath from the sky. The corn stalks move as though a ripple ran from root to top, and turn a living green. I start to go to one but again the voice says, 'Wait.' The breath comes again, and on each stalk is a tiny blade. At each breath the grayness has grown a little lighter. For a long time it is still, then the breath comes again, and from the blades shoot out long tassels of corn silk. It is now almost light but the light is blue. Again the breath comes, and the stalks sway and become alive. The air now is clear blue as though I were standing in a sphere of blue, itself enclosed in a blue crystal. The stalks bend over until they form a circular tent about me through which streams the blue light. I have a feeling of deep content as though I were enfolded in life itself, and in the lives of myriad creatures.

"This vision was in the afternoon. At night the vision returned again. This time the form slowly changed. The outer crystal withdrew somewhat. The whole was shot through with lines of clearer more luminous blue. These formed themselves into a double five-pointed star. The light of the rays was more intense at the points."

The meeting between the earth and the breath from heaven meant to this woman a meeting of masculine and feminine principles. This meeting quickens the dead corn to a living green. Then the woman is standing within a circle of living corn, a symbol of fertility. There is no hurrying this life process. As it gradually proceeds the light which has been slowly growing becomes manifest as a five-pointed star, the star of relationship.

The fourth vision conveyed a very different suggestion:

"In the high heavens I see a figure intoxicated with the joy of power. He is sweeping across the sky, his white garments swirl about him as though caught up by many winds. His face is lighted by an almost delirious ecstasy, his lips are parted as though he would shout with the wind, his orange hair streams upward and outward like flame, he brandishes a sword of light. In front of him is a monstrous cloud. He plunges into this joyously as a diver might plunge into the sea. Suddenly the cloud bursts into flame, the blackness becomes masses of suffocating smoke. From out the smoke grow repulsive, evil figures. There is one gleam of light from his sword as he sinks, and then the heavy smoke swallows him."

It was as though in this vision she saw a warning of what might happen if she believed herself to be one with these great images. Had she believed that these great powers that she had perceived were hers personally, she would have attempted tasks far beyond her own ability and would have met with disaster, even as did this Animus figure who tried to sweep across the high heavens, and was plunged into the heavy smoke of confusion.

The next vision brought with it a renewal of energy, of life.

"My self stood far above in an abysmal blackness and below was a gulf of impenetrable dark. The self was wrapped in sheath-like garments dark as the spaces. Slowly it unwound these and flung them off, yet this was not done in the manner of one who expected to attain freedom but of one driven by despair, making ready to plunge into the primeval void. But when the last enfolding garment was unwrapped, there emerged a slender shaft of light, and this moved through space, lighting its own way, until it came to a pillar with a narrow door. Through this it passed, and entered a tall tower, windowless and still. Up through this it made its way and the chamber grew ever narrower, but as it rose it became aware that, through this narrowing space, life was pulsing its way upward, even as the shaft was rising. Then a knowledge came that this was a living tree. And suddenly the imprisoned shaft burst out into foliage, stretched out into the light. Myriad-leafed was the tree and each leaf was of a strange white, like to a metal more precious than gold or silver yet the substance of it was living. The light all about was white like the light of the full moon, but more marvelously fair. Then the slender shaft lost itself in the life of a quivering leaf but in losing itself found itself more truly than ever before."

At the time when this vision came, she seemed to herself very far removed from the peace and security of the vision of the corn field, where she had stood protected by the living green and surrounded by the light of the star. That vision seemed so far from attainment that she now felt within herself a dark void of despair. This was the abysmal blackness that she saw below her. It was something like the blackness into which the Animus figure had plunged, but in this vision she entered into it, not in exaltation, but with a desire to accept what might be in this gulf.

In doing this all the garments that protected that inner self were cast from her. It was as though this single, slender shaft which remained was like the essential unprotected self, which is paradoxically both separate from life and yet a part of life. It entered into the mystic tree, that includes all life. When this vision passed there was the sense of the renewal of energy, as though force from some great battery were flowing through the being. There was no identification with this divine potential, only a sense that in accepting this new process within the self these currents of life could flow in and vitalize the being.

The next vision was as follows:

"I looked upon space and I beheld darkness. In that darkness moved mysterious forces. Not like the gods of man's conceiving were they, but strange primeval beings born before the gods of human form. They were hooded in darkness. Through their fingers they drew the threads of blackness and ever wove them back and forth. I saw the rays that they made like the rays that stream inward from a many-pointed star or the converging of the lines of a many-sided crystal, but these rays were not of light but of darkness, and the darkness seemed to draw all things into it. Thus I knew that they were weaving a great void that had no form nor boundaries.

"Then from the center of the void rose a single shaft, whether of stone or of a gray and lifeless tree I could not tell. As the shaft rose the creatures fell away till nothing was left but the void with the shaft standing in the midst. Then I saw that on the shaft there hung a human figure that held within itself all the loneliness of the world and of the spaces. Alone, and hoping nothing, the One hung and gazed down into the void. For long the One gazed, drawing all solitude unto itself. Then deep in the fathomless dark was born an infinitesimal spark. Slowly it rose from the bottomless depth and as it rose it grew until it became a star. And the star hung in space just opposite the figure, and the white light streamed upon the Lonely One."

This vision presents in a different form the same idea as that in the old myth of Odin hanging for nine days over the void, 'A sacrifice of myself unto myself that wisdom may be born.'

It was strange that this figure should come to her instead of the figure of the crucifixion, for the Christian atmosphere in which she had been reared would quite naturally suggest the symbol of the cross as the way of spiritual life. The star, which the lonely figure calls up by an act of contemplation, is the symbol of individuation rising up from the depths of the unconscious. The feeling that came from this vision was not that the woman had herself attained individuation, but that she had perceived a light by which she could find her own way of life.

Several later visions have been omitted. Then came one which in some respects recalls that of Ezekiel:

"And I saw a wheel with many spokes, and within that wheel another wheel, and men were struggling within the wheel, some pushing and some holding back; and on their faces was the terror of a mighty unrest, and as they struggled a great sun came up, red like blood, and the sweat of their unavailing labor poured from them. And then I saw a great veiled figure, still as a snow-crowned mountain. She stooped and took the wheel in her arms and laid it in her bosom. And those within the wheel struggled mightily and tried to push the wheel from her breast, but it availed them nothing. And then the wheel began to turn. As it turned, it tore her flesh. The blood spurted forth, and in the stream of the blood came serpents and strange monstrous things, half man, half beast. And those that were within the wheel cried out with terrible cries. Still the wheel cut, till I could not see those within that were within because of the blood that poured over them.

"And then, even as I looked, the blood was gone, and the wheel was bathed in a white radiance, and it lay still, deep within her bosom. Then the veil fell from her face and though I gazed upon it, yet I saw it not, but I knew that some yet-blind thing within me had perceived and known it. And it was of an infinite, living tenderness."

The value of this vision lay in the emotional effect which it had upon the woman who saw it. It therefore seems best to present no interpretation save that which she herself gave:

"And the woman was love, and the wheel was life. So love must go veiled and cold as the eternal hills unless she take life itself into her bosom. And life will rend her and bring from her breast all the evil that lives there, and this she must suffer willingly if life at last is to come into her heart.

"I stood in a sphere of grayness. This gradually became clearer and more luminous, until I perceived a plain bathed in silver light. In the center of the plain arose a great, gleaming gate. Upon this gate sat a shrouded figure. As I drew near, I felt an icy wind, cold, and clear as crystal, and I knew it to be his breath. Then I perceived that the gate was beset by a multitude of little cloud-like ones, and as his breath came upon them, some were dispersed into many little wisps and floated off over the great abyss, and others were gathered together and became as slender shafts of light shot like arrows from the bow of life across the gate and into the great spaces of eternity."

The slender shafts of light recalled the earlier vision in which such a form appeared. Although the gateway suggested the gate of death, it was not necessary to assume that this vision asserted the immortality of the soul. It was enough to recognize that it asserted the enduring value of that which had acquired real individuality.

Out of this vision, as out of the others, this woman gained a sense of having had an original experience of truth. Concepts and ideas which would otherwise have been trite and dead took on reality and life. The value of the vision is that it is a direct, individual experience. Not everyone has, nor need he have, visions. They are only one means of contact with inner realities. But a person to whom visions come should give them the attention which is their due, should recognize them for what they are, should accept the fact that they are an immediate experience of what is for him an undeniable reality.

XV. DRAWING

INTRODUCTION

ANOTHER WAY in which images may appear is in plastic form, in picture or in sculpture. The term "unconscious picture" does not necessarily mean that the maker is unconscious of what he is going to paint so that the process is automatic. It applies to all pictures dealing with the inner images which portray unconscious content which has not been subjected to conscious manipulation. The portrayal may be a matter of infinite conscious care, or it may be a sudden crude expression, but the *content* must be of the image of the unconscious.

In one case, one reproduces material which has *already appeared* in dream or vision or phantasy; in the other, the picture directs itself. Then the maker does not know at the start what he is to draw, but allows the picture to unfold at the dictates of an inner force. In this case, the image becomes visible on the canvas before it is perceived by the conscious mind of the maker. He seems to draw out of some slowly dawning inner perception and is often greatly surprised at the picture which results. Here the image hovers on the brink of consciousness. It cannot be expressed in words, but, even as one may draw a diagram to illustrate or to clarify an elusive point in talking, so one may draw a picture in which the unapprehended concept will appear.

Then the image can be examined; for the picture, like a snapshot of a wild animal, can be studied after the animal itself has made off into the forest. One cannot then say, "Perhaps that animal was only a shadow, or perhaps I just thought he was there." He is in the picture. So the unconscious drawing holds the image in visibility. Such drawings are not representations of factual realities but of inner realities. They portray the actuality of the hidden image.

The term unconscious, therefore, may apply to any plastic representation of an inner image, from the picture coming apparently "of itself," to the carefully elaborated portrayal of a vision or dream, which by its arresting beauty seems to demand a body. The care and devotion given to such portrayal gives reality and depth to the experience of the image. The result may or may not be a work of art; the creation is an inner one.

It is most important that the maker should not confuse these values. Even the subjective value of such pictures differs. They may be mere portrayals of personal problems, no more related to art than a personal idiosyncrasy is to genius. The object is an inner creation, a change in the person. When they deal with the personal, they have no message except to the person. Even a perfect technique cannot give universal meaning to a picture which is related to a purely personal problem. Indeed, to approach the whole matter from this standpoint of inner value, one must become as a little child, willing to produce material naive and childish—to labor for hours over pictures which have no objective value, but which are records of inner experience.

Even the crudest drawing, however, may reveal startling elements and release a dynamic force in the maker. It may be that there is a mere impulse to draw without direction. One may begin with almost formless lines or sweeps of color, which gradually take on a shape revealing unexpected content. Or an image may arise suddenly when emotion overwhelms consciousness.

A woman who was invaded by such tempestuous emotions, too unrecognizable to be put into words, began to draw. The first pictures were almost formless, or composed of disintegrated, disconnected elements. Then came the picture (Plates 28 and 29). With it rose emotions so violent that they swept away her conscious control. It might have been the work of a three-year-old child, so far as artistic merit is concerned, but as an inner revelation its value was as great as the most finished work of art. Here is her terror; herself as an embryonic child threatened by the primitive mother animal, a mere destructive force, so ages remote from our conscious life that one could not formulate the concept in civilized language.

This picture would reveal very little to anyone who happened to look at it; in fact, it seems a meaningless scrawl. It was her own connection with it which made it so important. There was an instant release of emotion, of terror, of hatred, in waves of primitive intensity. Suddenly there leaped into consciousness a sense of all that she had feared in underground instinctual forces that she had felt around herself when she was a child.

Here on one side is a monstrous starfish, a primitive form of life. Its center is a sucking void surrounded with teeth—primitive destruction where relatedness should be. It is reaching out to draw her in. On the other side is a figure which represented to her these same elements in her own mother's unconscious which as a child, an intuitive, intellectual child, she had always feared. Now this picture showed the remote but strangely immediate menace. She was a thinking type. Her inferior function, feeling, was undifferentiated. In the picture the unformed, embryonic child (a head with practically no body) represented her feeling, which by its own nature was at the mercy of these forces she had intuitively feared.

Plate 27 gives another concept of the mother. Here is a figure falling to destruction, but the hands—conceived of as the hands of the mother—represent a force of security and love which reaches down to enclose that figure and to lift her up from disaster.

Often the mood is betrayed by the color. Turgid, malevolent masses change to clear or brilliant hues, as the dark mood becomes understood as mood, as something to be met, and as new feeling values become integrated. At times, mere color serves as a release; it makes apparent the mood that is in control and gives it a tangible form. Just as a tone of music has its counterpart in color, so a mood has its color expression.

A man who had no art or color training was often overpowered by moods of despondency. He began painting masses of formless shadows, malignant purple-red or ugly black. These he had to accept as something within himself. This process—accepting the mood as his own and expressing it in an outer form—seemed to give him power to exorcise it. As he described it, "I have no idea why it should be so, but after such painting I seem to be released from an engulfing darkness. I find myself better able to turn from the mood and give my energy to my work. There is a sense of light instead of blackness."

Children often use this method quite naturally when left to themselves. A little boy * had kept himself apart from all the activities of the classroom, but watched with interest the children who were painting. One day he too began to paint. His pictures were of dark, shadowy monsters. They were "The Terrible Things in the House at Night," "The Terrible Things under the Sea," "The Terrible Things outside the Window." One day he chose gay colors, green and yellow and blue. When someone remarked on the change he said casually, "Oh! the terrible things are gone. I have put them all in the pictures."

This child was reacting as a primitive does when he makes images or pictures. He gave his terrors form and objectivity—that is, he put them outside himself, where he could not only look at them but also share them with others. In this way they lost their magic power over him as an individual; their secret connection with him was broken.

We can make no positive assertions regarding the ancient records which the archaic man left upon the walls of his cave, but from our knowledge of symbolic forms still in use in ceremonials of primitive people we can perceive the subjective element of these strange beasts and demoniac figures. To objectify the inner image, to carve or paint the fear, the power, the mystery, gives a feeling that here is the objectified god who may be propitiated by ceremony or taboo, or whose power may be obtained through an identification.

Such a process to the naive mind places the thing feared outside the self, where it can be seen and dealt with. A nameless, formless fear is a menace that cannot be faced. But when it can be given a tangible form, something can be done about it. When the modern man who attempts to meet his psychic problems sees similar images, he recognizes them as the result of forces within himself. He gives them form, not in order to project them, but to make clear the subjective element with which he must reckon.

Unconscious pictures, therefore, connect us with the personages of our own inner drama; first on the level of our personal

* This child was in the class of Miss Ruth Shaw, and the case is used with her permission.

life, then on deeper and deeper levels, until one is brought into contact with the symbols of the universal unconscious. In the early stages of analysis, pictures frequently appear which show the dissociated and warring elements of the personality—the confusion existing in the unconscious. They have no center, lines are split, figures unbalanced, there is no connection between different parts; even the colors may be at war with each other; each element—like the autonomous complex—exists without relation to the rest, and so militates against the formation of a center.

Often, these pictures cannot be analyzed; for they are mere portrayals of inner confusion. At other times, the various elements can be seen as the personifications or images of the elements which are destroying the conscious control of the maker. Through a recognition of these elements one changes one's attitude toward them; one takes responsibility for meeting them. The mere portrayal has in itself no significance.*

When there is an intuitive connection with the images of the unconscious, but a lack of integration in the conscious life, this condition will often show itself in pictures. A woman who seemed to possess a very forceful personality was really herself possessed by the forces that welled up in her. She had keen, intuitive perceptions, but felt impelled to use them in situations which she did not fully understand and into which she had no right to intrude. She was therefore in continual difficulty which she could not com-

* Quite definitely, the imagery of unconscious material as illustrated here has a purpose totally dissimilar from that of Dada or the Surrealists. Dada disintegration is accepted as existing in and for itself. Apparently, it takes no cognizance of the orderly and integrating forces also appearing in the unconscious. Surrealism, with its effort to give validity to the inner realities and the irrational, is a revolt against the limitations of the conscious, a protest against the absurd pretense that we can limit reality to that which consciousness decides to accept. It turns from the monstrous irrationality of the World War to the equally monstrous irrationality of the war within the self, but it apparently is content to remain with the disintegrated elements of that irrationality instead of becoming aware of them for the purposes of understanding and of integration. Although the material of the unconscious is real, it would be a mistake to give to all this material an equal value. For, as in the external world, objects which may have equal reality have different values—the garbage pail and the banquet have equal *reality* but not equal or interchangeable value—so, in the material of the unconscious, there are purely personal idiosyncrasies and disintegrations which cannot be confused with the original experience of inner images. One must examine these personal elements and by painting or modeling them give them visibility; but they are important only in so far as they have obtained some hitherto unrecognized authority over the personality.

prehend, because acts which seemed reasonable, even necessary to her, appeared to others as irrational and often destructive.

At length she was forced to ask herself whether there was not some profound dissimilarity between her life as it appeared to her and her actual reality. She tried to express her bewilderment in pictures, for she could find no words for it, and the resulting attempts showed the disorientation of both her inner and outer life.

These first were painted at a time when she had decided that she wished an analysis but had not yet begun psychological work. Some were only masses of broken lines and discordant color, in some, symbolic forms appeared, such as a malignant black sun, a mountain which was a monstrous breast, a blue magnet drawing to itself a strange nonhuman eye. One picture showed the split between the conscious and the unconscious; above the central line a portrayal of her attempt, not yet very successful, to find a form, a pattern for her outer life; below, a jumbled mass of line and color showed the disorientation existing beneath the surface of her outer adaptation. She did not understand these pictures and made no real connection with them.

When she began analytical work, it became evident that the idea or the fear which possessed her at any special time had an autonomous power over her and that the irrational quality of many of her acts was due to this. She could not see this herself because, in each instance, the particular image which dominated her was completely real to her. Her dreams and phantasies began to deal with these images and seemed at first to add to her fear. She realized the necessity for examining this material of the unconscious and accepted analysis as she would an operation, dangerous yet necessary if she was to achieve psychological health.

Then at a time of great tension she drew a series of eighteen faces, seven of which are given in the picture section (Plates 12 to 18). Some of these rose spontaneously, others appeared while she was trying to concentrate upon the irrational fear connected with some person or situation. By drawing them she could perceive that the image moving in the unconscious was very different from the objective reality with which her fear was consciously connected. Her *mind* accepted this, but it had little effect upon her emotions.

The last picture of this series, which she called "The Face at the Bottom of the Pool," filled her with a terror which she could in no way understand, for the face seemed to her both beautiful and peaceful. It appeared to her when, in phantasy, she was looking into a very deep, almost bottomless pool. It fascinated her and seemed to attract her into the depth.

It was impossible at this time to show her why this fascination was her greatest danger for she had a definite opinion that her identification with these supra-personal forces gave her an enhanced personal value. Explanation only roused the Animus, who must prove the value of the archetypal identification, so that everything disappeared in argument. She did, however, get some separation from these images through this drawing and this did diminish her terror of invasion by the unconscious.

In each case she felt she must leave the picture with the analyst, and in leaving it, seemed to leave some of her terror with another human being who could carry it. It was a process akin to that of the little boy who painted the Terrible Things till they were "gone," that is, "put in the pictures."

After she had drawn these faces there came a long series of dreams and phantasies relating to old experiences, old fears. At intervals she painted other pictures. They began to show more balance and form, but often a color or a line which she *consciously* felt did not belong would intrude. She gave herself up to the direction of the unconscious, in no way changing the picture to suit her conscious desire. As she frequently said, "I did not like it but there it was and so I had to paint it that way." Often she wished to deny the picture and manipulate it so as to show what she *wanted* to feel about herself, but she had too much integrity to do this. Through the analysis of dream and phantasy she was beginning to get not only a new relation to the images of the unconscious but also a new relation to her life in the world, and to people.

Then came the picture shown in Plate 20. It is a luminous white circle enclosing a cross. It was done in black and white with pencil and turpentine. In the original this gives a luminous quality which was to her the essence of the symbol which she perceived. It took hours to paint in this way, and though the picture itself seems so very simple, the devotion with which she painted it, so as to give this interpretation of living light, gave her a sense of its deep meaning to her.

The circle enclosing the cross is an ancient symbol of the self and this picture was to her an experience of integration. That the objective value is small is of no consequence. Its inner value was very great. After she had painted this cross she said, "I feel for the first time as though I had a quiet place within myself."

She then wished to look once more at the picture of the "Old Man at the Bottom of the Pool," but as the pictures were still with the analyst, and as her desire was immediate, she tried to draw it from memory. To her surprise she found that she could not (without violating her unconscious impulses) reproduce the former picture, although the face was clear in her mental imagery. As she reached the mouth she drew the stream of energy which flowed from the mouth of the first face of the series. The outline which this stream had taken in the former picture remained, but now the energy seemed to withdraw into a deep womblike crater, and on either side of this appeared the figure of a woman, one guarding the opening, the other turning away in fear.

It now seemed to her important to review the whole series of images she had drawn early in analysis and she brought the pictures home from her analytical hour so that she might study them. She put them up in her room one at a time and found that she could at first connect with them only as they activated phantasy. These phantasies all were experiences of the archetype. When she tried to find her connection with them she discovered their meaning to her and began to understand that her fears were not merely personal but had a collective origin. These phantasies are given in her own words but in very abbreviated form. The personal associations and deductions made from them also have to be much abbreviated (Plate 12):

"I was in a land of the past. Men were gathering—no women were to be seen—there was an air of suppressed excitement. I spoke to a man in the crowd but he answered, 'Be still, woman. It is the day of the coming of the High Priest.' Then the High Priest appeared. He stepped forward, a commanding character, his deep-set eyes like burning coals in his tortured, intense face, lit up by the wild light of the fanatic. Over his eyes hung deeply arched eyebrows, like two great, black wings belonging to a second figure formed by his nose, a figure, headless, but moving with a mighty force toward destruction and chaos. Below the nose a grim downward line marked the mouth, from which grew a beard so heavy that it seemed like the dark waters of a swollen river, rushing from his lips.

"There was in the face of this Priest a strange combination of forces, the magician bending over his crucible, mixing dark potions of evil; the earnest apostle of truth, confusing revelation and power; the zealot, a slave to emotion, bound hand and foot by visionary half-truths; and most conspicuous of all, the Messiah, who was the Chosen One to point the way in the wilderness of ignorance and sin.

"It was a gaunt face, strong and powerful, marked with deep lines of anguish that served only to intensify the burning conviction of an obsessed mind. No hypocrite this, but a man lost in the whirlpool of an idea, devoured by the very creature he had set out to destroy. He held the crowd as a spider holds a fly—with sure intent to kill, only he did not know, in his exalted frenzy, that he held aloft the torch of death—for was he not the Chosen One?"

As she reviewed this phantasy, the stream of energy flowing from the mouth of the High Priest assumed an important meaning. It was the "word"—the masculine principle here directed by the dark forces of the unconscious so that its power became only the power to destroy.

At first she tried to connect this with her father, whose impassioned argument had often held her fascinated and whom she had feared in her childhood. But as she talked of her terror it became more and more clear that it was this force within herself that she should fear. For she could by the force of argument convince herself that a half-truth was absolutely true. She could argue herself into a place where she appeared, to herself and others, to be completely sincere. It was this archetype which she had projected upon her father, while all the time she herself was caught in the trap. For the first time she could see this and begin to understand why, when she was under this domination, her rationalizations appeared so unreasonable to other people.

A few days afterward, when she had been studying the next

picture, the following phantasy (also abbreviated here) arose (see Plate 13):

"I saw before me a priest with the inhuman face that I had drawn. He said, 'I am the Priest of the Lower Regions.' Suddenly we sank down, down, down into a cavelike room that was bare except for an appalling altar; across a long, rough board were strewn three skulls and some bones. In the center burned a tiny flame over which hung a crucified dove. 'The Holy Ghost,' he said as he knelt before it. I dropped upon my knees opposite him. His face was like a death mask from which peered two cruel, cold eyes. Over them hung abnormally arched eyebrows, like two dark sheds hiding the evil within. Relentless, inexorable, I knew that to touch him was to die.

"And then, as if apprehending my thought, he looked straight at me and said, 'Enter, but do not eat; kneel, but do not worship. This altar is consecrated to the soul which has become consumed by its own fire. Go now, for you do not belong here.'"

As she talked this over, the Priest became to her the Priest of Death who had crucified the truth, here the dove, the Holy Ghost. Its meaning became clear only gradually as, through the discussion of many associations, she perceived the working of this force within herself and its relation to the High Priest of the former picture. It was the obsessive intuitive idea which, taking possession of reason and emotion, ruthlessly destroyed all facts or all forms of truth which might threaten its supremacy. Under the domination of this idea she was indeed "the soul consumed by its own fire"—the fire of fanatical conviction.

Here the illogical, creative quality of phantasy appears. The Priest, who serves this altar of Death, and who would logically hold her to the same service, tells her that she does not really belong there. The phantasy therefore shows her the difference between her condition when she first drew this face and her present situation.

Her interpretation of the next picture (see Plate 14) was a mixture of phantasy and memory. She saw herself as a child standing before her father, and terrified by his severity. Fearing his invective she tried to appeal to his feeling. At once his masculine image became obliterated by a female face rising from within himself, and superimposed upon his own.

"It is the face of Medusa. I see the horrible ringlets curled like inverted snakes around her head; from her eyes dart the cunning and evil of a serpent, coiled to spring; and on her forehead is a diagonal black line, the shaft of a crooked, poisoned arrow that forms her mouth. I stand before her as I stood before my father, a strange blackness enveloping me, the pain becoming so intolerable that it blots all else from my mind, and as I stare at the snaky head a heaviness creeps over my limbs. I become drowsy. Slowly and coldly I am turning to stone."

It is as though she actually *saw* his Anima in one of its archetypal forms, in the Medusa image which, ruling in his unconscious, could rise in a cold emotion and paralyze all feeling in himself and others. This Medusa quality seemed still to overcome her whenever she felt in others a withdrawal of feeling. Hence it made her completely irrational in judging and acting in situations where she inferred coldness or severity.

But this was not the only interpretation which this phantasy bore for her. Studying it, she could see that there were times when—without her having any sense of withdrawal or coldness on the part of other people—her own feeling would suddenly become frozen. She was then identified with this Medusa image, and, in order to obtain power over others, would deliberately chill *any* warm feeling that was trying to live in a situation which she wished to dominate.

The phantasy activated by the next picture (Plate 15) was as follows:

"I was tied to a pole in a circle of savages. Wildly they danced about me the ceremonial Dance of Death.

"Suddenly from the circle one of the most inhuman and ferocious of them emerged. Two long, black snakes seemed to fall from the top of his pointed head, and with a shudder I realized these were his eyebrows. His eyes were like serpents' heads. An arrow marked the shape of his fierce, cruel mouth, and the tribal mark on his forehead gave the illusion of feathers at the end of the shaft.

"A knife flashed and buried itself deep into my breast. The howling circle of beasts closed in, I saw my own blood stream into a jug they held beneath me, and as I lost consciousness I felt the spearpoint, now blood-tipped, plunged like a branding iron into my forehead.

"When I awoke, an old, old woman was sitting beside me. 'You will live,' she said, 'but until you burst asunder the bonds that held you in that circle, and subdue the savage with his own magic, that mark on your forehead will be a torture and an agony to you.' Then coming closer she bent over me and whispered, 'Fear not—your spirit is strong—that mark is the birth symbol.'"

The key to this phantasy lay in the words of the old woman, who, she felt, was the wise woman of the tribe. The woman had said, "Until you subdue the savage with his own magic, that mark will be a torture and an agony," and again, "That mark is the birth symbol."

The "magic" of the savage was derived from the intensity of unrestrained emotion which gathered a supra-personal force from an identification with collective forces. The savages in the phantasy were infected with a communal emotion which, as it increased in intensity, gave their acts a ceremonial magic. The fearful mark that they made on her forehead was a mark of initiation. Such an initiation could not take place unless there were forces within herself which made her akin to the savage and which, so long as they possessed her, had an almost magically destructive influence in her life.

In order to understand what these forces were she had to reconsider the times when her emotions had possessed her. She remembered how, as a child, she had been "torn to pieces" because of her rebellion at demands of civilization that ran counter to her own impulses—a rebellion that she did not then dare to express. This attitude of rebellion had persisted. She recalled times, not so far distant, when, "I felt that my emotions must be expressed or else I was denying my inner truth. I therefore felt a supreme rightness in taking what my emotions demanded. It gave me a feeling of guilt to restrain my emotion." Thus she was always being held responsible for destructive acts which she felt were not her fault, since they had been caused by inner necessity. And so she found it almost as difficult to live in the civilized world as a savage would, and it was, indeed, a "torture and an agony" to her.

Now for the first time she could perceive the meaning of

possession by the affect, and how this differed from conscious choice. She saw, too, how possession by the affect had delivered her over to a form of *participation mystique*, for she would also be swept away by the emotion of others, and this participation she mistook for depth of feeling. Emotion, therefore, whether it arose within herself or assailed her from without, delivered her over to her primitive side.

While she was possessed by the emotion, she was one of the savages. But if she herself possessed this magic, that is, had conscious control over it, she could subdue the savage within herself. In this way the second remark of the old woman in the phantasy —"That mark is a mark of birth"—became clear to her. For the separation of herself from the affect, and the understanding of it, was the first step in integration.

As she looked at the next picture (Plate 16): "I heard a man's voice which I knew I had heard before. Suddenly I was swept out into wild waves. I was in a tiny raft in midocean and a glorious wind tossed me about on the white-capped sea. A fierce exultation overcame me, a sense of infinite power. I was strong and unafraid; Christ walked upon the water, so could I. Then, as suddenly darkness fell, a great wave swept over me; I was struggling, impotent.

"As I sank I seemed to see the face of this *me* that was swept under. It was the face of the Mad Madonna. Every feature was distorted, all perspective lost. The eyes were turned inward, brooding on the madness within. The cross on her forehead was no longer the cross of spiritual insight but the black cross of madness, for she had abandoned herself to an impersonal force that, like a whirlpool, sucked her down."

As she discussed this phantasy she saw that it had been actuated by the memory of an early experience. The voice was that of a man whom she had met in her youth. He was convinced that man contained within himself the infinite power of God, and that this power was infallibly good. Finding her an eager disciple, he had spent hours with her, exhorting her to trust this power, to give herself completely to it. Under his influence she had become intoxicated by a religious ecstasy which swept her out of all reality and which was followed by a profound depression.

On discussing this she realized that she had never really given up her secret belief that she could return to this experience and someway live in it continuously without disaster. This belief had its roots in early childhood when, afraid of the outer world, she had retreated to religious phantasy. As she grew older this had been a form of escape from the task of meeting life and understanding her own part in it. It was therefore that false introversion which leads only to inflation.

The phantasy arising from the next picture (Plate 17) was this: "I seem engulfed in a flood of blind suffering. I am like a defenseless city open to air raids. The bombs of all human suffering rain down upon me, causing chaos and disaster. In the intensity of suffering I seem to live a heightened, a Christlike life. Yet this Christ that I have followed is blinded, and cannot see the cause he serves nor the values of the life he abjures. As I study the picture of the Blind Christ I see one crucified for a crusade that has little value. The motive has been Christlike, the anguish almost intolerable, but there are dark blinders on the eyes of the leader, the mark of the hangman is on his forehead. He has become the public executioner."

Through this she became aware of a deeply buried identification with martyrdom. Self-sacrifice as an end in itself had so strong an appeal that she lost all discrimination as to the results produced. The intolerable ecstasy of pain had become a goal of life. *Participation mystique* with all suffering was to her a mark of the Christ. The Blind Christ becomes the public executioner because he kills life. He is the direct enemy of the Christ who came that we might have life and have it more abundantly. She saw how the split between the love of life and the desire for crucifixion and the various forms of *participation mystique* had warred against any possibility of establishing her own individual center.

Next she looked at the picture (Plate 18) which had before filled her with such terror. This "Face at the Bottom of the Pool" was the face of a very old man whose eyes were closed as though in sleep or deep withdrawal, and yet she had felt that it could draw her down with magnetic power.

After studying this face again, she wrote down her interpretation of it. "I had always liked being alone because I could enter a world that was closed to me in my life with people. When I was by myself I often closed my eyes and listened to an impelling voice calling—calling. I had heard it ever since I was a child; it seemed to have a power of guidance, a complete authority. When I concentrated upon it I could literally feel something going on within me, like the great, unseen tide of the ocean. Sometimes I felt as if I were a hollow form through which a mighty force seemed to pass, and then again it was as if I was that force itself, and all else that existed was but a phantom and a shadow. I knew that this inner life was rich in beauty and truth, but there were shadows in it that I did not understand.

"But giving oneself up unreservedly to any force carries with it perhaps more danger than value. On the one hand it brings one very near the source, but on the other, the self is lost and with that loss discrimination also goes.

"When I drew the picture of 'The Face at the Bottom of the Pool,' I did not understand the difference between being lost in this deep source of wisdom, and being able to gain strength from it, and yet at the same time establish a resistance to it and to be separate from it. When I look at this face I realize that the wisdom here is sleeping. It possesses no consciousness. It is in the depth of the unconscious and is itself unawakened."

She had now come far enough in her own integration to understand the terror which this face at the bottom of the pool had caused in her, for she realized that until she had established some center *within herself*, she had no power to withstand the lure of the unconscious. She now recalled the blue magnet of her earlier paintings. At the time she had interpreted it as spiritual power; now she saw that it depicted the hypnotic force the unconscious had always held for her.

The mandala of the cross in the circle (Plate 20), painted so long after these pictures, showed that she had, through long analytical work, begun to establish an inner center. It was her sense of this inner security that enabled her both to revaluate the pictures, and to enter into her archetypal phantasies without losing her own identity. The appearance of the archetype was no longer a mere invasion which destroyed individuality but, through the intervention of consciousness, it had become a real experience, one which gave her a new adaptation to life.

This change within herself, she felt, must have shown itself in the changes which had seemed so imperative when she tried to reproduce from memory the face of the old man of wisdom. She now studied the face (Plate 19) which had resulted from this attempt at reproduction. This picture suggested to her masculine creative energy directed *within*, so that it poured into the womb of the unconscious (the Great Mother), there to produce new life. It symbolized the creative power of the unconscious, the power which is continually reforming and reshaping the individual.

As she studied the two women standing at either side of the craterlike womb she realized that they were sides of herself. One woman, the regressive infantile side, now shrinks back in fear. This is the side that hitherto had retreated to the unconscious as a child retreats to the mother to avoid personal responsibility, and that relies on the authority of the wisdom of the unconscious to avoid the responsibility of individual choice. It is the side that fears the fruit of knowledge, that would remain ignorant of the reality of good and evil, lest it put upon the individual the burden of responsibility. So in the picture this woman shrinks back in fear of rebirth.

On the other side is a figure of individual strength quietly awaiting what life will bring forth. She knows herself to be part of this life and yet apart from it. She develops through acceptance and understanding. It is a figure of the newly developing self—perceiving rebirth as a continuous process of life.

An intimation of this process was shown in the next mandala (Plate 21). Here a luminous five-petaled flower appears within the circle. This was to her a feminine symbol—the flower of relatedness. It seemed to connect her with her center *as a woman*. A final mandala which could not be included here brought together the two others. Here the four-petaled flower of individuation appears in the circle, but its color is the red of the Eros principle.

Intuitions which are hardly conscious often appear in unconscious drawings. In the series of archetypal faces just described was one (the Medusa) which showed the daughter's perception of her father's Anima. In the series (Plates 34-38) which were drawn by a young man the mother's Animus appears.

This youth thought of his mother as gentle, defenseless, almost a child. Even though he resented her clinging demands, he never realized that they were power demands. He felt a rather sentimental pity for her. But when he started to draw her picture it took the form of a cat creature (Plate 34), with embryonic legs that could not hold her erect and long arms reaching out with cat claws to hold him. Then the Persona appeared with crown of thorns and halo (Plate 35). Then he tried to draw a picture of her "suffering self," which, to his surprise, emerged on paper as a *masculine* face, weeping crocodile tears (Plate 36). Then he drew a picture of her as a young woman (Plate 37). She was enclosed in a locked fence of steel—an unsexed and a self-imposed isolation. Suddenly he felt an intuition of a reality hitherto unperceived. Almost automatically he began to draw a picture of her as he now saw her (Plate 38). Here the Animus, a complacent figure, had taken over the very center of her woman's being. She was no longer a woman, but a Persona shell enclosing the Animus.

These pictures made clear to him an irrational fear of his mother which he had projected upon all women. After analyzing these pictures he drew the face of the unawakened Anima (Plate 39), a face that could not rise to consciousness until he had drawn the other pictures.

The Animus and the Shadow both appear in a woman's drawings, only a very few of which are included. Plate 63 shows the Shadow blinding the right eye—destroying the conscious vision. Plate 64 shows the destructive libido, a wild horse who holds her in his mouth. Plate 65 shows her sense of impotent fear as the negative Animus looms above her. In Plate 67 a young boy—the new Animus form—appears between the Shadow and the negative Animus, while she stands beseeching them not to shut her from this value. Plate 66 appeared to her to be the sacrifice of the superior function. Here she drew a figure plunging from its heights —the function which before had been too high. Plate 68 was drawn long after these and shows the birth of the new potential. The aesthetic value of these drawings is such as to suggest that they were done by a trained artist. This is not the fact. The woman who drew them was wholly without experience or training in this field. It was only in her portrayal of the material of the unconscious that the artistic quality became evident.

A woman's awakening to the value of the instinctual side of herself is shown in Plate 30, where in the rocky cave arises the dark woman of the flame with the symbol of life upon her breast. At her feet is the five-pointed star, the star of relationship. In the foreground the woman herself appears lifting up the serpent—the old instinctual life—which in this place of transformation is becoming the blossoming rod. In the next picture (Plate 31), the fire has become a flaming tree; at its top appears the four-pointed star of individuation.

The tree appears repeatedly in unconscious drawings. Plate 75 shows the Tree of Life. Its roots are living fire; its top is the chalice of life, the Holy Grail; one leaf has been broken and from the wound fall drops of blood. This, to the maker, signified the human life not yet made whole. Plate 76 shows this symbol of the tree in a very different aspect. A figure is kneeling before a tree with fire around its roots and at its top a folded bud of flame. The figure is facing the serpent, very evidently a serpent of sexuality, and between them is the mixing bowl, a symbol of the bringing together of different elements, that is, a symbol of experience.

Instinctual forces often appear in pictures that are far less evolved. One of the pictures from a series made by another woman (Plate 32) shows the creative energy emerging from the waters, and, as it emerges, breaking the yoke of the unconscious. The yoke is a classic symbol of submission. It was the low gateway through which the captive or prisoner passed. Here the energy pushes up the bar and rises to freedom. Plate 33, drawn by this same woman, depicts an eyeless serpent, unconscious feminine earth wisdom, awakening to the sun, the symbol of the dawning of new life.

The experience is equally valid whether appearing in dream or drawing. In the chapter on the self, there is cited a man's dream of the fire and the crystal, the fire symbolizing the inner energy destroying the old adaptation but leaving the crystal, the symbol of the individual value. In the series of pictures (Plates 69-74) drawn by a woman, a process essentially the same is represented. To this woman there came, as a sudden vision, a great circle of almost impenetrable blackness. Then upon this appeared very brilliant spokes in the form of two crosses, one of red and one of blue. A voice said, "This must now be considered." Later this image arose again but this time there were circles about the crosses, one red, one blue. Then from the bottom a flame broke out and swept through the entire circle, piercing the circumference. Now she began to paint the three pictures from memory. The first two pictures (Plates 69 and 70) seemed to have an archaic quality, very remote from the maker. Yet since the voice had been imperative they had to be considered. Then, as she was painting the third picture, the flame seemed of itself to change form and to become like a great bud of fire, and in the flame there appeared the face of a man, the spirit within the flame. At the center was a small fragment of blue which had not been destroyed by the fire. When this picture (Plate 72) was painted it seemed imperative that the background of the whole should be darkness—and the picture conveyed a sense of the approach of death and was so interpreted. But these three pictures (Plates 69, 70, and 72) gave to their maker a sense of some incompleteness which made them seem like an insincerity—as though evidence had been given which repressed important facts. So the picture of the destructive fire was now painted as it had first appeared (Plate 71), and as the pictures were placed together so that their meaning might become clearer, it was, of inner necessity, the third of the series. Slowly it became apparent that this death might easily be, not a physical death, but the death of the old adaptation; and that the fire, the inner energy, which destroyed the old form, contained within itself the living spirit which might animate the new. A new picture began to form itself (Plate 73). This evolved very slowly and grew a little at a time as it was painted. In the center of a sea of grayness lies an egg guarded by two fish. The sea conveys a feeling of undefined life and movement. About this gray sea winds a dark gray river which, too, seems full of potential life. The waters of the personal unconscious are here enclosed by the great stream of the collective unconscious. From this stream forces of new life break and are shown in the colors at the four points of the picture—the blue of the Logos, the red of the Eros, the green of new life and the yellow of the earth. These in their time will penetrate to the egg, which the fish now guard until this impregnation can occur. That is, a period of quiet and withdrawal must be accepted if a new value is to be born. The spirit which had appeared in the flame is now confined in the egg and must find a new form of life. Such pictures put upon one the burden of an inner necessity; nothing can be hurried, nothing manipulated. Much later, after a number of intervening pictures the mandala (Plate 74) was painted.

She saw a great circle of violet light. A thousand petalled lotus appeared enclosing the four petalled Golden Flower. A four pointed star of blue rested upon the golden petals. The center was hidden by violet mist. Then it began to glow until it became an inner circle of pure red light surrounding the figure of a woman. Her mind had expected a Buddah encircled in white light to take form within the heart of the lotus. Instead this figure of woman rose by its own authority and claimed central place. As she contemplated it she realized that this red had a warmth and quiet of its own and that its rays were of radiance rather than of restless flame. It was a fire that warmed rather than consumed and the woman at its center was the archetype to which she must now give devoted attention.

She was in a place of transition. Her life was taking on new form. At times of change it is so easy to stray from the center because a sense of nonfulfillment, or a success that holds out ambitious promises makes one seek new goals. But these are times when one must stay quiet within the center, deepening the connection with the central law of one's own nature. She pondered upon the woman law, the law of Eros manifest in love as lover, in material creativity, in friendship, in its ever broadening aspects of impersonal love that reaches out into the world in understanding of relatedness, and also in the dark shadow side of Eros in personal and impersonal life. She asked of the woman, "What have you to say to me in this place where I now stand? How shall I as woman meet these present problems? What will the shadow try to do? What counsel will you give?" Slowly the woman at the center gave answer, directing her toward a still distant goal. A mandala like this remains with us throughout life, for the archetype does not change but our relation to it changes with our inner growth.

Drawings and paintings done during analyses furnish records of important crises in the individual's analytical history. This is shown in the three sections which follow.

PART I

THE FOLLOWING series of pictures, which succeeded one another with great swiftness, forced themselves so dramatically upon the screen of consciousness of the man to whom they appeared that there was no escaping their deep significance. There were no dreams. The pictures took the place of dreams and furnished material for equally illuminating associations.

Though I speak of these pictures as coming of themselves, the door to the unconscious had been opened by conscious choice. The man who drew them had for many years conscientiously lived in accordance with a selfless ideal and had tried to meet the increasing difficulties of his life in a reasonable and controlled way. With the growth of these difficulties, he felt a greater and greater inner tension, until he felt compelled to seek some sort of relief. No rational approach to the problem helped at all. He decided, therefore, to see what was really happening within himself.

Without this decision, these images would probably not have come through to the conscious. They might have remained vague fears, gaining in destructive power, drawing away conscious energy, but never appearing with a clarity which would permit them to be recognized. The conscious did not decide what images should appear, but by permitting their appearance and by giving them attention, made them reveal their meaning, at least in part. Although he acquired almost at once some sense of the significance of the images he drew, he could not until much later make a vital connection between them and the life that he had to live.

The man was of an artistic, sensitive nature. In his early life he had been overshadowed by the forcefulness of a masterful and managing mother. He had taken refuge in daydreams, withdrawing from the pressure of forces which he feared within himself and which he felt pressing upon him from without. He tried quietly to go his own way and to attract as little attention as possible. There was something of the identification with the martyr in his patient endurance, his desire to turn the other cheek.

This early attitude continued to be his refuge in middle life. While it gave him a sweetness and charm and a sympathetic attitude toward all who were dependent upon him, it did not develop his more aggressive forces. He found himself inadequate to face certain situations. The strength and commanding qualities necessary for his own manhood were repressed, showing themselves only in occasional outbursts that seemed to belong to some other being. Life had forced him into the business world, where his artistic, irrational sides were denied expression except as they could find it in professional work. It seemed selfish to demand a time and place for them. It was more in keeping with his ideas of duty and sacrifice to give them up than to fight for them.

His deepest affection had been given to his youngest daughter, a tempestuous, power-loving, dominant child, recognizing no law but that of her own desires. Toward this child he had an infinite patience; he had made many sacrifices for her, and it was her difficulties that led him to consult an analyst. His own problem, however, needed more immediate attention. Nevertheless, he could get no dreams. He was aware of a chaos of emotions concerning his situation, and these had first to be dealt with.

His first intimation of forces trying to break through into consciousness was that at night he began to hear the telephone ringing, when in reality there was no sound. Part of him knew that this was a subjective experience, yet the sense that someone was trying to communicate with him from a great distance was so strong that several times he took up the receiver and asked who was calling, only to be told that there was no one on the line.

Then, equally clearly, he seemed to hear the footsteps of someone following him. This person, he felt, would overpower him from behind. The analyst told him to try to get a visual image of what this being was, to turn in phantasy and face what he saw. This picture (Plate 22) was what he saw—himself and the beast-man that had arisen from his own unconscious, the Shadow, now powerful and close at hand.

This beast in the picture was old, far older than the man himself; it represented to him primitive instinctual desire, lust, animal strength, and all the Shadow side to which he had denied life because he feared that it would destroy greater values.

He had been conscious of the beast only at those rare intervals when his gentle reserve had broken, and bitter resentment and anger had come through; and at times when sexual phantasy beset him. Now he saw this beast-man as part of himself, a part which was going with him wherever he went, which was living on his own inner energy, growing strong at the expense of his conscious life, but from which he himself was gaining no power. He saw that this beast was not something peculiar to himself, but that for him it was peculiarly powerful because it had been repressed.

In the examination of his emotional life there was brought to light much that had been hidden in the relationship which had seemed to him quite ideal. This was his devotion to the daughter who was in such need of his love and understanding. His own emotions, his sexuality and virility, were all dominated by this strange unconscious relationship. It had masqueraded as only protective, paternal love; but in reality it had sapped the energy which, as a man, he should have given to other relationships and it even fed upon his creative talent as well, for his daughter had usurped the place of his Anima. In many instances it had made him unfair to others, afraid to assert himself where assertion was needed, aggressive only in protection of that relationship which secretly fed the beast.

All this had been hidden so deep within himself that he had really been unaware of its existence. He had to see this element of his love in its stark reality before he could realize how strong a part of his inner life it was. Now it had a form that he could recognize. He could, if he would, become aware of it, and by seeing it objectively could face it, as he could not face this vague, shadowy, formless terror that had followed him. For this relationship had in it a strong element of sexual desire, inadmissible to consciousness. He could quite truthfully say he had never thought of such a thing. The vague intuitions had translated themselves into fear; yet the desire could not be conjured away, because the child was actually living out masculine elements that he had repressed, and so had captured his libido.

When the strength and force of the instinct become associated with an unacceptable idea, they are repressed, for fear the undesirable element may take over the dominance. To admit the masculine strength and desire would be to admit its existence in this relationship, which was unthinkable. He therefore tried to cut himself off completely from the unconscious, and by so doing repressed not only the beast but all the creative energy in the unconscious. So when this man could admit that below the threshold of his consciousness his instinctual sexual energy was all being given to a relationship which he would completely repudiate in his conscious, then he was able to examine this situation, ask why these things should be so, and begin to see what the unconscious was really trying to accomplish.

Often the real, though futile and twisted, purpose of such emotional urges is the fulfillment of an inner necessity which has been early thwarted by life. It may be a long task to unravel such a purpose, but as long as this man could say, "This is quite impossible. I could not possibly feel a sexual desire toward a child of mine," he was at an impasse, for every association which would cast light on the situation was repressed. But when he admitted this fact to consciousness, he could say, "What is there in this child that has such an unconscious hold over me?"

If we can discover back of the present conflict the original urge, we can see the thing in its right relation to the present. Here was a so-called "incestuous impulse," an almost compulsive emotional demand consciously accepted as duty toward a dependent child, but really arising from inner confusion through the need of possessing what she had, that is, her emotional and masculine strength. Labeling this as incestuous is misleading and does not reach the real motive. One felt in this girl an energy and force always seeking expression. Such a being was a challenge to the beast, to the instinctual dominant force of the male. But it was more than that. It was an image of a force which existed in his own psyche and which, rightfully developed, grown-up and civilized, would enable him to command his own life. This he was trying to take into himself through a kind of *participation mystique* with the girl; it was when she was most destructive in her self-assertion that he seemed most fascinated by her.

For him to see this force in its primitive, unconscious power as an undeveloped side of the self, is what is meant by accepting the beast, taking it into oneself. It involves a recognition of the instinctual, unlived side. It is like adopting a savage, untrained child and educating it so that it can live without destroying the values of the conscious cultural life. This man needed the strength of the beast, but not in beast form. Things are remade when blind obstinacy becomes determination directed by conscious choice; animal sexuality takes on a different meaning when united with feeling.

For so often the ideal or theory of life suited to one phase can no longer serve its purpose in another. The sensitive, artistic, irrational type needs to protect its own creative values by refusing to be forced too early into an aggressive masculine adaptation. The problem of the average man is to accept his Anima. But with a man like this, the danger is that he will become identified with his Anima, and then his problem is to break this identification and live out the masculine elements which have been buried in the unconscious.

This did not all unfold itself from the drawing. Such understanding comes gradually. But from the first picture he got so much that he felt he must continue to draw. In the next one he was looking into a deep pit. There he saw a sphere of white, and over it leaned demoniacal monsters who seemed to be conferring about this sphere of light which they held in their power. One closely resembled the beast that he had turned and faced. The others he could not at the time recognize, but they afterward became more real to him and were associated with terrors and weaknesses within himself.

As he looked at this picture, he felt that this abyss lay within himself, that the sphere which he saw was his own unique value, now in the power of those demons; and great surges of fear and weakness came over him. He almost abandoned so perilous an adventure. He had a great temptation to turn his back upon the whole thing and to try to thrust it all down again into the unconscious. But another side of himself realized that he could never do this. Having once seen these things, he knew he must find a way to meet them. It is such a time of peril that is the test of one's courage and honesty. Having seen the danger, he accepted it and again began to draw.

He found himself standing in a great field of ice. A desolate plain stretched before him. Far beyond were mountains, also of ice, but back of these was a deep red glow, as though fires still burned. Now in front of him rose a great figure, terrible and forbidding, shrouded in black, with a face hidden under a black cowl. Before this figure he was as a tiny pigmy. He saw no way of passing, yet an inner voice that he had begun to hear told him that he could not turn back (Plate 23).

He could no longer see his relation to his daughter as something warm and simple. Nor had he yet developed any new connection in which he could consciously use his feeling. This gave him the sense of being in a region of ice, and though in the distance he could see the red glow, telling him that the warmth still existed as a possibility within himself, the way to it was barred by this black, threatening figure.

As the determination to understand and to go on grew within him, he made another drawing in which a great figure appeared, this time that of an old man of wise, impersonal majesty (Plate 24). He himself, still infinitesimally small, stood among mountains of ice, and this great figure that towered high into the heavens reached out its hand to take the pigmy man as a pawn and move him wherever it would. He felt that these two figures were really one, and that their deep significance for him lay in their immensity and his insignificance.

As he thought this over, he became conscious of one of his most deeply buried attitudes to life. He had always been overshadowed by a sense of doom; there were times when he had almost no realization of himself as a self-directing individual. He felt that men were pawns, moved about in the strange game of life. Sometimes the figure of fate might be dark and menacing and destructive, and sometimes wise and impersonal; but always something against which man was really powerless, no matter how he might struggle, or how cleverly he might pretend that he was shaping his own life.

At first, these pictures merely served to intensify his conviction of doom, but in the discussion of them he had to defend this conviction against an opposite point of view. He cited instance after instance from the past in which he had found himself helpless at a critical moment. As he discussed these, he began to wonder whether, after all, with a little more understanding, he might not have handled things differently.

In the next picture, he had crossed the plain and was standing before the great mountains of ice. In front of him was a doorway which, though it led straight into one of these ice mountains, was surrounded by a pale, gold light. High over his head, as in protective covering, was stretched the great hand of the old man of wisdom. The way seemed to lead only into limitless regions of ice, yet he knew that for some reason he must pass through that door.

Passing through this door meant to him entering an unknown land, his own unconscious, a region yet to be explored. Up to this time, he had had no conception of the dual nature of unconscious energy. Since he had always tried to repress everything which did not conform to his conscious ideas, he had only experienced the unconscious when it broke through and overpowered him with irrational fears or violent and hysterical emotions. Therefore, the idea of voluntarily exploring the unconscious really seemed to him the most perilous of all ideas. But a *voluntary* exploration was clearly indicated in the picture. The figure of fate had assumed, for the first time, a protective quality; but its protection did not extend beyond the entrance to the mountain. If he chose that way, he must enter alone. Yet he knew that this was the only way of discovering what forces within himself had been instrumental in making him feel that he was only a pawn.

Then in phantasy he entered the mountain, and found himself in a cave in the bowels of the earth. Before him was a huge rock which, he felt, contained the treasure. At first he had not enough strength to win through to the treasure. Then he had a sense of energy descending upon him and, looking up, perceived the hand of the old man of wisdom stretched above him. From this hand streams of energy were descending, and entering into himself and also into the rock. Immediately after this phantasy had come to him, he painted it (Plate 25). The experience was translated into his outer life, and he was able to complete very rapidly and very effectively a creative piece of work. He realized that the energy which he had brought to bear on this piece of work was irrational, that it arose from the unconscious, and that, if he could keep his connection with the unconscious, it would remain available.

After this he drew a picture in which he was standing by the side of a river. Across this strode a huge, naked man. Here was another archetypal figure, the figure of masculine energy. He was lifting up his arms to this figure, as though entreating it to give him some of its strength. This picture was a great surprise to him. He had expected and feared that the next picture would be a picture of monstrous and destructive forces. Instead, he was confronted with an image of masculine self-determination.

Then there rose in him a desire for a relationship with a woman which he could consciously accept, and in which he would assume the masculine role. He had had a vision of such strength, but had as yet no understanding of the things still to be conquered within himself. When he tried to draw a picture of an embrace of man and woman, he was amazed to find that the figures expressed nothing but a mutual dependence that had no hint of strength or purpose. Here were no man and woman, only two figures, undifferentiated, clinging to each other in an embrace that was not even passion, only spineless acquiescence.

The emotion roused by this picture was more intolerable than the fear which had been aroused by the picture of the devils. He saw that much that he had thought of as unselfishness was actually weakness. This picture was no more an expression of his entire emotional life than was the beast an expression of his whole self. It did not say, "This, you see, is what you are." It said, "Be careful, this weakness is present in your way of life. It is part of you. Look at it, face its reality." At this time, however, the whole idea of this picture was so completely unacceptable to him that he attempted to block the flow of the unconscious by consciously producing a series of petty and rather facetious pictures, in which he tried to make light of the whole matter.

But he could not interrupt this process, except momentarily. He was about to draw another of those satirical pictures when there rose in front of him a huge temple, so vivid and so impressive that the small picture of his conscious imagination was blotted from his mind. He began to draw the temple. It appeared like a rectangular block of black marble. From the center rose a high tower whose top was bathed in red light. Great shafts of shadow rose from the ground and penetrated the sky like a dark aurora. The temple was manifestly phallic; it was the archetype of the phallus, the symbol of the masculine principle, virility, creativeness, not mere sexuality. He knew that here was the portrayal of a force much greater than himself, but one which could energize him because he was a man. For the first time he felt that force as really within himself.

After this, he drew a picture of himself standing alone and looking straight ahead. He felt able to do this now for the first time. From this perception, the next picture grew. A man and a woman stood facing each other, and in each figure was a sense of independent being. If he could stand alone as a man, he could also make an adult relationship. This, of course, was only a concept of what might grow in the future, but it was a concept which differed so greatly from the old unconscious desire, the desire to find in another the energy he should seek in himself, that it gave to him a new sense of purpose.

Then again he was on the great plain, but now the ice had gone, and the plain was illuminated by a huge blue sun that sent shafts of light far into the sky. This picture gave him a sense more of great solitude than of connection with the light. This sun with its shafts of blue light connected in association with the old Gnostic symbols, in which the blue is the color of the Logos, the abstract masculine principle. It was an abstraction of thought and spirit which is part of the life of man. But he was still involved in the emotional aspects of his masculinity, and therefore this picture could have, at most, a remote meaning for him. The only real immediate affect was a desire to be more alone, so as to get a deeper contact with the unconscious.

In the next picture was a fountain of gleaming water, which seemed to rise from the depths of the earth, while at the back great, black shadows hovered. He associated this water with the spiritual energy in the unconscious, which one cannot obtain without going through the shadows and obscurities which are also elements in the unconscious.

In the next picture, this duality in the unconscious was more closely connected with his personal life. Here he pictured himself as a man, half black and half white, who faced the rising sun. As he considered this picture, he had an intuitive perception that only in his acceptance of the dual sides of his nature as portrayed in this image could he really face life. A change had taken place in the unconscious. In the first picture, the beast and the man, his

Shadow and himself, confronted each other. Here they were united.

In the final picture of this series, he stood before the naked figure of the old man, who this time seemed a combination of the old man of doom and the masculine figure he had seen striding across the water. Now this figure was leaning down, accepting him, while on his head fell its semen (Plate 26). When he looked at this picture he felt as though he had been a witness of some strange, primitive initiation rite. The semen he felt to be a symbol of energy through which, in this primitive baptism, he was received into manhood.

A picture like this is not a final picture. It does not mean that he has become miraculously wise, but only that he has reached a place where he says, "I am responsible for working out my own life."

Now came a period when these pictures stopped and he turned to his outer life. He found a new strength and virility coming into his work, and a very different attitude toward his old relationships. But he was even more conscious that much confusion remained, that there was still much to be done.

Then there came another picture. It did not follow on from the climax of the other series. Instead, it seemed to throw him back to the place where he had started. Again the monsters of fear appeared, this time laughing and rejoicing. But now, instead of feeling that he himself was in their power, he was an observer of this scene, wondering what it meant to him and what he should do about it. So he turned back to find the reason for their joy.

Then there rose before him a great tree that bore both pear-shaped fruit and one from which issued these same forms of fear. As he drew this, he heard the sound of rushing winds. He was back in his childhood. He recalled nights when he had lain awake listening to the wind, fearing vague presences of evil. And now this wind connected with his mother's voice, as he had heard it at times when she had been swept by her own emotional storms.

Here again the tree was a mother symbol. The pear-shaped fruit is an old symbol of the womb. This tree was the tree of unconsciousness, and the fruit of the womb was fear.

He still disliked high winds, and felt disturbed when in the night he heard the sounds of a gathering storm. Now he remembered other nights in his childhood when he had awakened to hear his mother's voice, tense with some stormy emotion, and these storms of the outside world were connected with the emotional storms which had swept through his mother. A very intuitive child, he recognized forces in her unconscious which might destroy the security of the home. He also feared her dominance, and so kept secret any interests and ambitions which he felt might not meet with her approval. He shielded his phantasy life and his artistic aspirations from her; and yet, in all his contacts with the outer world, he was extremely dependent upon her. The aggressive side of life was left to her; and this side of life which she had lived for him he afterwards tried to find in his own daughter, who was temperamentally so like her.

As a child, he could not have done differently; for he would only have entered into a losing battle with his mother, which would probably have resulted in her forcing him to accept values which were not really his, to the destruction of his own unique value.

So this picture of the Mother-Tree brought him to the analysis of his own personal material. The picture series had prepared the way for this, and had given him a strength and understanding to meet it. Usually, the personal analysis comes before the great archetypal images make their appearance. But one can never predict the sequence of the unconscious. One must accept the material as it comes.

PART 2

THE FOLLOWING pictures arose in the form of moving phantasy —that is, when the first image appeared, the man concentrated upon it until, through the intensity of attention, it became activated and began to move with a life of its own. Sometimes the phantasy moved through a succession of events, and afterwards he painted images that had appeared with the intensity of vision, as one would illustrate a story, selecting the vital elements. Sometimes a single vivid image so arrested his attention that he painted it before continuing the phantasy.

In this chapter, two series of pictures are described. From the first, the man obtained the excitement of a great adventure, and an increase of energy in his creative life. But he substituted excitement for experience, and his personal life fell into deeper confusion. The second series was accepted as an inner experience to which he tried to find his own relation. This is the difference, the vitally important difference, between the two series.

It is not possible to give either series in full. Parts are selected which seem especially illustrative. In the first series he followed a guide to "a world below the world." Here in his journeyings he came to a wood of fungus growth and, exploring it, found a sarcophagus in which was buried a woman wrapped in a red and green mantle (Plate 43). He awakened her, and she gave him a diamond wheat ear. He turned from her, and, still following his guide, took his way to a great cave, vast, somber, impressive. Then before him rose a tremendous figure of great majesty and stillness. The face was covered by a dark mask. He felt in the presence of a mystery before which he knelt (Plate 45).

He laid the wheat ear at the feet of this god as a sacrificial offering. Immediately a green vine sprang from it, which grew until it encircled the face of the god. He climbed up this vine until he stood on a level with the black mask. This he snatched away, and there was revealed a face of living green, so full of light that he could not look upon it (Plate 44). Then the figure vanished, and the man became enveloped in a dark vapor of energy which whirled rapidly and more rapidly about him, acting like a great drill, until he descended, whirled in its vortex, deeper, deeper, past strange visions of terror, until he reached a cave in the innermost recesses of the earth.

In the center of the cave, living flame shot forth, and he perceived himself bound to a black shaft in the center of the fire. Then the chains that bound him fell away and there emerged from out the fire a great primeval beast.

This brute which had so strangely and unexpectedly emerged from the flame, set out upon a journey of its own. The man saw it standing upon a sea of black glass, worshipping and drawing power from the crescent moon (Plate 46). Then he came to a great temple of white marble. On either side of the doors and on either side of the windows were marble columns with crescent moons upon their tops. He felt it to be the temple of the mothers (Plate 49).

"I enter this central room. From above me a row of great beasts look down with gleaming eyes (Plate 48). On the other wall is a strange frieze of figures which I feel to be connected with birth (Plate 50). Above me in the air a batlike monster darts to and fro. To the right and left of me I see domed temples of mellow white marble, each adorned with four white pillars. The two temples are connected by a closed colonnade of marble. A red thread leads straight into the middle of a cross ornament in the center of the space and vanishes. I examine the interior of the right-hand temple. In the center is a great shallow bronze bowl of blood in which floats the severed head of a child. I pass through the temple on the left—the floor is a mosaic of round white pebbles. Four golden-winged suns are inlaid about the center, where a clear effervescent spring is perpetually sparkling and foaming. On the ceiling I see a great golden star" (Plate 42).

This second temple contains the living water, the well spring of life which is eternally welling up in the unconscious. It is life, as the temple of sacrifice is death, and both are aspects of the Great Mother.

He passes from this temple of the mothers, where he has seen both the sacrifice of the child and the promise of the renewal of life, and out into the open plain. Before him looms a mountain of white marble with the face of a woman (Plate 51). From her lips comes a windlike breath which utters the letters A-I-O-N—aion—age. It is the ageless Anima here appearing as an eternal mountain, remote and made of gleaming stone.

He starts again upon his journey. Throughout this journey there is a separation between the two sides of himself. From the flame emerged, not the spiritual self, but the beast. Yet he never connected with this beast—never accepted it as his Shadow that held his masculine strength in an undeveloped and unacceptable form. It was to him an interesting phenomenon, an artistic concept. It had its adventures, then quite irrelevantly the spiritual creative self became the hero of the drama. This hero appears as Galahad, as a beautiful fawn, as a man lifted up beholding the movement of the stars and seeing the winged horses whirling through infinite space. Descending to the earth this hero self is drawn into a great rock through which he passes and from which he emerges as a youthful slave with a golden ring about his neck. This youth is "slave to the selfless life." "He must give twice what he receives, he must create values which he may not share." He painted a picture of the face which he saw emerging from the rock (Plate 52). It is the face of a nonhuman, terrified woman. That is, he has remained unconscious of what the experience means, so it is the Anima in an undifferentiated form who emerges from the rock. At one point the hero self finds a great moonstone guarded by a serpent (Plate 53). He slays this, cracks open the stone and finds there a sleeping woman. Again he is unmindful of the values of the Anima. He does not awaken her but goes on with his endless adventures.

The beast, too, penetrated into the earth. He wandered into a grotto of strange, fleshly red; tentacles like umbilical cords reached down to encircle him. These cords clung to his navel. Then suddenly they broke the confines of the cavern and reached to the sky, connecting the beast with the stars (Plate 47).

As he painted the picture he was excited by the idea but completely remote from it, and the stars appear not in the heaven but in a pattern of red about the beast.

The phantasy reached a culmination in the drawing of a great star, a star whose numberless radiations always proceeded from a four-pointed center and continued to develop in multiples of four.

Its painting created within him an intense, burning excitement. Surely, now, "the thing had happened," the unique self was born.

Yet he made no connection between all this and his personal analytical material, regarding these visions as of value in themselves. He put all his energy into the task of making them beautiful pictures. The star therefore was in a short time another remote vision. And the phantasies began in another cycle as though there had been no appearance of the symbol.

In a general way, of course, he could interpret the images of this first phantasy series. The woman in the underworld, the deep unconscious, is robed in red and green, the colors of love and new life. This figure of the Anima gave him energy only as an artist; he could not yet connect her with his life as a man. She gives him the diamond wheat ear. The diamond is the symbol of the perfect crystal, the diamond body, the redeemed self. When he lays this before the god, it becomes a living vine on which he can mount and behold for a moment that intolerable force. This, according to an ancient legend, is the living god upon which one may not look; it is Chidir, the green one. This vivid green is the color of the spring renewal, its sudden revelation is like an uncensored glimpse of the great archetypal image of the intolerable dynamis of life.

Then a change takes place deep below conscious life. The old self is sacrificed, but there emerges from the fires not the beautiful spirit self but the beast-man, the repressed lower self, the part that as an artist he had feared. He felt no conscious connection with this beast after the excitement of the phantasy had passed, and the adventures of both beast and hero were to him like a fairy tale quickening his imagination but otherwise unrelated to himself. The star, too, became a beautiful picture. The long process of concentration without which a symbol has no activating power was exchanged for excitement and a false sense of achievement. Consequently, nothing happened within himself.

It is often impossible to bring home to a person under the fascination of the great images of the collective unconscious the fact that it is not enough merely to have such phantasies, that they cannot be taken as statements that great inner changes have actually taken place. This man was energized by the intense inner excitement which the phantasies had aroused. But when this excitement faded, he found himself no better off than before.

His experience was reminiscent of the old fairy tales in which the hero, who has wandered into the enchanted palace, tries to eat of the fairy food, when suddenly the splendor vanishes, and he is back in his desolation. So this man found that his sense of achievement did not last. Having made an incorrect assumption, he was bitterly disappointed when the results of the error appeared.

He resolved to have nothing more to do with the unconscious. But this solution was not possible. His whole temperament, his creative life, made him too near to the unconscious. When he attempted to separate himself from it he was inundated by it. He became full of fears, haunted by doubts, his personal life fell into greater and greater confusion. So he returned to analysis to see if anything could be done about this personal situation.

For some time the analysis was entirely concerned with the exploration of the personal unconscious and the examination of certain unassimilated experiences of his childhood. Then he had this intensely vivid dream, which alarmed him because it seemed to take him right back into the archetypal world of his former phantasies:

"I go up a steep hill between two rows of houses. I leave behind me two women dressed in black who are, I feel, dear to me, and enter a rocky cliff at the top of the hill. I pass through a cleft. I am in a dark cave. In a window niche cut in the western wall of the cave sits an old man bowed over a crystal ball which he holds in his two hands. Over his back are folded two great wings. I see cracks in the floor of the cave. A strange rosy glow shines up through them. I peer down through one of the cracks. I become aware that far below me, underneath the rocky floor, is another world. Incredibly ancient winged beings of flame come and go. This world below my world is full of a tremendous life. Can I go down there?"

In the dream he leaves behind for a time the women who are dear to him, who are known and yet not known, and the rows of houses where ordinary people live. That is, in his journey into the depths of the unconscious, he temporarily leaves the Anima in her personal projected form behind.

What is this strange adventure upon which he has set forth and what is this flame which he has seen below the rock? The old man in the cave is again the archetypal figure of ancient wisdom, another form of the god that he had seen in the first series.

Here the old man gazes into the crystal. This crystal, he feels, indicates the creative potential of the future. The wise old man is himself in contemplation, waiting for what may develop. On the great black table is the sign of individuation, of the self. The window, phallic in form, also suggests creativeness, the generative power of the vision. It associates not only with the joy of creation but with old ideas of fear of birth, that is, fear of coming out into life.

In the strange light that streams up from the cave, the winged beings, creatures of this hidden fire, also bring a sense of terror, for they are not only flaming and beautiful power, but they are inhuman. The quotation came to mind, "Indeed the rousing of this fire is full of peril; and woe to him who awakens it before he has purified his being into selflessness, for it will turn downward and vitalize his darker passions and awaken strange frenzies and inextinguishable desires. . . . Again and again I would warn all who read of the danger of awakening it, and again I would say that without this power we are as nothing. . . ."

As he discussed this dream, the picture of the cave became more and more vivid in his mind. He wished to paint it, but he was almost afraid to, because he feared he might be drawn back into the archetypal world which had before proved so dangerous for him. It was suggested to him that this form in which the archetype had appeared must have some vital connection with his own individual life, and that in painting this picture he might discover this connection. He spent all day on this painting (Plate 54), and when he woke the next morning, a quotation came to his mind: "First cometh sleep before awakening. First cometh darkness before day. First cometh dark before light."

Suddenly he seemed to be back in the room where he had slept as a child. He remembered evenings when he had sat up in bed, long after he was supposed to be asleep, reading with intense excitement. Then he had a feeling that the picture which he had painted the day before was connected with a picture in one of these books of his childhood. As he thought of this he recalled a favorite illustration in Howard Pyle's *The Garden Behind the Moon*. Here the child goes behind the moon and finds the Moon Angel, who makes old things new. In the illustration in the book the child stands in the same attitude as the figure of the man in his own drawing and the tops of the angel's wings have the same vaguely phallic form as the window in the dream.

The comparison of the two pictures and the associations aroused showed that he was emotionally in a situation akin to that of his childhood. He was seeking for a new reality, for an understanding which would help him to meet his fears and accept the values of his personal life. The dream did not come because he had once seen this picture, but because the quest of childhood was still his, and the questions of childhood were the ones to which he was still seeking an answer.

He had moods of despair which he felt "came upon him;" he now remembered that such moods had been part of his childhood life. Then he had tried to solve them through the excitement of phantasy and the elation arising from heroic day dreams. The archetypal phantasy was a repetition of this same attempt. He must now relive and conquer the fears which long ago he had tried to repress, or to evade in phantasy. Old images of terror returned to him. These had to be met and connected with the fears which were still deep within him, and which stood between himself and the acceptance of his personal life. Then flashed into mind the quotation, "When we dead awaken, we see that we have never lived."

So the dream was saying to him, "You are now seeking the thing for which you sought as a child, going back and asking the questions which you then feared to ask, going back and living the old emotions and trying to find in them a new personal meaning and satisfaction. What is it that you never found as a child, the lack of which makes life still seem to you futile? For this old figure of the ancient god is the source of wisdom within the self, which is as closely related to your childhood quest as to the tremendous, impersonal, creative energy which has been set free in you."

After he had painted the picture of the cave, he recalled the vision of the star which had come as the completion of his first phantasy series. At the time, he had dismissed this as irrelevant. Now he felt a desire to paint it, and a very curious thing occurred. It seemed to demand its own form. It was no longer the intricately beautiful star of the first series, but much smaller and simpler; and yet it seemed to be more his own. He again looked for personal associations, and again recalled the story of *The Garden Behind the Moon*. He remembered that David, the child, polished his own star until it shone with a living light; this star which he had now painted symbolized to him his personal life to which he must give real attention.

From this point onward he began to perceive that the archetype could have a meaning for his individual life. His former confusion had not come from the fact that he had had an archetypal experience, but from his attempt to substitute the archetypal for the human.

His analysis now followed two lines. He continued to give great attention to his personal dreams and their bearing upon his immediate problems; and at the same time, in his waking hours, archetypal images would arise and he would follow them into phantasy. Because he was building up some security through facing the reality of his life as a man, the phantasies no longer exerted such a fascination over him, nor did they fill him with such terror.

A new phantasy began and is given in abridged form, omitting many episodes and pictures:

"I stand with my back against a pillar of black basalt on which is engraved a mysterious Hebrew word in letters of gold. Winged beings of fire stream upward through the red sky from horizon to zenith (Plate 59). I am filled with wild excitement and also with terror. I feel that this pillar is barring my path. I overthrow it and turn my face toward the east, where a new light is breaking. Then I am kneeling before a red obelisk on which rests a golden bowl. Three great cones, like cones of incense, stand at the foot of the pillar (Plate 60). I throw these into the bowl, and as they are destroyed, feel suddenly that I am destroying my old worship of false gods."

Two episodes of this phantasy—that of the black pillar of basalt and of the red obelisk—stood out so vividly in his mind that he painted them. The black pillar, bearing the ineffable name, stood to him for his old concept of God—Jehovah—the center of strength, but also the God of Wrath, one to be feared. The figures of flame associated with his childhood terror of the everlasting fire.

As a child he had felt the fascination of these fears, and could now recall early phantasies connected with them. They were still active in him and shut him off from life. That is to say, the image of the Jehovah God in his unconscious had been invested with a terrible authority, and this authority had manifested itself in his obsessive idea that a retribution would follow any act which he really enjoyed, however harmless it might be. The personal analysis, however, had dealt successfully with many of these old fears; and the overthrowing of the black pillar meant that his idea of a jealous and vengeful God had lost its autonomous power in his unconscious.

Now he could turn toward the east, "where a new light is breaking." He finds himself kneeling before the great red obelisk. The obelisk is phallic, and symbolizes the sexuality hitherto forbidden to him because of his fears. But the color, the glowing red, which suffuses both sky and symbol, is traditionally the color of the Eros principle, which is greater than mere sexuality. The three cones of incense which are destroyed, "go up in smoke," were three attitudes towards the Jehovah God, attitudes which had been dissolved in his personal analysis. Here he sees himself as sacrificing them on this new altar; and once the sacrifice has been completed, he is free to continue his journey toward the east.

This was a picture of changes taking place in his unconscious. Such changes often occur long before they are used by the conscious; and, indeed, do not become an actual experience until they are worked out in life. To do this he had to go through a long period in his personal analysis.

Then, one day, in phantasy he found himself descending upon a crimson rope deep into the earth. He was at a crossroad in this underworld, and he was turning his back on hosts of winged beings that streamed upward through the glowing air. And he questioned, "Are they the Harpies, the Faces in the Smoke; are they the Watchers of the Living?"

In turning his back upon them, he felt that he was turning

his back upon lovely promises of mystical vision in order to set out to find a deeper truth, the truth about his own life as a man. But why had he called them Harpies? The Harpies were the vampire birds, with women's faces, who swooped down and stole the food of their victims. These figures in the phantasy were beautiful, flamelike beings, yet he felt he must turn from them because they represented that side of the Anima which snatches from man his human food.

As he considered the necessity of turning his back upon these figures, at once fearful and fascinating, he drew a picture of a beast standing in front of a fireplace which had been in his own nursery. This beast strikingly resembled the one above the door in the second chamber of the temple which he had seen in the first series of phantasies. This suggested only too clearly that this beast was not something magnificent and remote but something connected with his own early experiences, a form of sexual phantasy which had seemed to him beastly but to which he had retreated in his fear of actuality.

A long time passed in a personal analysis before another phantasy came, a phantasy of the reborn hero setting forth in a ship on his quest (Plate 55). In this, the sun, which is rising, is green like the face of the green god in the first series. But now this experience of the green sun seems to him to be a living reality, because this journey is actually being accomplished in his own life as a man and is being related to each step in his own progress. Then the ship moves toward the right and enters a harbor. It approaches a great cliff in which a door is cut. Above the cliff rises a hill, not a natural hill but one built of wood.

As he moves toward the door a monstrous, blind, bull-headed creature comes over the brow of the hill as if to prevent his entering the door (Plate 56). Nevertheless, he does pass through the door guarded by the bull-headed monster. This bull-headed creature he felt to be his instinctual side, now blind and grown to this gigantic size because of its constant repression into the unconscious. He now dares to pass this monster and goes through the door. He is then confronted by a series of sliding doors, that are like two-edged razor blades (Plate 57), showing the peril of the experience through which he is passing.

He passes through these doors, and as he penetrates the last of these he finds himself absorbed in the great primeval rock (Plate 61). Then in a strange way he realizes that he is not only within the rock but that the rock is within him; he has absorbed its strength into himself. In other words, the strength once projected into the old idea of the black column, had now been taken back into himself. From the actual experience of the phantasy came a sense of amazingly renewed masculine strength, as though he had become part of the eternal strength of the earth.

The contrast between this picture and the one in the former series, where nothing had emerged from the rock but the undifferentiated Anima, is highly significant. The former picture showed that he was still under the spell of the unconscious. Now he could make a real connection between the two sides of his life.

He then comes to a series of doorways cut in the solid rock, going down further and further into the earth. Each doorway is guarded by a great eye (Plate 58). He felt the eye to symbolize a watching god who guards the treasure of the temple, protects the person who comes in reverence, but detects any evil intent, and brings immediate vengeance upon a despoiler.

He goes down past these gateways and finds himself in a long, horizontal rock tunnel, leading toward the east. At the end of the tunnel a great crimson rose hangs in space. In the phantasy he sees himself crawling through the tunnel, mounting the space, and finds himself stretched out in the shape of the cross and lying in the heart of the rose (Plate 62). Here the rose took on for him a double meaning: on the one hand, passion, earth, life, love of woman, acceptance of the renewal through love; on the other, that of the Rosicrucian rose, the spiritual rose that lies at the center and the heart of the inner essence of life. With this phantasy a real sense of peace and fulfillment came to him.

In the period during which this second series of phantasies had appeared he had done two things. He had seen them not merely as pictures to be painted, but as inner experiences in which he had a real and difficult part. He had, at the same time, connected them with the problems of his external life. As a result of this double effort the separation between the life of the imagination and the life in the outer world had ended.

PART 3

THE PICTURES discussed in this section were done at intervals over a period of several years. Sometimes they came in groups, sometimes singly; there were long intervals in which were many dreams. Often the meaning of a picture could not be understood until after painful struggle to accept and experience material which appeared in dreams. Almost all of the dreams are omitted because it was as though the unconscious, like a discriminating artist, selected the dramatic moments of a long story for illustration, and chose so cleverly that the reader can follow the movement of the life history without the text furnished by the dreams.

The dreams, however, with their constant reiterations and insistence on personal detail made the analysant able to realize the living meaning of the pictures. They kept a very necessary connection between the archetypal and the personal material. Occasional dreams had such vivid imagery that they took almost the form of pictures and were afterwards painted. Several of these are included.

A series of four pictures began this woman's long period of unconscious paintings. The first came when she was listening to music and began to draw sweeping rhythmic lines. She felt something growing out of the rhythm. It came as a surging force rising within herself, directing the line, almost forcing its own form onto the paper. The colors, too, seemed directed rather than chosen. In this picture (Plate 1), the octopus, the classical symbol of the Terrible Mother, looms above her, ready to draw her back to the dark womb of the unconscious, to annihilation, to death. The woman is plunging toward it with an orgiastic joy. The vivid tones of her sweeping garment express intoxication and excitement; the whole figure sweeps forward, not with reluctant acceptance but in a delirium of power and desire. The octopus is closing in, its tentacles are cutting the garment; that is, it is attempting to cut her off from the energy in which she is clothed.

In the second picture, the mad death pursuit is arrested;

something has now come between herself and the octopus. This is indicated by the sweep of the garment which shuts her from the path to the octopus. She lies desolate in a bleak, gray land. There is no color, no movement about her. The octopus has withdrawn a little, and the curve of her garment comes between them. This garment has now taken the form of a crescent moon, here, as often, a feminine symbol. Consciously, she felt "something connecting me with a woman is coming between myself and the octopus." She assumed that this was her trust in the analyst; but this is not what the picture says. It is her own garment, that is the unconscious energy in which she is clothed, which in the first picture sweeps her on to death and has now become redirected. Assisted by the analysis, it moves between her and the octopus.

At this time she saw the octopus only as a personal mother symbol, not as something in the unconscious pulling her into death. Actually death and suicide held a fascination for her. She was in a very perilous place, but it would have been foolhardy to press its full meaning upon her at this time, for there was no positive desire for life which would free her from the death image. It was almost as though, in escaping the clutches of death, she had lost her last, blind, unconscious joy. Without death, there was left to her nothing but a gray void.

This often happens, for the lure of death is like the lure of life, intoxicating and exciting, a loss of the burden of the self and of personal responsibility. Though the way to death had been cut off by a change in the unconscious, the desire for life was still so small that it could not keep her from falling into the grayness. This was so dreadful to her that she tried to do something about it consciously. She said, "Now, I *ought* to face the octopus. I *ought* to be strong enough."

In the third picture she does face the octopus. The drawing of this picture had not come with the same feeling; it did not seem to force itself upon the canvas as had the two previous pictures. Although she had a conscious sense that it must be drawn, so little life energy went to this task that she could never finish the picture. She could make only an outline of the woman. The woman who *could* face the octopus had not yet been conceived even in her unconscious and therefore could not be painted.

(If, by a conscious act of will, one attempts to portray something which, it seems, *ought* to be in the unconscious, the resulting picture has no life of its own.)

In the fourth picture, the woman stands looking down at the octopus, which, small and shriveled, lies at her feet. But this picture gave her no sense of reality; it also was something that *ought* to be painted. It was what she consciously felt she should do; it turned into a design with no life. The octopus lies in the road of grayness now beneath her feet, but the woman and the mountains are both clad in a somber purple. There is no greenness of spring on these mountains, no suggestion of a renewed life. It was quite evident that a mere sense of duty was not going to give her a new energy.

In reality, she fell into the void; that is, the grayness which she had painted in the second picture. "Shortly after painting this fourth picture, I had the actual experience while at the theatre at a Sherlock Holmes play, which by its character suggested analysis, of suddenly losing consciousness and falling into grayness. There was nothing but the grayness around me and a terrifying fear. It happened once again while I was in a picture gallery."

Now begins a series of pictures which were almost those of madness. Physical death was not the only threatening quality of the octopus; there was that other form of death, a loss of the self in insanity. The pictures now lost any consecutive design. They were broken and disoriented. In one she appears struggling for a way out of monstrous masses of almost formless plants. In another she is crawling through the grayness, while she tries to gather strange fungus growths of sinister red that loom high above her. In another picture her head is rising from waters over which many of these curious red growths tower, while hovering above her is a great snake which encircles two monstrous blue leaves. All of these pictures were so disconnected that they could not be interpreted save as showing disintegration. The painting of them was a necessity at this time; she had to project her terror and disintegration onto paper. But it would have been a great mistake to have strengthened her own connection with them through a discussion of their meaning. Emphasis, therefore, was laid upon the dream material, and upon strengthening her conscious connections with life.

Then a picture came in which she is toiling up a black hill (Plate 2). From behind she is pursued by a huge fish, the devouring monster of the unconscious. In front of her the way is barred by a tall misshapen bird who seems to be growing out of the earth like a plant that blossoms, not into flowers, but into a bird of prey.

This picture, though monstrous, is no longer incoherent. It has at least a definite meaning. Here she is caught between two forces. The bird symbolizes the masculine principle, the Logos, thought; her thoughts have become monstrous and prey upon her. They are even more terrifying to her than the fish of the unconscious which would swallow her.

The full meaning of this picture could not be shown at this time, but she could be told that it did not depict her real situation but a distortion brought about by fear which made her unable to see anything but the negative aspects of life.

During this period she had many dreams. Through discussion of them she began to gain some connection with life and greater trust in the analytic process. This trust made it possible for her to paint such pictures without being devastated by the hopelessness of the situation which they portrayed. There was at least something to hold on to, some growing sense of not being completely alone with these perils.

After more pictures of this same character, she drew a picture of the Animus as a powerful masculine figure, blinded by a scarf, pursuing its way unaware of a tiny hand which is held up in a futile attempt to snatch the scarf from his eyes. This scarf was the color of the woman's garment in the first picture, vivid orange. What had in one picture suggested a power which had swept her toward death, now covered the eyes of the Animus, making him only a blind force.

Almost immediately after this Animus picture she drew one in which she was bound to her father's tombstone by ropes of snakes (Plate 4). Her mother, a figure of death, stood back of the grave. Though she was struggling to free herself, the picture showed that the ties, the sexuality and instinctual feeling that had bound her to her dead father, were still important, for the open grave was at the edge of a precipice and below was nothing but the sea with a monster rising from it. Should she, at this time, succeed in breaking this instinctual connection with the dead father, which later on had to be broken, she would only plunge into the depth of the unconscious, and become the prey of the monster.

Such a picture has to be treated with caution lest the explanation be destructive. The technique of the picture made very clear the necessity of such caution. She was unable to draw the sea and the monster as they had appeared to her. Instead, she drew an ornamental sea with a very conventional monster. Any attempt to depict the reality filled her with overpowering fear. The unconscious was still a peril because she had so little connection with life and with any deep relationships. Her connection with the father image was most important, for through her memories of him she had a realization of the value of love and tenderness. She had much to understand in the unconscious bonds that had bound her to him and until she could separate the true from the false, it was dangerous to break these bonds. Also she must establish some present reality on which she could stand.

She made this attempt through a false type of introversion. She shut her feeling away from people and tried to be able to stand alone, to become self-sufficient. The result of this is shown in the picture (Plate 3). Here she stands, indeed alone, upon a lifeless peak. Her whole attitude shows, not acceptance of life, but defiance—both of earth and moon. It is a place of complete negation.

She accepted this meaning and struggled against the forces that were impelling her toward such isolation.

Then came a long period of dream analysis from which she gained a slowly increasing connection with her own inner energy.

The image painted in the next picture first appeared in the following dream: "I was living in the old home, but it is now on a wild frontier. I had tenderly said good-bye to the man who was both my father and husband—I should never see him again, and with this knowledge he became the father. Then I knew he was dead. A doctor told me that he had left me a value. I went into an inner room to find his picture. The picture was definitely that of my father, yet in features it bore no resemblance to him. It was that of an old man with a long white beard and eyes of infinite wisdom. This, then, was my father—and he had left me a value."

The picture in the dream was like a photograph in black and white, but when she started to draw it she saw the colors so vividly that it had to be painted. The most vivid color was in the eyes, which were of clear living blue. She did not understand this picture until long afterward. She had found it in the inner room, that is, within herself. It was one of those intuitive dreams that are prophetic in that they show the value which may develop. That is, she may find within herself the masculine image of wisdom so that though the old father image must die she could retain the value. By painting this picture she could make real this image and as one may look on a symbol which awakens perception, so she could return again and again to this picture to understand the value it represented to her.

Next she drew a picture which was quite incomprehensible to her. She is standing in a cave with the Animus—an androgynous figure with the body of a man, but with no penis, who is pointing to the pool of the unconscious and bidding her enter. A great animal, impassive and Sphinxlike, sits by the side of the Animus. She is terrified, and, blinding her eyes from this sight, is trying to creep to the back of the cave, where there is a small inner cave. In this sticks are laid for a fire and, at the back, the rising sun appears.

She felt from this picture that she was being called upon to go deeper into the waters of the unconscious, but she was still too terrified to follow this injunction. Consciously she was anxious to go, but again it was necessary to realize how real and right her unconscious fear was; for she was not yet ready to take this plunge. Too much of her own personal material had still to be worked through. Her childish fears and resentments were still too great a burden. This took much patience; for the material seemed to her petty and irritating.

She had a theoretical knowledge of the Animus as a spiritual and creative force in the unconscious, but that her concept was merely theory was shown by an unconscious picture of the Animus, who appeared as a horrid, distorted little man, like the disintegrating, insinuating thoughts and intuitions that continually destroyed the fabric of her conscious rational life and kept her from the experiences of the unconscious that she desired.

Then came a picture of herself lying upon a beautifully manicured hand, while all the strength of her being was sucked away by a mad distorted growth which bore hands that threatened her (Plate 5). The manicured hand was like the hand of her own mother.

All this time she was working at another type of drawing, and doing some quite interesting work in applied design. But she came to a strange block whenever she was asked to draw a tree. A cloud of resentment rose in her. She interpreted that resentment as a feeling of frustration, caused by an inability to get the technique of drawing a tree. She struggled to conquer this difficulty by a conscious determination, by telling herself that this was absurd, that she *must* do it; but there she stuck or, rather, she went deeper into confusion. She hated trees, hated to look at them even.

Then, in her analysis, it was suggested that she should stop looking at trees or trying to draw them, and instead, retire into herself, and draw her *feeling* of a tree. Plate 6 was the result. Here was a startling revelation, a chronicle more vivid than words. Her idea of a tree was a woman, blindfolded, supporting and nourishing by the sap of her own being the monstrous burden of the mother breasts.

Here subjective facts were expressed in an objective form. Had you said to the woman who had come to this block in her drawing, "Perhaps you think of your mother as a tree," she might have replied "How ridiculous!" or she might have talked about the mother image very intelligently without connecting it with her emotions (in the same way that she had discussed the Animus), and afterwards dismissed it all as an interesting but not very important idea. Or, had it appeared in some dream form as an archetypal image, she could still have turned away from it, and persuaded herself that it had not happened, or that it was not so important, or that it was possibly a passing phantasy.

The first effect which this picture had upon her seemed anything but life-giving; for there was loosed a flood of resentment, suspicion, and negativity. This was projected both upon the analyst and upon her own work. Then she went back over events of her childhood and saw how early these same emotions had not only destroyed the results of her childish creative impulses but had continued to block all her creative activities, so that whenever she attained a degree of success she destroyed her own creation by a negativity which made her abandon all effort. Sometimes she even destroyed the actual object which she had created or had nearly completed—sometimes she lost interest, or again decided that she would "never get anywhere," and with those decisions her work began to deteriorate instead of improve.

These same emotions had stood between her and all human relations. In any relationship she could get just so far, and then, either she would destroy it by some negative act or else she would seem to have no energy to give to it. She felt unwanted, as unable to create life values as she was unable to create values in her art. Now this drawing revealed one source of this negation of life. She saw the tree as a mother symbol, a hideous object. She had hated her mother. She recalled times when her mother had shown pride or interest in some developing talent and how immediately she had given it up. Rather than give the mother any gift of achievement, she preferred to destroy it. This same feeling had been projected upon her teachers and also upon the analyst.

But the tree was also a symbol of her own developing life. The blindfolded woman who formed the trunk was herself. She had been weighed down by the burden of the futile conflict with her mother. When she perceived this she realized how much of her energy had been given to supporting something that was not a natural growth out of her own life. When, through this drawing, she was able to see a creative effort as something of her own which should be separated from a hated mother image, she understood why she had again and again abandoned or destroyed the very thing she had worked furiously to accomplish. Such pictures deal with the emotional content connected with an image and also show how great is the divergence between psychic and factual reality and how great is the power of the unconscious to draw to itself energy belonging to the conscious.

This released new energy which was apparent not only in her technical work in design but in increased enjoyment of all forms of art. This release of her artistic energy was, however, only one product of the process. It started also a release of emotional energy which she could use creatively in all sides of life, for human living is in itself an act of creation. This drawing constellated, clarified her special problem. It brought it up where she could see and begin to handle it. Also it expressed the problem in such tangible, permanent form that she could not forget it. For it was as though the understanding of the tree picture had destroyed some dam in the unconscious which had turned the stream of energy into a destructive channel. It was as though the force expressed in the garment in the first picture might now flow toward life. The octopus no longer threatened.

But though energy was released, no miracle occurred. In her work she was more aware of the causes of her failures and discouragements. In her personal life she had much more desire to connect with people. But the deep-seated negativity was still an active factor in every attempt that she made to enter into life. Quite irrationally, her impulses turned from death to life. She had, through the picture of the mother tree, become conscious of the personal mother image which had sapped her strength and left her blindfolded. In the ensuing struggle with her analysis she relived many of her infantile experiences. Through a positive transference to the analyst she began to develop positive feelings within herself. Having now something positive to sustain her, she could investigate those elements within herself which had stood between herself and life. As yet she could only feel vaguely that this "something" existed, but she determined to look for it until its image became clear.

She began to be overpowered by bodily weariness that could not be accounted for by any physical exertion. Resting did not seem to diminish her extreme lassitude. Then she began to hear something padding, padding about behind her. She found herself reluctant to open the door of her apartment, fearing to find some strange presence there. What was following her on soft, padding feet? What was waiting for her at her own threshold?

She tried to see the thing as an inner image. Then the impulse to paint came to her and she began without knowing just what she was painting; but, as it took shape on the canvas, she knew it to be the beast within herself. As she painted it, she felt a loathing of it. It was full of stealthy malignity, a great slothlike beast with small, evil eyes. Even its color, slimy, bluish gray, suggested stealth and treachery. It was inertia, stealing the creative power. It was easy to see how it would slink out and kill every new living thing.

She had an impulse to tear the picture up, to deny its reality. Instead she put it upon her wall and lived with it. It is not pleasant to live with a beast like that, to accept it as a part of your own self that must be met and studied and acknowledged. It is far easier to feel that you have seen an image out of the collective unconscious, interesting but separated from you by several million years. You say, "How wonderful the collective unconscious is. It shows you things that happened in the remote past." And if you do enough of that sort of thing, pretty soon you begin to feel that you saw that beast because you were such a fine, imaginative person yourself and the whole meaning of the image has vanished. The picture becomes an interesting psychological record, and the beast slinks back inside you and goes right on stealthily destroying values.

But this woman was in deadly earnest. She was not so much afraid of facing dangers, as of remaining in ignorance of them. She knew this beast was her immediate business. Whatever values she had, or could develop, depended very largely on what she did with this beast, now that she could actually see it. So she kept it up in her conscious world and talked to it, and learned all she could about it. It is this kind of concentration upon the inner image that activates it and makes it reveal itself. She began to discover its connection with her own inertia, how it had fed upon her dawning enthusiasms and left her with only a sense of futility; how it had destroyed impulses to creation, leaving her with a feeling of hopeless inferiority; how it had stealthily devoured small beginnings of love and left her with only suspicions of a feeling that she herself could never receive love.

All her energy was now given to this inner conflict. She felt that quite literally she was fighting for her life. She began to see concrete instances in which these forces had worked destructively. Then memories of her relationship with her father arose. The old picture where she was tied to her father's tombstone came back to mind. She realized how blindly and instinctually she had clung to him, allowing no real discrimination to come into her feeling, because it was the only human connection which she had really accepted. This explained why it would have been perilous to attempt to break these bonds when the picture first rose from the unconscious, for one must have human feeling, however blind and instinctive, to save one from being drowned in the unconscious. Now she looked at the picture again and realized why the deep-sea monster looked so unreal, a sort of rocking horse sea dragon, fitting into the design rather than the inner meaning. She had pushed away the real dragon that she saw, for it was one she had not then been ready to face.

Suddenly and quite unexpectedly, she felt that she had to find an image of beauty to interpose between herself and the beast. She clamored for a vision as a child might clamor for a lollipop. She resented her own unconscious because it gave her no redeeming symbol, no image of beauty from which she might paint a picture which was her own original experience of rebirth.

One morning as she woke she saw in front of her a landscape and felt that a vision was arising. Then across the landscape stretched an automobile license plate—No. 746. The background was of muddy red and the numbers were in white. A voice said, "You can get all the information through this number." Her first reaction was anger. Was this the inner revelation, was this the saving vision which she could paint to hang on her walls to confront the beast?

The anger passed and she decided that if this was the vision vouchsafed to her she would try to understand it. She tried to say the number aloud but all she could say was, "D 46." Then she tried to put it down but only "D 46" appeared on the paper. Instantly she said, "D stands for death and 746 was the train my father took to the city." The train connected in her mind with the directed energy that carried him to the office where he lived his own life as a man. Her automobile had come into dreams over and over as a symbol of her own life energy (libido). Now the license (insignia of authority under which she might drive her car) was the same number as that of her father's train, but when examined more carefully it became a combination of death and his libido. What did death signify in this connection? She knew intuitively that it could not be literally interpreted as his death, but that it was death in relation to herself.

First came a sense of desolation, her deepest feelings had been given to him. His death had been also the death of her feeling. Then she realized that the connection lay deeper. His libido and hers were expressed in the same terms (i.e. by the same number). She had not permitted her energy to find its natural expression but had identified with him, taking over his ideas and attitudes, thinking as he thought. Temperamentally they were very different, and therefore identification with him killed her own growing reality. Truly the "picture" now before her told her what she needed to find out.

At this point she reconsidered the two earlier pictures which had portrayed this relation with her father. She had previously seen why she had been tied to her father's tombstone and why it would have been perilous to break the bond until she had made a connection with her own energy. Now she recalled the dream in which she had seen the portrait of her father as the wise old man and tried to discover the value which her father had left her.

The first thing that she remembered was his calmness in the midst of emotional storms—he could enter a room where the atmosphere was disturbed and it would become quiet. She had looked to him to quiet her own fears and emotions. Had she a potential of quiet like this? Could she find it within herself instead of feeling that death had robbed her of the security of his calm? Other qualities of his came back to her. She had looked to him for them instead of developing them within herself. She had also taken over his opinions and beliefs so that her feeling and thinking were predetermined and therefore in the power of the negative Animus. By looking within herself and seeking wisdom within, the image of the father could change to that of the spiritual Animus (inner wisdom). This unacceptable vision of the license plate which she had so nearly rejected was indeed one which might enable her to confront the beast.

While all this was happening she wished to paint another tree. She painted it with wide-spreading branches. Underneath stood a mother with a new-born baby in her arms. When she started to paint the shade beneath the tree, she quite instinctively painted a circle of light instead. It was as though this tree cast light instead of shadow. This made an immediate association in her mind with the miraculous birth of the Redeeming Child. This tree was the tree of life, which also had its roots in the unconscious.

Her need to paint it at this time was undoubtedly a very real one, for it gave a sense that things were growing toward a new value. As she looked at the picture, however, it did not carry with it that sense of immediacy and reality that she still felt when she looked at the beast. She would have liked to say, "Now everything has come right, I am the eternal mother and I have brought forth a child in a circle of divine light." But she had no sense of conviction. There was not the slightest emotional connection with the picture. This quiet was still a concept, not a reality, as was shown by a series of dreams.

In the first, she had a beautiful strong baby. She left him in her mother's house while she went to a dinner party. When she came back he had shrunk so that he was now asleep in a pill box.

In the second she had two babies. She loved them but found it too much trouble to go down stairs to get their food. She called out to her mother and was incensed because the mother disappeared unsympathetically.

In the third she went driving with some people and left her little baby at her mother's house with nothing to eat. When she returned home she found it dying of starvation. E had tied her baby to a cold water faucet. . . . He had shrunk almost away. (E was an Animus-ridden woman whom she often met in her mother's house.)

Although in every case the dream showed clearly that she refused to be responsible for her child, she more and more insisted that the trouble was with her mother. It was in her house that the disaster happened. It was she who had destroyed her early values so that now she could not find energy to care for the potentials she still might have within her psyche. Then the following image arose in a dream:

"I was in a huge, archaic boat, which I thought I was steering myself, but I saw at the curving prow a great, shadowy figure who was in some strange way directing the course over shallow and muddy waters. I knew it to be my mother."

In the picture which she painted of this dream (Plate 7) she was at the tiller—that is, she was making a conscious effort to go her own way. But the figure which was actually steering the boat was the great archetypal figure of the mother, the image which was really directing from the unconscious. The picture and the dream both showed her that she was unconscious of the fact that she was still caught in a typical situation. She had not broken from the archetypal mother (that is, from the dependence upon her), and her resentment and bitterness toward the actual mother only blinded her to the fact that she herself was keeping to shallow and muddy waters because she still chose to remain a child. She was in the power of an archetype, that is, of an unconscious force which really ruled her choices.

Her own explanation was ingenious in the extreme. In some way her own mother exercised a mysterious power even over the archetype; in fact, if the actual mother had been a more understanding person the archetype would not have behaved that way. Even this archetypal situation was *all her mother's fault*. Consciously she saw the humorous aspect of this idea, but unconsciously she clung to it. This projection was one from which she could not as yet escape. She had still very little belief in her own values and without that she could not take over the burden of her own responsibility.

Presently, in a dream, the unconscious once more presented her with the image of the child she had left with her mother: She was looking for a place where her new-born child would be cared for. Her mother offered her a room in her house. She had a foreboding that if she took the child there he would contract infantile paralysis. Nevertheless, rather than take over the responsibility herself, she accepted the offer and left him in this room. When she came back she found him paralyzed. Slowly she began to see that this child so constantly appearing was her own, and that she was constantly trying to take it back to her mother. It was her own potential for which she would not accept responsibility. She *had* a value within herself, but it was a value that she must herself care for. But how could this be done?

Then from the unconscious came an answer. Quite unexpectedly, impulses toward life surged up within her, like warm fires kindled inside herself. Then this warm, red, pulsing life seemed to encircle her. She felt herself in a tremendous red cave. There was the actual experience of feeling warm, pulsing life all about her in this great cavern. As she began to paint the cave

(Plate 8) it took on the form of a living womb, red with life. A path of light led through it, and in this path stood a woman lifting up her hands to a cross. This cross was not a crucifix of suffering and sacrifice, but a glowing symbol of life, for it was made of vibrantly living red roses. The red rose is the symbol of love, of passion, and of the mystery of the living center.

This picture showed another aspect of the archetypal mother —the mother to whose womb man returns for rebirth. The cross, as a symbol of individuation, here was a cross of life. It was life that must be accepted and her rebirth must be found in an understanding of the symbol of the red rose. She had projected the negative image she held of her own mother upon the shadowy archetype who had stood at the prow of the boat, but in reality this had not been a negative image—it was merely archetypal. It was a menace if she projected upon it her own responsibilities and if she insisted upon remaining a child; but on the other hand, it was a symbol of rebirth if she could realize that she must accept her own life, with all its potentials and limitations and responsibilities. She alone could decide whether it was to be a menace or a symbol of rebirth. But even if she decided that it was to be a symbol of rebirth, she could experience its real meaning only by relating it to her own personal life.

This she could not do. Instead, she was filled with excitement. She allowed the archetype to carry her into a perilous place, a place of inflation. She felt "one with the experience." She had now had a great collective experience and need no longer worry with her personal problem. She must be a very remarkable person to have this and to paint such a picture. She *was* reborn, it was a *fait accompli*. From now on her experiences would be suprapersonal.

But that the way of rebirth was still unknown to her was shown in the ensuing dreams, all of which dealt with the instinctual life which she had neglected. She dreamed that she had allowed a man to take away her little dog and drown him. This dog had appeared many times in her dreams as instinctual feeling and trustfulness. Then she dreamed that a cat and a dog tried to get into her car. When she pushed them off they climbed in and began to fight, and since she could not cope with the situation she jumped out of the car, and it dashed ahead madly without a driver. Though she kept a record of these dreams and discussed the animals in them as the instinctual elements which were disregarded and at war within herself, and with which she refused to cope, she made no emotional connection with them, nor did she feel that if she made friends with her instincts they might prove helpful. She persisted in thinking of them as trivial, as taking her away from her great experience. She tried to withdraw from life, imagining that in this false type of introversion she would come into touch with the images of the collective unconscious. Her personal life therefore became more and more unsatisfactory and the dreams continued to show all the irritating personal problems which she so persistently ignored.

Then came the following dream: She was standing by a pool covered with ice, watching the skaters. She saw a child venture out into the center and break through into the icy waters. Then another child followed and also sank down. She felt that she must save these children and went out to the edge of the ice. But when she looked into the dark waters she saw a Christmas rose at the bottom of the pool and said to herself, "While that rose is there I can do nothing to save the children."

Here again appears the symbol of the rose. This time it is the rose that blossoms in the snow, at Christmastide, the time of the birth of the Redeeming Child, the new value, the symbol of love. Yet in the dream this saving potential is only a peril. While it is at the bottom of this ice-covered pool she cannot save the children —her individual values. They will be drawn down below the ice and perish. The idea of being caught under the ice, of coming up through the dark waters and finding that transparent barrier through which one could not pass, seemed to her a most terrible death. What was this ice which cut off any return to life and why should the rose be only a lure to death—like a magnetic force? What was the power of the rose when enclosed by ice?

Her first association with the Christmas rose was that she had seen it only in her mother's garden—and because it grew there it had never seemed beautiful to her. But now as it lay in the center of the pool it had strange beauty, and yet it filled her with terror. Then she realized that her own personal associations with the rose gave it a negative meaning to her and until she could break the projections which held her in childish fears and resentments and dissolve the icy barrier—her own coldness and lack of feeling—it was dangerous for her to try to go down into the deep waters of the unconscious. For her the collective unconscious would be death to her individual values, because she would only be drawn away from life, and the way of return cut off. So the very treasure she desired—the experience of the archetype—would be death unless she first dealt with her personal problems.

Now she determined to deal with the material of her dreams, however trivial they might seem to her. The dreams went back to the instinctual plane. A dog suddenly went mad and tried to bite her—an animal shut in the cellar howled in terror—the people appearing in the dreams were all ones who had shut themselves away from life—they had in many cases power over these imprisoned animals. These negative images she studied carefully, trying to see their counterparts in her own unconscious, and to discover what gave them their power.

Then she was walking down a road and stopped to watch two snakes which were on her left. One, a large brown one, seemed half-dead, yet was making a loud hissing noise. He was being dragged about by a black one, whose body was withered but whose great black head was alive and strong. She realized that the brown one was poisonous and could kill her. She tried to get away but her limbs became paralyzed. She seized the snake's head and held its mouth shut. She called, "George." Then "George" appeared with an axe and killed the snake.

As she thought of George (a real person whom she had known many years ago), she wondered why it was he who could kill the snake. He seemed to her a very ineffective person and one for whom she had never cared. Then suddenly it came to her. He had always loved her, even though she did not love him. To love, to have real feeling within oneself, was the important thing. She had always felt that being loved made one superior; now she saw that it was being able to love that gave one strength. It came to her with all the force of revelation, as so often these self-evident truths come. It was the beginning of her understanding of differentiated feeling.

Again she turned to her dreams. They now depicted, in confused profusion, events and desires both past and present. There seemed no starting point for the new life which she wished to bring through. Then, whenever she was alone, she saw the face of a great, dark animal. It was not an unfriendly beast, simply an animal of force, with unconscious, brooding eyes. Yet at first she was afraid of it. She did not know what it would do to her.

Then in phantasy she saw a woman go to this great animal and lift up her arms, and encircle its mouth, and the animal blew its breath into her. She painted this as she had seen it (Plate 9), and as she did so she knew that this was a deep, primitive force and that its breath gave the woman new life. She waited quietly for this to happen inside herself and became aware that this was the breath of rebirth on the instinctual plane. It was from such a simple beginning that her own rebirth would come. She felt the quiet of a child. She became willing to see herself and accept herself. She knew that the other beast (the one who had once followed her) was not dead. He had his life in a force older than her personal self, but she knew that she had something real and living to oppose to him, something that drew its strength from another force as old as he, for the animal often represents the supra-personal, the deep instinctual force.

As she lived with this second animal, he assumed a very personal aspect, that of a creature who was very simply and always himself. And she began to feel in this same way about her own life, that she, too, could be very simply herself, and did not have to be apologetic about her real interests and desires. All through her early life she had been identified with a very conventional Persona. During the analysis this Persona had become increasingly unsatisfactory; there had been complete division, so that she lived her own reality secretly, not able even to assure herself that it had a value which she could acknowledge, and stepped back into the old Persona whenever she went into the world. Now at last came an acceptance of her own nature, a pleasure in things that were in her daily life; and her need for the false Persona was dissolved. The acceptance of herself as she really was gave her a new security. She lost her fear of going down into the unconscious; it was also easier for her to meet the external world.

The next picture was one of a gigantic bull who appeared in a dream. In the dream she was seated on a high bank. Below her in a field, a man and woman were seated. Standing in front of them was a young bull, gigantic in proportion, but in some incongruous way appearing to be an incarnation of playful energy. This seemed so far from her idea of a bull that she leaned down to look in his face. There he was—a real bull, red-eyed, physically terrifying in his strength and animal energy. Yet, though visually so frightening, he gave her no sense of fear. In spite of his enormous size, he reminded her of a playful puppy.

The man got up, and the bull put his hooves upon the shoulders of the man. Though he towered above the man, he seemed only to be playing some game with him. Then the dream changed, and she found herself walking with this creature. She pushed him into a great lake which arose in front of her, but thereupon she found herself running down the road much impeded by wet garments, though it was the bull and not herself who had been pushed into the lake. Then she heard the beast coming behind her. At first she ran, then, going slower and slower, she stopped running and allowed him to overtake her. Suddenly she lost all fear, and thought of him as a companion. Now she did not see him, but felt his presence, and knew that he was going with her. A sense of joy welled up in her. She had a feeling of life and strength.

When she painted the bull, the picture had a great gaiety, and he was surrounded by flowers. This made her associate him with Taurus, the sign of May—the symbol of spring, of fecundity, and of creative energy. She had at first feared him and had tried to push him back into the water (the unconscious) but found that it was herself who was impeded by wet garments, for the bull was an impersonal, archetypal image, an energy that she could not so easily dispose of. Then, when she accepted him, she felt the renewed energy come to her. This was what actually happened. She began her own creative work and wished to go out into life.

Then she felt a desire to paint a picture of the city as she saw it from her window. Consciously she began to paint the buildings as she saw them before her. The city rose in the towering masses of the modern skyscraper, yet, strangely, it did not seem to be a portrayal of the actual city at which she was looking. It thrilled her with a sense of life within the buildings and in the streets. The picture began to take a form which she did not anticipate. The buildings were bathed in strange mist, and light streamed from the windows. There was a lake in the foreground. She had a feeling of exhilaration as though she had found something for which she was looking, as though almost unconsciously she had found her home. Then she recalled a dream which she had had in the beginning of her analysis, almost three years before.

In this dream she had wandered out of New York and lost her way. She could not see the city even in the distance. Then she came to a little house where an older woman was living. This woman seemed to her like a wise woman. She said she was lost and wanted to get back to the city.

The woman looked at her very quietly, and said, "You have a very long way to go. You must go down the road to the left."

The left she knew was the way of the unconscious. Before her stretched a country road which looked very lonely. It was desolate and went through waste lands. She was afraid and thought one could be murdered on that road. She said, "Why can I not go back the way I came, which is to the right?"

The woman answered, "You can, but it is not your way."

Then she looked down the road to the left and saw ahead in the distance a city of shining lights, and she felt a thrill, and as she started out the woman said, "Take every turn to the left."

When she awoke, this city seemed to her to be the new Jerusalem, the city of the soul. She had almost forgotten this dream but as she looked at the picture she knew that quite unconsciously she had painted this city that she had seen far in the distance in the dream of three years ago. Yet it was also the actual city in which she was living. It was at the same time the tangible, actual city and yet not that city, but a city of the spirit, for in this picture there appeared the pool at the center. She remembered the pool of healing where those who were ill waited until the angel "troubled the waters" and then, entering the pool, received the gift of the spirit which was a healing of their sickness. The pool was also the living water, the place of baptism and rebirth. So, as though in the center of her own present life, was the pool where she could find rebirth. She had once hated the city, and had felt she could not be happy there, but now she saw it differently. Now she realized how little difference it made where she actually lived, if she was at peace with her own realities. She saw again the stretch of dreary road but now she looked back upon it. She did not feel that in coming to this city she had come to any final stage in her development. It was the acceptance of her reality situation which contained the potentials for new life, a life which must be, as in all creative lives, a continuous process of rebirth.

This actual picture was lost a year or so later but the inner connection with it was unbroken. She felt a desire to have the picture as part of her objective record of the entire experience and started to repaint it. But such pictures are too deeply connected with the inner condition to be reproduced in old form if the life has taken on a new aspect. This new picture (Plate 10) was more abstract, it had an archetypal aspect. In the foreground a great rock had split, giving birth to the city. The rock and the city had begun to take a form almost like a mandala. The deep blue seemed the only color in which it could be painted. The fire in the central building which first appeared in the rock was like the living Eros principle at the center of the city of life.

She was surprised at painting this city blue, because she had associated blue with the Logos principle, and, since her first experience of painting the city, she had been deeply connected with her life as a woman—it was on the Eros principle that she had pondered. Her own feeling and her relatedness to the life that came to her had been her concern. But this new city was blue, the color of the Logos and of the spirit. When she came to the painting of the central fire, which she knew to be an essential part of the picture, she felt a great fear. This fire seemed not only to be at the center of the dwelling but also under the great rock. Almost reluctantly she painted the little flames that she saw emerging, as though fearful that, in so doing, she would admit this force within herself and have to reckon with it.

She was still studying this picture and painting it, when, one morning just as she awoke, a vision flashed upon her. The figure of a man arose as from a great depth and stood before her with arms outstretched in the form of a cross. Then from beneath his feet two double-headed serpents uncoiled themselves. They moved swiftly, with great energy, and encircled his body. Their heads, which were raised above him, were plumed like the Plumèd Serpent of ancient legend. From the man's head a flame sprang, as though the great energy which he contained had sprung forth.

The whole figure possessed such force that it overpowered her. After the vision had passed she drew this figure, and as she drew him she perceived that he was enclosed within a circle. She felt that she must also paint it as she had seen it, but was not yet ready to do this; so she went back to the painting of the city. Still her fear of the fire persisted. It seemed to her that if she could study her vision, try to connect herself with its meaning, she could understand her fear. She started to do this, but when she turned to the canvas, another picture arose of itself and she painted with great rapidity.

First she painted a wide circle of deep blue. Within this circle of deep blue a transformation is taking place. From the bottom of the picture a fire bursts forth. A man is bowed over this, plunging his hands into the flame, gathering the fire. Above him appears the head of a huge archetypal bull who touches the man's head with his tongue. The bull is quite different from the embodiment of youthful energy, the Taurus bull, who had gone down the road with her in one of her dreams and who had to be painted decked with flowers. This bull is ancient, ageless. His eyes are green, like the plumes on the serpents' heads. They are kind and quiet, like the eyes of the wise beast who had once breathed into her the breath of reality so that she could discard the false Persona and become a woman. In this picture the bull seems to be guarding the man, making it possible for him to meet his ordeal by fire. On each side of the flame is blackness, and, above the black, soft green light radiates, like the bursting forth of new life.

As she pondered this picture, it seemed to her an initiation which could take place when it was under the protection of the instinctual force here symbolized by the bull. For it is not in the daily life but within the inner center—the sacred place—that a true transformation takes place. It is in that tremendous moment of the meeting with the archetype, when life becomes more than the personal event, that initiation and rebirth can come.

She felt a deep connection between this picture and the earlier one. Both seemed to her an acceptance of reality in its instinctual form. In the first, it had been an acceptance of her life as a woman. Now the other side, the masculine creative principle, born of the fire and accepted by the bull, appears in this rite of initiation: and this side, too, must be accepted. In fact, the picture presented a new problem, the problem of the Animus; and she must meet this without destroying the connection which she had made with her own nature as a woman. If she could accept the active creative principle which was arising within herself and could let this principle find its own form and expression, then new values could be born which she as a woman must serve with real devotion.

She felt that, in some strange way, the bull had given her new courage by showing her the strength and quiet which were also in the unconscious. This instinctual strength had twice appeared to her—in the wise dark beast, and now in this archetypal bull. If she could keep her contact with this, she need not fear that the sacred fire would destroy her.

Then she returned to her picture of the city, and her fear of painting the fire was gone. Again she wished to paint the vision which she had seen. It grew very slowly upon the canvas. In a great sphere of blue appeared an eight-pointed star containing a circle of fire (Plate 11). Within this fire is a quiet center. The man of the vision appears against this background, as though arising from the depths. He is at the center of the picture, but not at the center of the star. Artistically, there is a balance of design; psychologically, the picture appears still uncentered. A new force is arising: it must be accepted and understood.

All the dreams now dealt with this unconscious energy, tremendous but not menacing. The star that she had painted gave her deep feeling and reassurance, but it seemed to her an intuitive perception of something which she would know at some future time, when she had come to another place of integration and could understand better how to use the creative energy arising from the unconscious.

She realized now why this new city which she had painted had appeared bathed in blue light and with the flame at the center. It was not merely that city of the outer world of reality, but far more deeply a city of the world of inner reality—the city of the spirit. Within that city life is lived on a deeper plane. It is not the city of rest, but of growth and development.

She had indeed travelled upon the road to which the wise woman had directed her; she had taken every turn to the left;

she had traversed the waste lands which she feared; and she had come to the city. But it was not the end, but only a place of new beginning, of new effort, of new integration. Her personal life now took on a deeper significance. She saw why this new city had assumed the form of the mandala, the place of protection. For the time of integration is a time of great fear. The unknown intrudes and the present security is threatened; it is a time when the personal and the impersonal are brought together. At such a time one finds a relation to one's own myth of life—that is, into the daily personal life enter the deep experiences which have been lived over and over throughout the ages. One is not only connected with personal events but with individual destiny. One lives in connection with the archetype, and yet remains an individual. No wonder that this experience can take place only in the protection of the inner circle.

This city, therefore, which had taken on the mandala form, was a place where, through the acceptance of new problems and the understanding of her relation to the inner images, she could increasingly maintain a connection between the inner and the outer worlds. In this way, life could be continually reanimated and reborn.

4

5

6

7

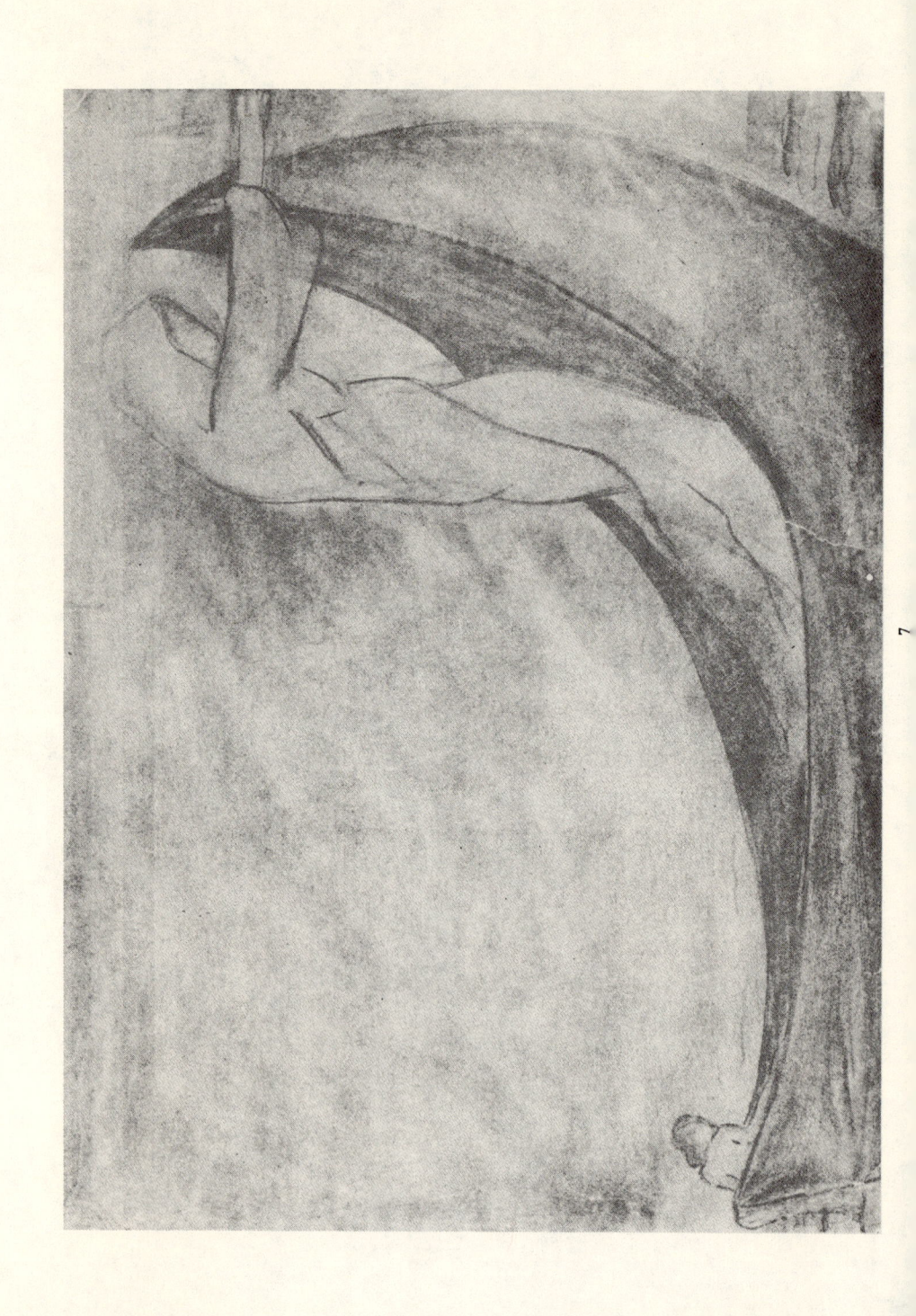

8

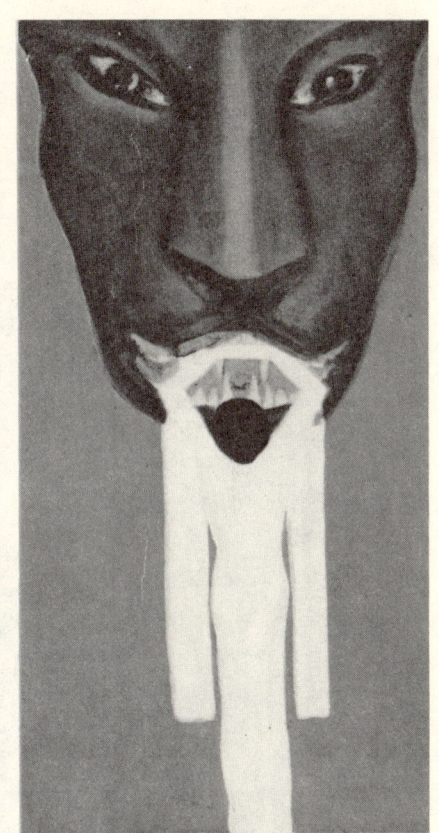

9

10

11

12

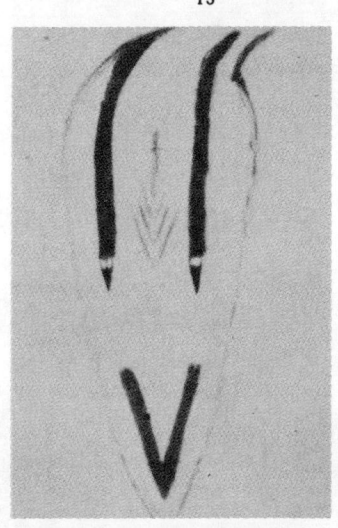

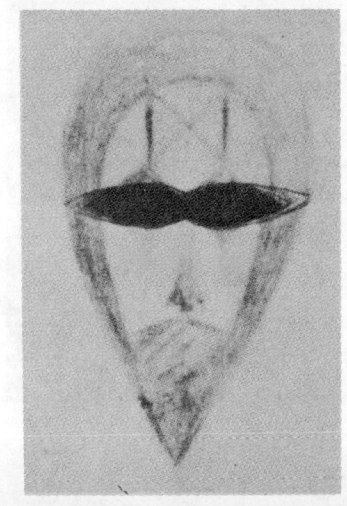

13

14

15

16

17

18

19

20

21

22

23

24

25

26

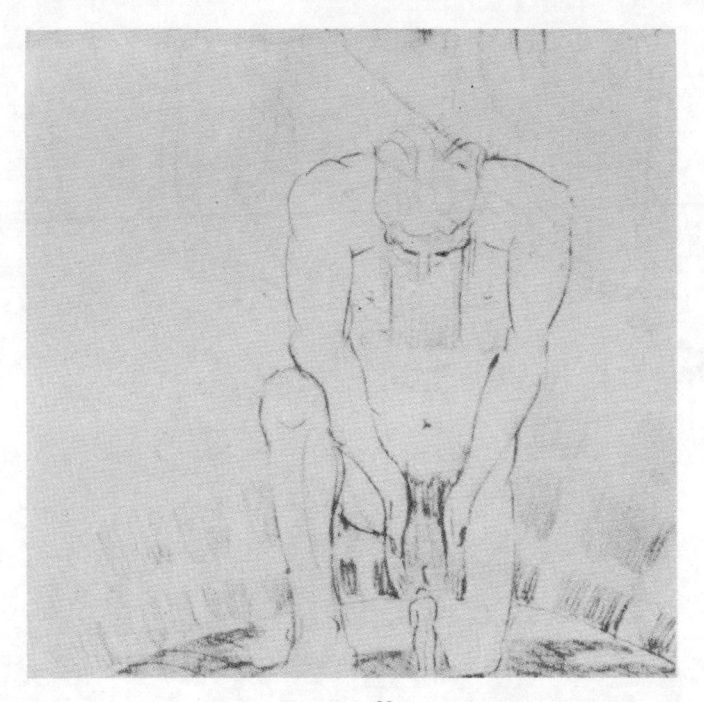

27

28

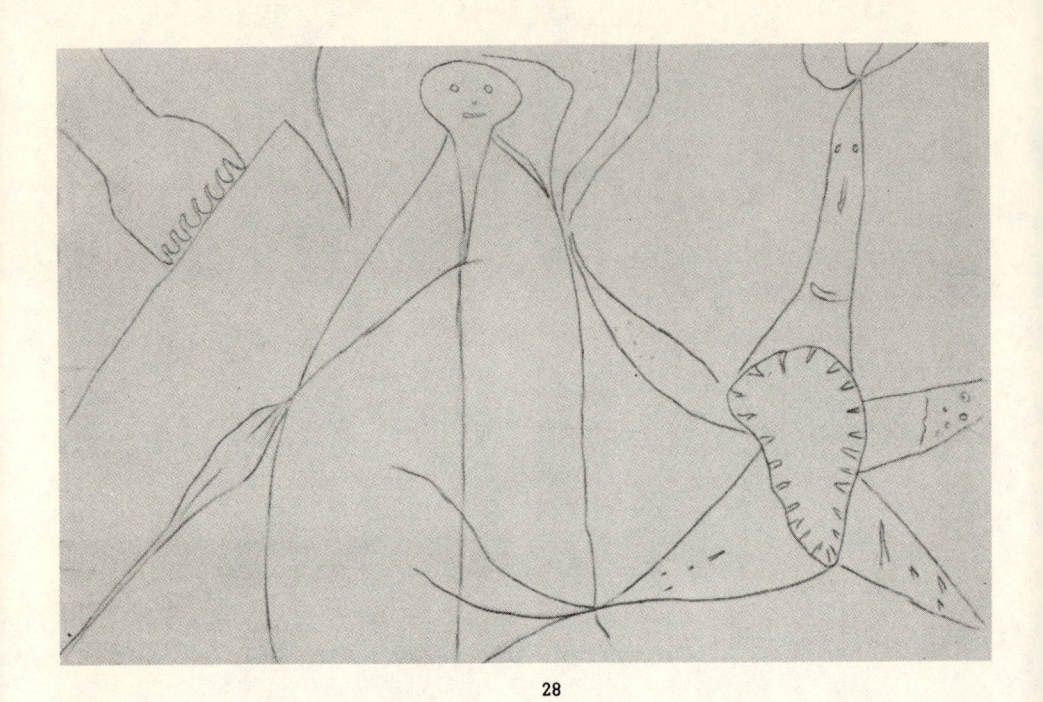

29

30

31

32

33

34

35   36

37   38

39

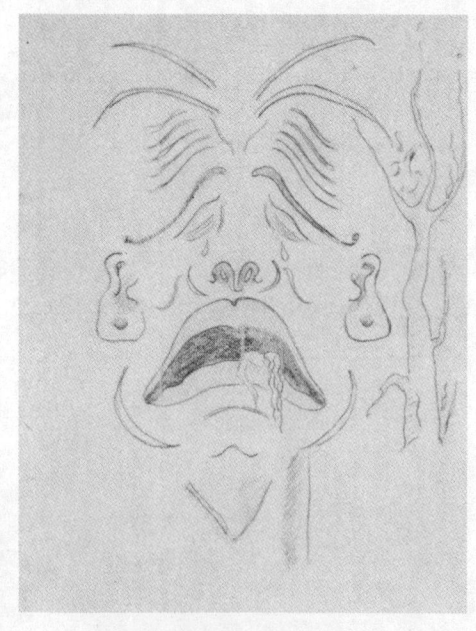

40 41

42

43

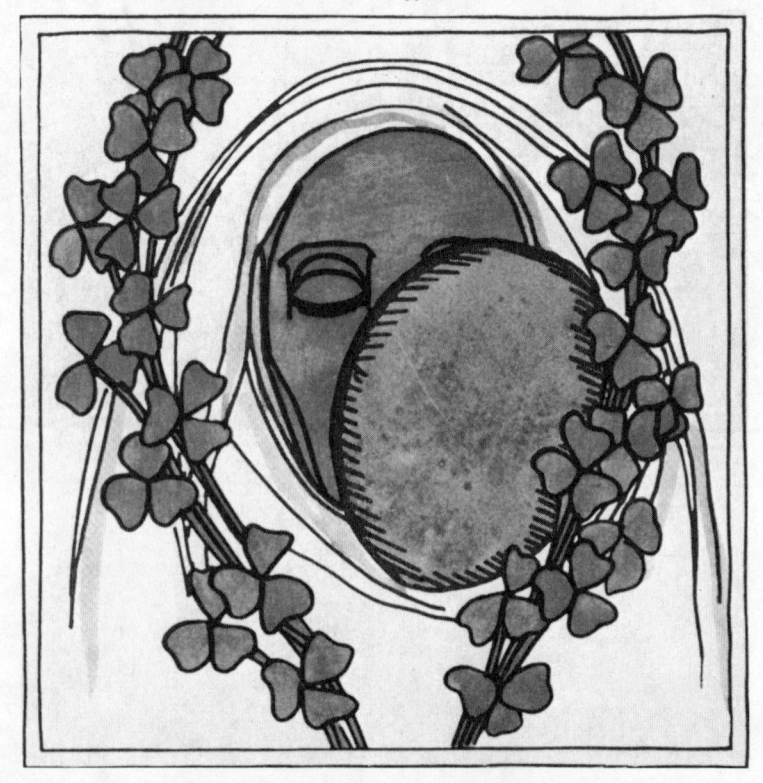

44

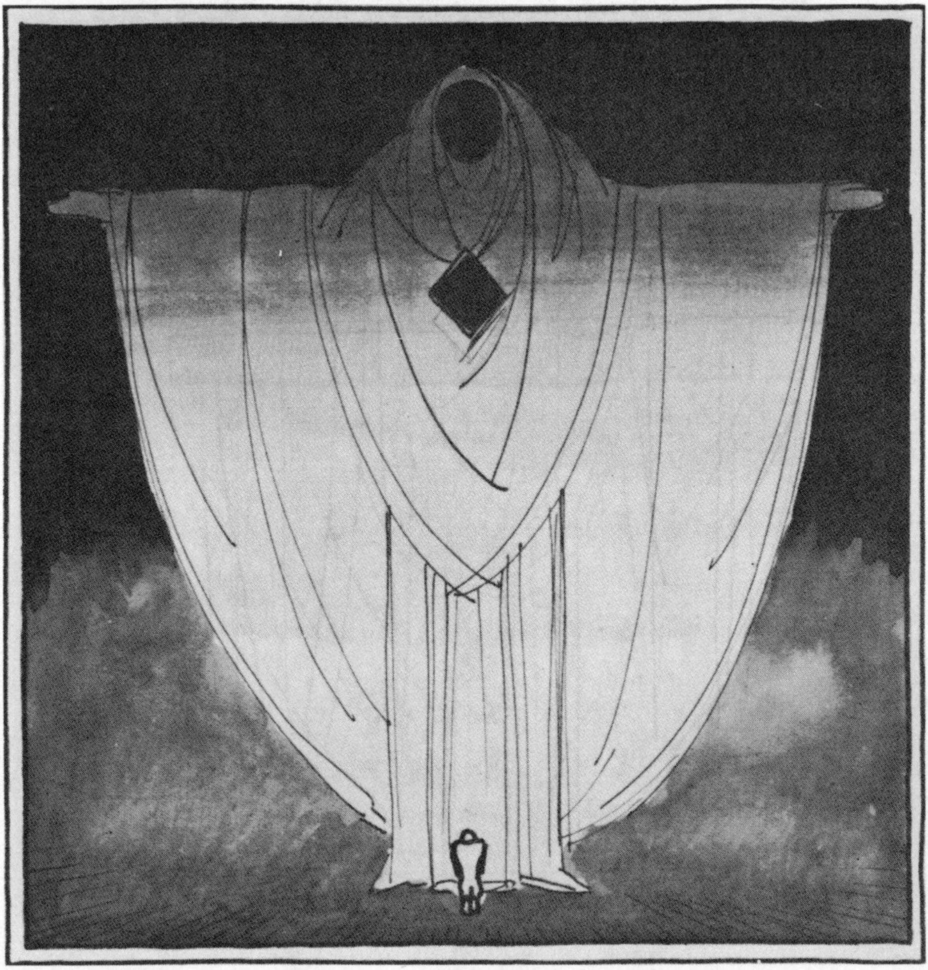

46

47

48

49

50

51

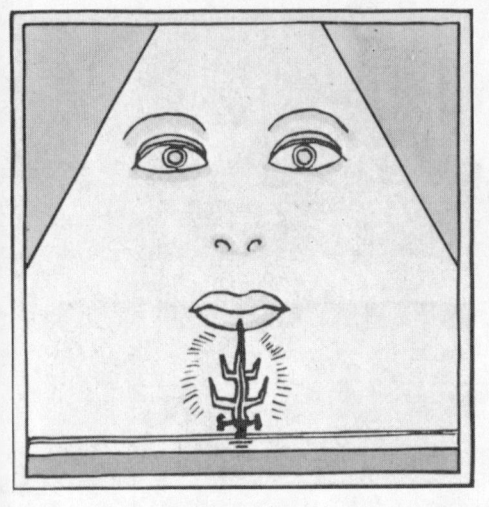

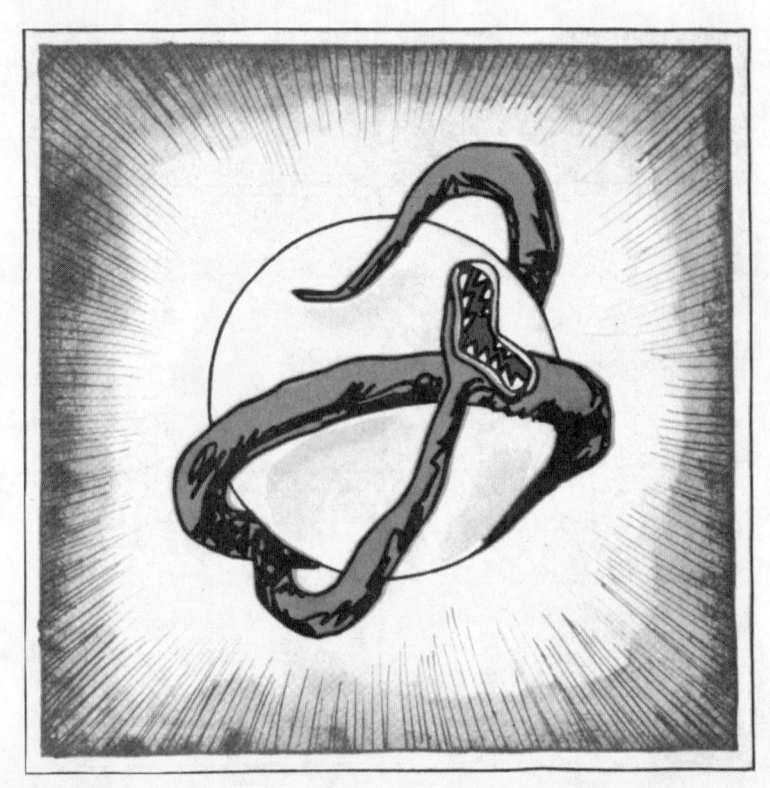

52

53

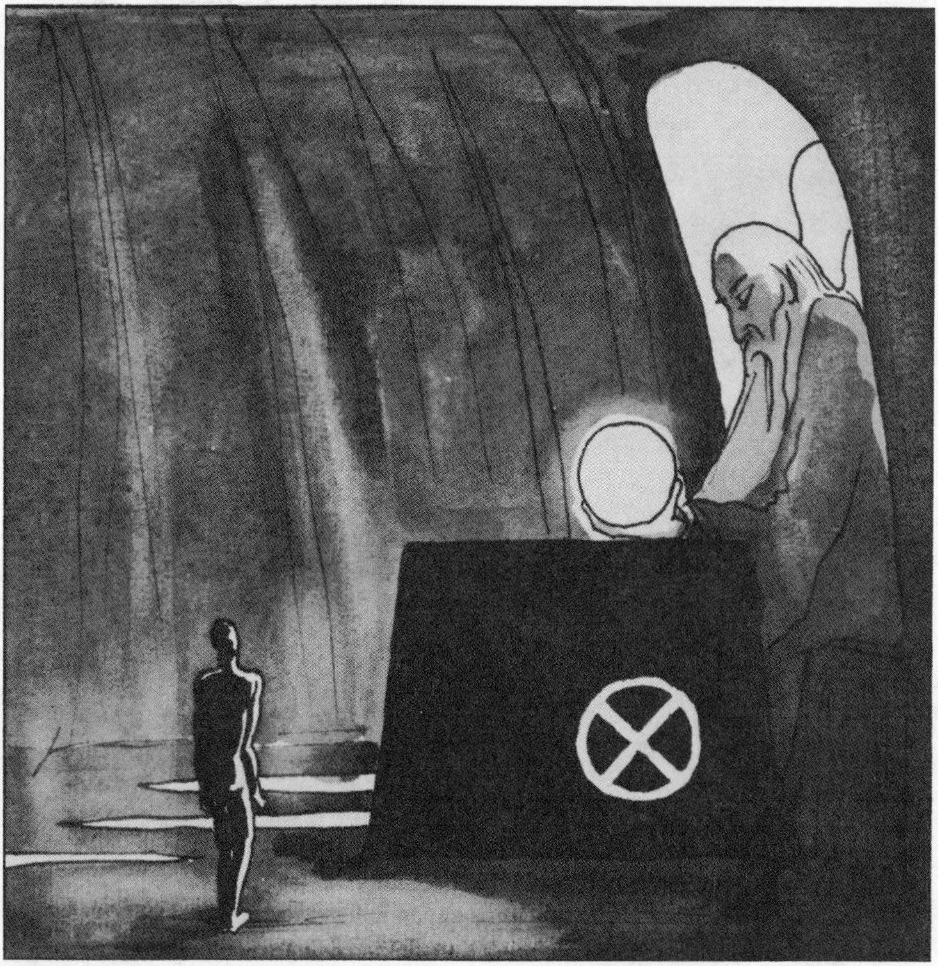

55

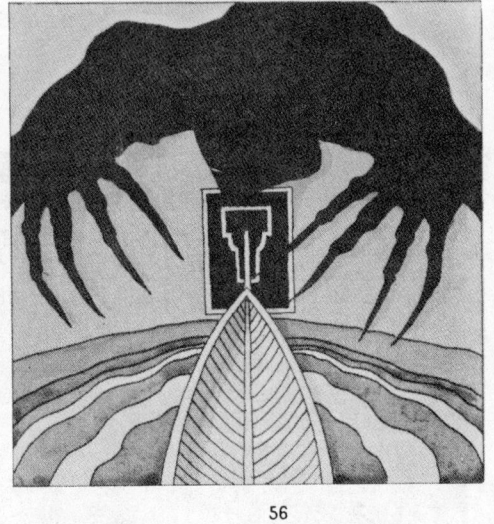

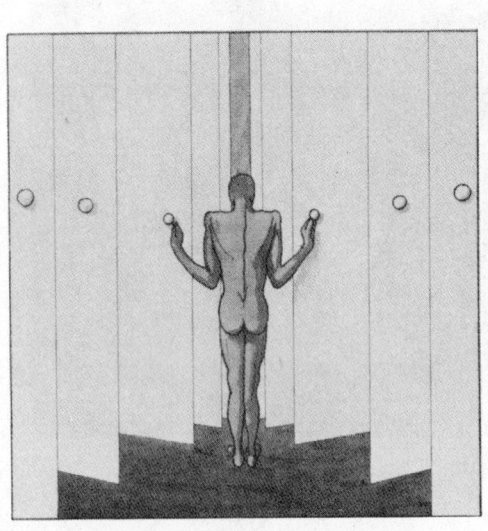

56

57

58

59

60

61

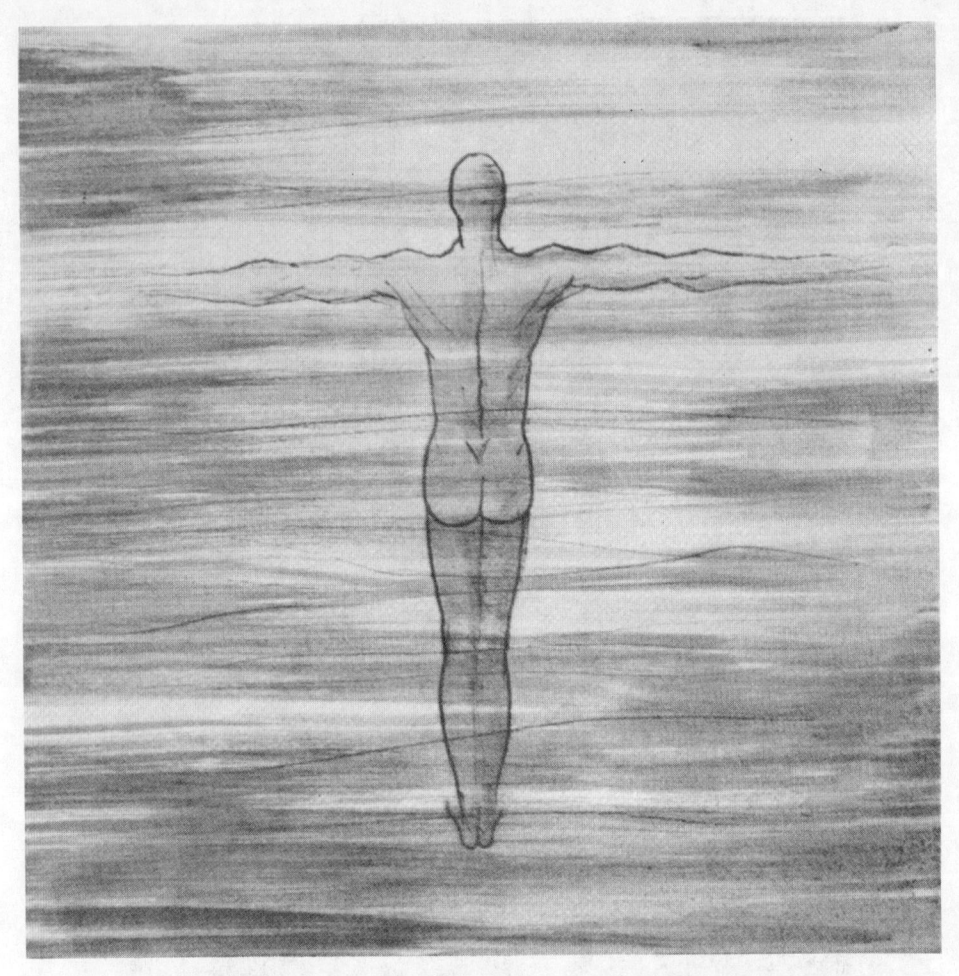

62

63

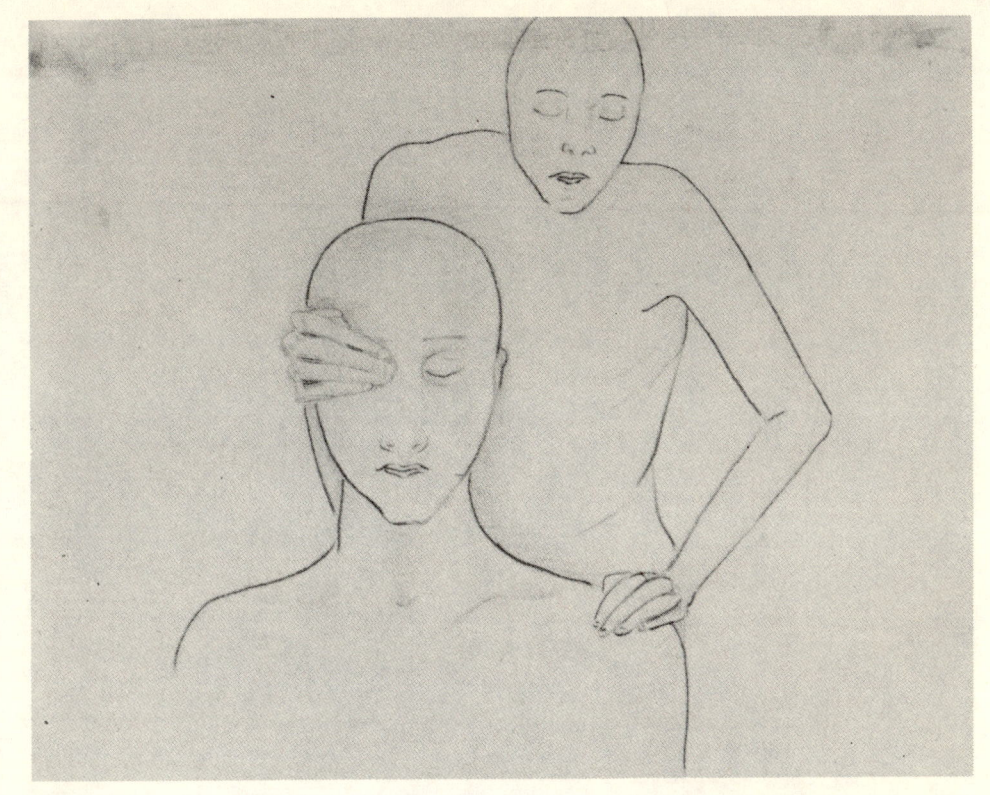

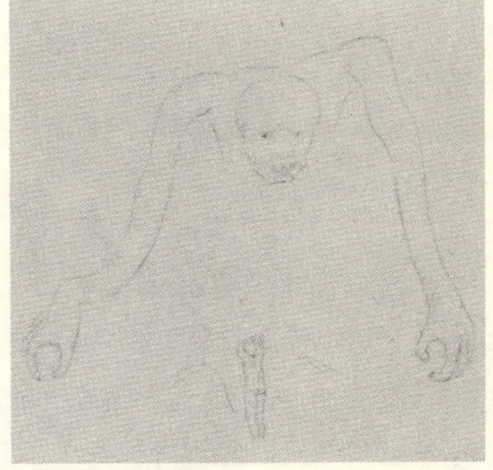

64
65

66

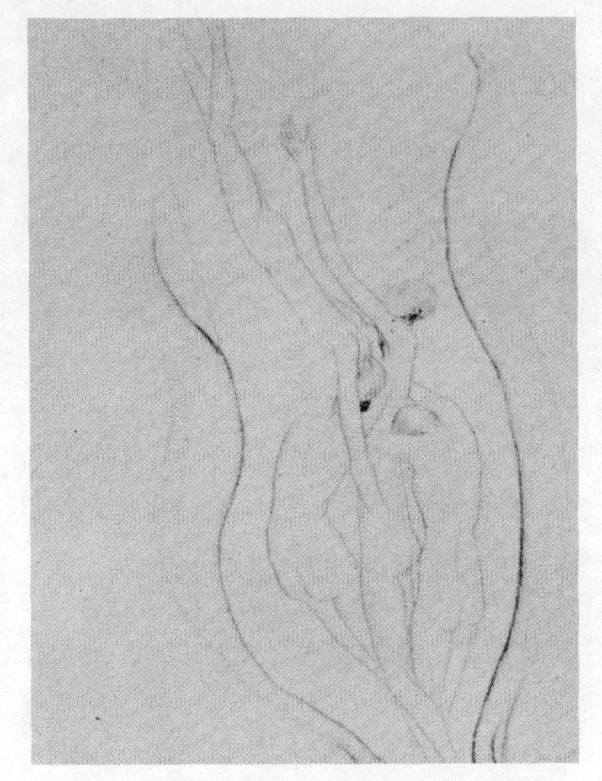

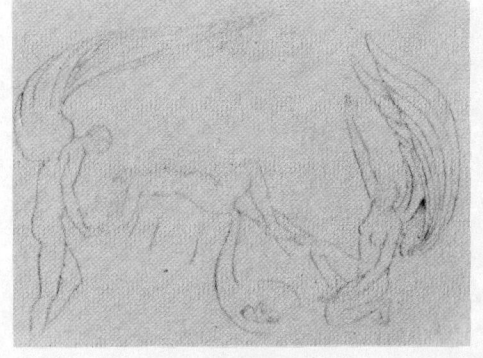

67 68

69

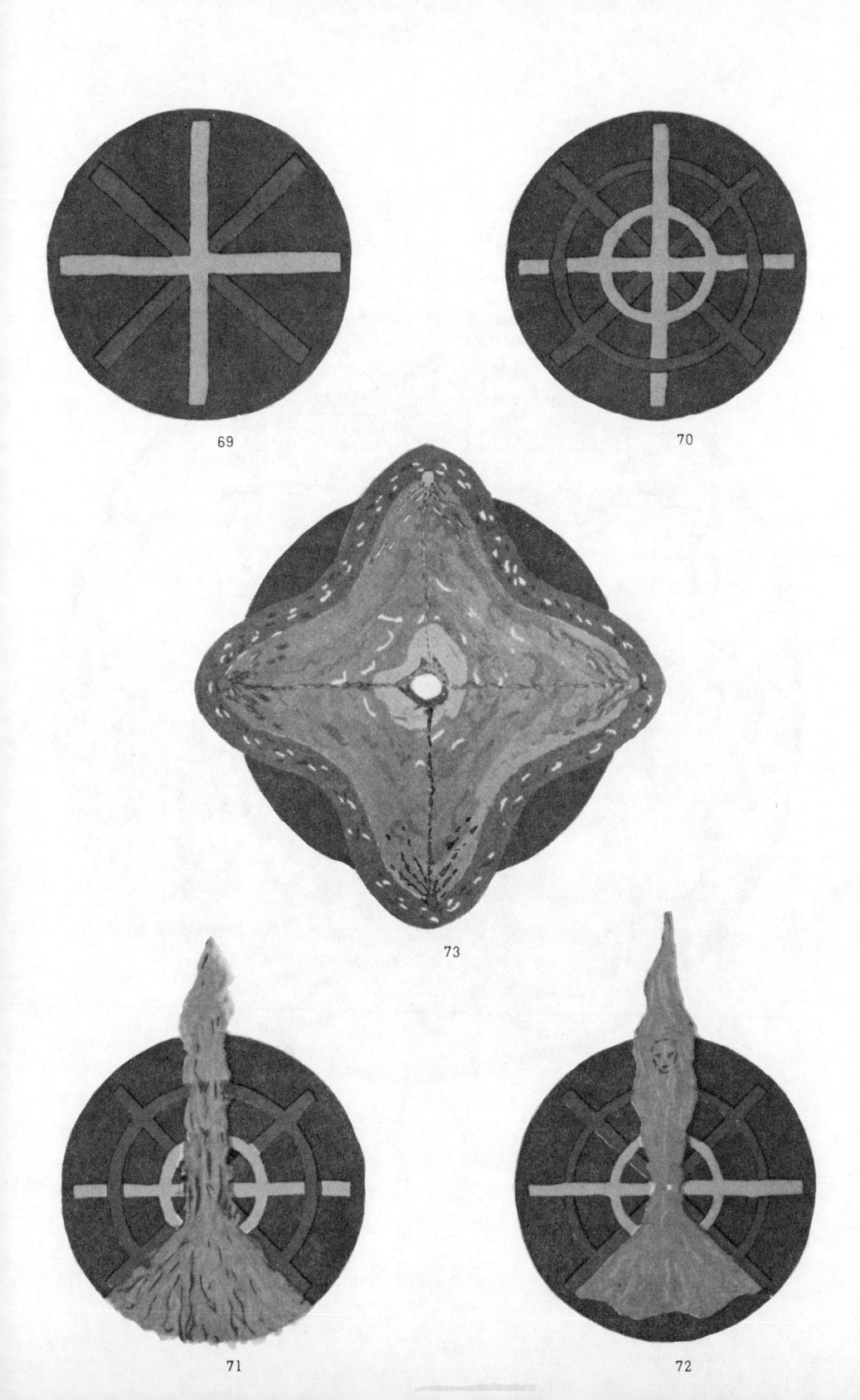

70

73

71

72

74

75

76

77

78

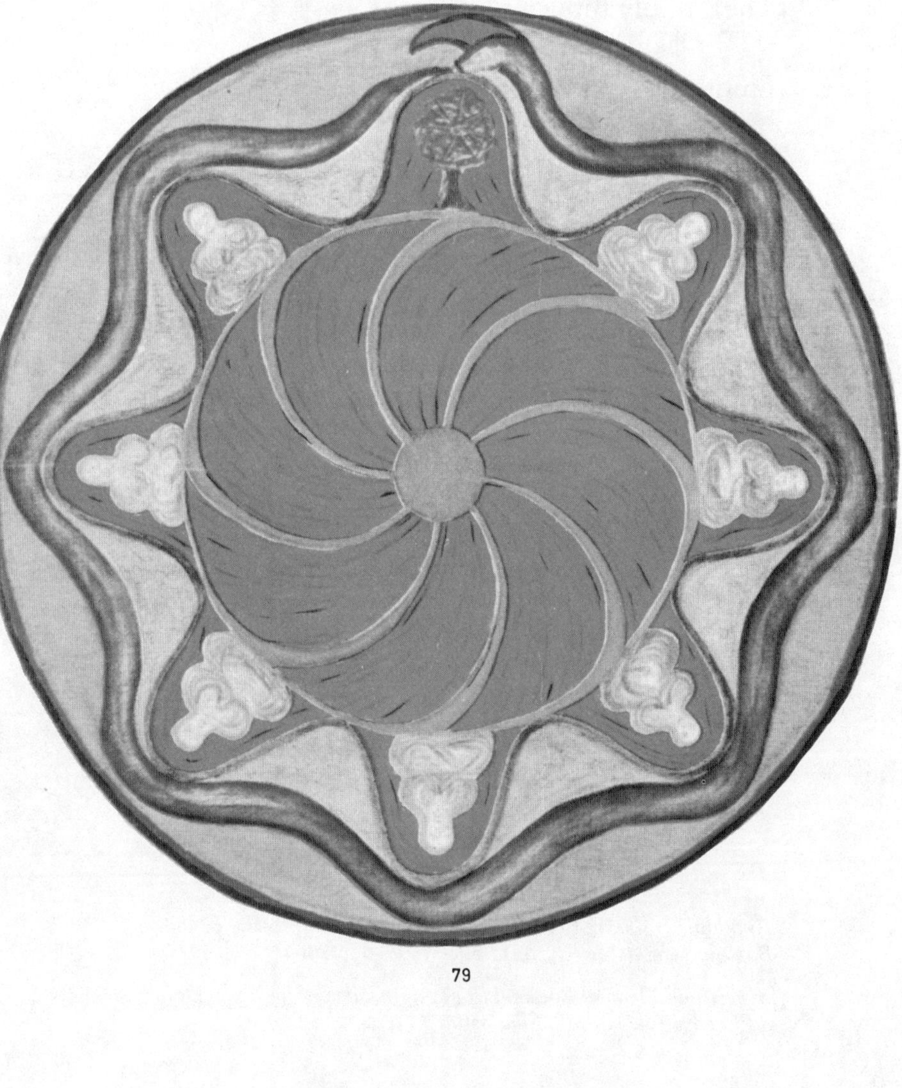

Other Titles from Sigo Press

The Unholy Bible *by June Singer*
$32.00 cloth, $14.95 paper

Emotional Child Abuse *by Joel Covitz*
$24.95 cloth, $13.95 paper

Dreams of a Woman *by Sheila Moon*
$27.50 cloth, $13.95 paper

Androgyny *by June Singer*
$24.95 cloth, $14.95 paper

The Grail Legend *by Emma Jung & Marie-Louise von Franz*
$35.00 cloth, $15.95 paper

Inner World of Childhood *by Frances G. Wickes*
$27.50 cloth, $14.95 paper

Inner World of Choice *by Frances G. Wickes*
$27.50 cloth, $14.95 paper

Inner World of Man *by Frances G. Wickes*
$27.50 cloth, $14.95 paper

Puer Aeternus *by Marie-Louise von Franz*
$32.00 cloth, $14.95 paper

Sandplay *by Dora Kalff*
$14.95 paper

The Secret World of Drawing *by Gregg Furth*
$35.00 cloth, $16.95 paper

Available from SIGO PRESS, 25 New Chardon Street, #8748A, Boston, Massachusetts, 02114. tel. (508) 526-7064

In England Element Books, Ltd., Longmead, Shaftesbury, Dorset SP7 8 PL. tel. (0747) 51339, Shaftesbury